China's Emergent Political Economy

This edited volume represents the first collaborative effort to explicitly view China's rapid international ascent as associated with the same process that catapulted Great Britain, the United States, Germany, and Japan to international prominence – the emergence of a capitalist political economy. Each chapter therefore applies the capitalist lens to analyze aspects of China's monumental social, economic, and political transition. Topics addressed range from examinations of China's industrial capitalism and its new multinational corporations to studies of China's changing polity, state-media relations, and foreign policy.

With contributors writing from highly varied backgrounds each chapter approaches the subject from a slightly different perspective, but the underlying findings show considerable common ground. China is developing a unique form of capitalism by combining elements rooted in Chinese history, such as the prevalence of networked forms of capital and the continued dominance of the state, with the growing influence of global capital, including the rapid adaptation of recent organizational and technological innovations. Concluding chapters draw out what capitalism in the dragon's lair implies for our 21st century world, cautioning that China's rise is likely to challenge the present world order along both political and economic dimensions.

Dr Christopher A. McNally is a Research Fellow at the East-West Center in Honolulu. As a political economist, he studies contemporary varieties of capitalism, especially the nature and logic of China's capitalist transition.

Routledge Studies in the Growth Economies of Asia

China's Emergent Political Economy

Capitalism in the dragon's lair

**Edited by
Christopher A. McNally**

Routledge
Taylor & Francis Group

LONDON AND NEW YORK

East-West Center Studies

East-West Center Studies books present significant
new research and policy analysis on issues of
contemporary concern in the Asia Pacific region.

First published 2008
by Routledge
2 Park Square, Milton Park, Abingdon, Oxon OX14 4RN

Simultaneously published in the USA and Canada
by Routledge
270 Madison Ave, New York, NY 10016

*Routledge is an imprint of the Taylor & Francis Group,
an informa business*

Typeset in Times New Roman by
Newgen Imaging Systems (P) Ltd, Chennai, India
Printed and bound in Great Britain by
Biddles Ltd, King's Lynn

British Library Cataloguing in Publication Data
A catalogue record for this book is available from
the British Library

Library of Congress Cataloging in Publication Data
A catalog record for this book has been requested

ISBN10: 0–415–42572–7 (hbk)
ISBN10: 0–203–94058–X (ebk)

ISBN13: 978–0–415–42572–8 (hbk)
ISBN13: 978–0–203–94058–7 (ebk)

To my wife, Pauline Ping Bai
And in memory of my late father, Michael McNally

Contents

Figures

Tables

Contributors

An Chen is Associate Professor of Political Science at the National University of Singapore. Previously a Research Fellow at the Chinese Academy of Social Sciences, he received his PhD in Political Science from Yale University. His current research focuses on China's rural reform.

Christopher Edmonds (PhD, University of California–Berkeley, 1998) is an Economist, Asian Development Bank, Manila, Philippines, and an Adjunct East-West Center Fellow. He has extensive experience working on economic projects and research in Asia for several organizations (e.g. International Rice Research Institute). His books (e.g. *Reducing Poverty in Asia*) and articles cover many topics related to economic development in Asia.

Dieter Ernst is Senior Fellow at the East-West Center. He was senior advisor to the OECD and research director at the Berkeley Roundtable, University of California-Berkeley. His research covers global production and innovation networks and implications for industrial and technology policies. His books include *Technological Capabilities and Export Success in Asia, What are the Limits to the Korean Model?, International Production Networks in Asia,* and *Innovation Offshoring – Asia's Emerging Role in Global Innovation Networks.*

Jian Gao is a Professor of Entrepreneurship and Innovation at the School of Economics and Management, Tsinghua University, Beijing, PRC, where he also received his PhD in 1996. He has been a Visiting Scholar at the Sloan School of Management at MIT, a Price-Babson Fellow at Babson College, and a Visiting Scholar at the Graduate School of Business at Stanford University.

Maryanne Kivlehan-Wise is the Deputy Director of the CNA Corporation's Project Asia. She is coeditor of *China's Leadership in the 21st Century: The Rise of the Fourth Generation* and *The Chinese Media System: Continuity, Chaos, and Change* (forthcoming). She holds an MA from the

George Washington University, and is a graduate of the Hopkins-Nanjing Center for Chinese and American Studies.

Sumner J. La Croix (PhD, University of Washington, 1981) is Professor of Economics and Population at the University of Hawaii. His research on China has analyzed foreign direct investment; the political economy of economic reform; energy use; intellectual property rights; and international aviation markets.

Yao Li is currently a Degree Fellow at the East-West Center as well as a PhD candidate in the Department of Economics at the University of Hawaii-Manoa. Her research interests include international trade theory, trade policy, and regional development.

Christopher A. McNally is Research Fellow at the East-West Center in Honolulu. As a political economist, his research focuses on contemporary varieties of capitalism, especially the nature and logic of China's capitalist transition. He is also studying the implications of China's growing economic power on East Asia's regional order. Most recently, he authored publications in *The China Quarterly* and *Comparative Social Research.*

Barry Naughton is Professor of Chinese and International Affairs at the University of California, San Diego. He is an economist who specializes in China's transitional economy. His study of Chinese economic reform, *Growing Out of the Plan: Chinese Economic Reform, 1978–1993* (New York: Cambridge University Press, 1995), won the Masayoshi Ohira Memorial Prize. He has also edited two volumes on China and his textbook, *The Chinese Economy: Transitions and Growth*, was published by MIT Press in 2007.

Yinhong Shi is Professor of International Relations and Director of the Center for American Studies at Renmin University, Beijing, PRC. He spent years in research and teaching at institutions in the US, Germany, and Japan. He has published 11 books and 340 articles. Many of them have had wide influence in China and some have become internationally influential.

Ian Storey is a Visiting Fellow at the Institute of Southeast Asian Studies, Singapore. His areas of specialization include Southeast Asian security issues, ASEAN-China relations, and maritime security. He has held positions at the Asia-Pacific Center for Security Studies in Honolulu (USA), and at Deakin University in Victoria (Australia). He was educated in Great Britain, Japan, and Hong Kong.

Paul Vega is a Consultant with the Asia House of McKinsey & Co., which specializes on cross-border topics relating to Asia. He holds a PhD from the University of St Gallen and an MSc from the London School of Economics. He was a Doctoral Fellow at INSEAD and Wharton-SMU in Singapore, and completed his thesis on venture capital finance in China.

Steven White is Associate Professor at the China Europe International Business School (CEIBS) in Shanghai, PRC. He studies two major issues related to fit: *strategic fit* focusing on organizational change and innovation; and *relational fit* focusing on control, cooperation, and value in interorganizational relationships. He holds a PhD in Management from MIT.

Peter J. Williamson is Professor of International Management and Asian Business at INSEAD in Fontainebleau, France, and Singapore. Author of seven books, his latest, *Dragons at Your Door: How Chinese Cost Innovation is Disrupting Global Competition*, will be published by Harvard Business School Press in May 2007. Formerly at The Boston Consulting Group, he acts as consultant and serves on the boards of several listed companies. He holds a PhD in Business Economics from Harvard University.

Kang Wu is Senior Fellow at the East-West Center, where he conducts research on energy and economic policy issues with a focus on the Asia-Pacific region. He also leads the Center's China energy research and is the author and co-author of numerous journal articles, project reports, professional studies, conference papers, book chapters, and other publications.

Ming Zeng is Professor of Strategy at the Cheung Kong Graduate School of Business, Beijing, PRC. He has conducted extensive research on the growth strategies of Chinese companies and published widely in the world's top management journals. His book coauthored with Peter Williamson, *Dragons at Your Door*, will be published by Harvard Business School Press in 2007. He was also a faculty member at INSEAD from 1998 to 2004.

Wei Zhang is an Associate Professor at the School of Economics and Management, Tsinghua University, Beijing, PRC. His research interests focus on entrepreneurship and venture capital. He was a visiting scholar at the Stanford Graduate School of Business and Price-Babson College Fellow (SEE-20).

Preface and acknowledgments

This volume grew out of a long journey. Perhaps the starting point was in 1985 when I arrived in Hong Kong after growing up in Switzerland. I was starry eyed by the thriving metropolis and in love with Chinese food. But this was also the time when the People's Republic of China's reform and open door policy garnered steam. The seeds for two fascinations which have since shaped my career were planted during these first years in Hong Kong. First, I became deeply involved in studying the political economy of modern China. Second, I developed a keen interest in the inner workings and outer manifestations of the socioeconomic system we call capitalism. Indeed, it was the contrast between thriving Hong Kong, staid Switzerland, and chaotic China that impressed upon me the importance of the comparative study of modern capitalisms.

One consequence of these two fascinations is this edited volume. It aims to explicitly interpret the enormous transformations taking place in China as associated with the same process of capitalist development that shaped the rise of the world's great powers. In this manner, it provides a big picture analysis that is historically and comparatively grounded. It also enables a synthetic examination of various facets of China's transition, including China's evolving business systems, changing politics, and emerging role in the world. In the end, the hope is that this volume can integrate insights across disciplines to arrive at a more realistic and unclouded analysis of China's emergent political economy.

The production of this volume benefited from several major sources of inspiration. First, I came across two wonderful little books by Robert Heilbroner in 2001, *The Nature and Logic of Capitalism* and *21st Century Capitalism*. Heilbroner here masterfully merged key insights from the history of economic thought with knowledge about how modern economies work. In my opinion, these two books provide one of the most readable *and* most insightful expositions on the nature and logic of capitalism. These two books also prodded me to combine their insights with my prior studies in comparative politics and institutional political economy. A fertile ground appeared from which to understand modern capitalisms. Chapter 2 of this volume has grown out of this ground.

A second source of inspiration has been my wife, Pauline Ping Bai. As a cellist she comes from a background very unlike my own. But having grown up in the early reform years of the People's Republic and having developed a keen eye for observing human nature, she has become my favorite partner in conversation. Her wisdom, passion, and astute perceptions have allowed me to gain a consummate understanding of China's wrenching transformations, especially as they affect the livelihoods and emotions of the Chinese.

Finally, I owe a deep gratitude to my erstwhile collaborator on the China's capitalist transition project, Elizabeth Van Wie Davis. My discussions with her over glasses of wine proved to be invaluable for moving this project along. In fact, it was the broad range of topics we covered that inspired me to undertake this perhaps somewhat foolish sweep of China's contemporary affairs. Looking back, though, I am grateful to Elizabeth for urging me to integrate insights on China's business systems and domestic political economy with analyses of China's future role in the world.

One reason for the unique constitution of this book has been the institutional goals of the East-West Center. The Center aims to foster collaborative research that includes both interdisciplinary and, more importantly, cross-regional research teams. The result: a unique team of collaborators spanning three continents, three disciplines, and three fields of analysis. I would also like to thank the East-West Center for its generous financial support that enabled us to hold two workshops in August 2004 and 2005 that led up to the production of this volume. In particular, I would like to thank Charles E. Morrison and Nancy D. Lewis, who believed in this project and made it possible.

A collaborative effort such as this volume is self-evidently the work of many hands. To begin with I am therefore grateful to my contributors for being such superb collaborators. All of them displayed immense enthusiasm and commitment to this project. They also provided precious advice at critical junctures, something I deeply appreciate. Without their hard labor and dedication this volume would have not been feasible.

During the workshops in Honolulu we were also blessed to have two excellent teams of project advisors. Each of these advisors offered pertinent observations and criticisms concerning the conception and implementation of the China's capitalist transition project. Special thanks thus go to David M. Lampton, Richard Baum, Philippe Schmitter, Miles Kahler, Jieqiu Wan, Xianguo Yao, Dru C. Gladney, Cindy Y.W. Chu, Wei Wang, David Finkelstein, Elizabeth Economy, Sarah Tong, and many others who have contributed to the workshops. Without their input and review of chapters, this volume would have never attained its present range of coverage and depth of analysis.

In the process of my own research and writing, I further benefited from several vital opportunities. First and foremost, I would like to thank Victor K. Fung (PhD), Chairman and CEO, Li & Fung Distribution Group, who invited me to undertake research on China's emergent political economy in the winter of 2004/2005 in Hong Kong. This research stay was sponsored by the Hong Kong Forum and the Centre of Asian Studies at the University of Hong Kong. Especially David Dodwell and Professor Siu-lun Wong provided helpful personal support, including assistance in organizing several research seminars at the Hong Kong Forum and the Centre of Asian Studies. Jean Hung at the University Services Center, the Chinese University of Hong Kong, also kindly helped me to arrange an additional research seminar there. During these seminars I received a wealth of comments and suggestions, the origins of which I cannot fully acknowledge. Nonetheless, I would like to thank Victor Fung, Edgar Cheng, Vincent Lo, David Zweig, Gilles Guiheux, Cindy Yin-wah Chu, James Tang, and Peter Cheung for their insights.

During my years of research and study in China I also encountered a myriad of individuals who proved extremely willing to help. Alas, I cannot name them by name here because of promises of confidentiality, but would like to recognize them anonymously. Two names that I can mention, and who have become good colleagues and friends, are Hong Guo and Guangwei Hu of the Sichuan Academy of Social Sciences in Chengdu.

My sincere gratitude goes to my support staff here at the East-West Center in Honolulu. Above all is Brenda Higashimoto, who has provided invaluable assistance during the production of this manuscript. I at times felt that I would drive her crazy with my repeated demands for proof-reads, adjustments, and reference searches. I also would like to thank Jane Smith-Martin and Carolyn Eguchi who aided in the organization of the two workshops. Finally, I would like to recognize the help of several graduate interns, including Shi Fu, Ian Zhao, and Vitoria Lin.

My final thanks must go to those without whom I would not have come this far: my wife, Pauline Ping Bai, and my late father, Michael McNally.

Christopher A. McNally
Honolulu, Hawaii
February 2007

Abbreviations

3G	Third generation (Mobile Telephony Standard)
ASEAN	Association of South East Asian Nations
CASS	Chinese Academy of Social Sciences
CCP	Chinese Communist Party
CEC	China Electronics Corporation
CETC	China Electronics Technology Corporation
CNOOC	China National Offshore Oil Corporation
COE	Collective-owned enterprise
FDI	Foreign direct investment
FIE	Foreign Invested Enterprise
GAPP	General Administration of Press and Publications
GDP	Gross Domestic Product
GEM	Growth Enterprise Market (Hong Kong)
GIN	Global innovation network
GPN	Global production network
IP	Internet protocol
IPO	Initial public offerings
IT	Information technology
JMSU	Joint Marine Seismic Undertaking
LNG	Liquefied natural gas
MBO	Management buy-out
MFN	Most Favored Nation
MNC	Multinational corporation
MoST	Ministry of Science and Technology
NGO	Non-Governmental Organization
OEM	Original Equipment Manufacturer
PC	Personal computer
PLA	People's Liberation Army
PLAN	People's Liberation Army Navy
PPP	Purchasing power parity
PRC	People's Republic of China
PTA	Preferential Trading Agreements
SARFT	State Administration of Radio, Film, and Television

SASAC	State-owned Assets Supervision and Administration Commission
SCO	Shanghai Cooperation Organization
SLOC	Sea lines of communication
SOE	State-owned enterprise
SOM	Strait of Malacca
TVE	Township and village enterprises
VC	Venture capital firm
VoC	Varieties of capitalism
WTO	World Trade Organization

Part 1
Setting the stage

1   Introduction

The China impact

Christopher A. McNally

Of all the competing forecasts for the 21st century, most agree that China's international ascent will have a defining impact. Nonetheless, most serious forecasts seem at a loss concerning how to capture the exact nature of this impact. China's ascent might be the harbinger of international turbulence, or portend the rise of a vast consumer market, ushering in a new era of global prosperity.

Whatever view one might lean toward, China's impact will spring from the massive transformations its political economy is experiencing. Analyzing these transformations is the purpose of this volume. We will explore the domestic origins of China's emergent political economy and its global ramifications.

The People's Republic of China (PRC) underwent a period of industrialization, nation-building, and military buildup after its founding in 1949. However, the starting point of China's contemporary ascent is most widely set in late 1978. It was then that Deng Xiaoping and his fellow reformers initiated the policy of reform and openness. The launch of these economic reforms triggered a breathtaking transition toward an internationally open market economy, in turn engendering an economic boom with few parallels in modern history. By now, this boom is putting Chinese workers within reach of middle-income status and potentially creating the biggest consumer revolution the world has seen.

Concurrent with economic change, a host of new social forces were unleashed. These include the creation of distinct professional interests, the move of human capital from the countryside to the city, and the stratification of China's social order. Enormous differences now exist in the life opportunities of Chinese citizens, especially along regional and urban/rural lines. China's reforms have therefore created severe imbalances that are threatening stability and pressuring Chinese leaders to establish more socially responsive institutions.

Even in terms of China's political system, often seen as a laggard in the reform process, changes have unfolded at a rapid pace. Whereas prior to 1978 China was characterized by a centralized system with almost absolute control over its populace, the reform period triggered a transition toward a more open and pluralist polity. New interest groups, new avenues of expression, and new spaces for political influence are opening up despite the efforts of China's authoritarian political system to control these trends.

Throughout this reform process domestic dynamics and international forces have mutually conditioned each other. For instance, as international trade and financial flows increased across China's borders, Chinese economic policy became more constrained by global economic events. In tandem, international integration has catapulted China to become a major global economic player. The Chinese economy was in 2006 the fourth largest global economy, the third largest trading nation, and the most dynamic buyer of commodities. Perhaps most telling, China is now widely perceived as the world's factory for a large variety of consumer goods.

As a result of these concurrent and monumental changes, China has started to impact the world's economics and geopolitics. The country's growing interdependence with the global system is encouraging its leaders to take initiatives to engage and influence their international environment. Initiatives such as the pursuing of a free trade agreement with the economies of the Association of Southeast Asian Nations and concerted efforts to secure energy supplies are all altering regional and international political balances. Evidently, as China's international interactions increase, so will the country's impact on world affairs. The "China Impact" is likely to become more prominent as the 21st century progresses.

Scholars have responded to China's dramatic transformation by producing a large variety of works on its economy, politics, society, and international relations. While during the Cold War information on China was scarce and anecdotal, this new body of literature has allowed the world to gain an in-depth appreciation of contemporary Chinese affairs. In a sense, this burgeoning analysis has truly opened China to the world.

Nonetheless, China is often seen as standing on its own in this literature, somewhat distinct and special in terms of its historical experiences and contemporary circumstances. Even as China possesses vibrant markets, its economy remains permeated by the influence of state organs. And even as Chinese society is clearly on the move, the country continues to be dominated by a communist party. Indeed, China often appears as a contradiction within itself. Somehow the country's circumstances just don't fit the universe of social scientific concepts used to describe modern societies.

For sure, there have been many attempts to situate China within social scientific theory. In the political economy of development, China has been conceived of as a case of a developmental state, crony capitalist state, or post-socialist transition economy.[1] However, all of these conceptual migrations do not sit quite comfortably in the China of today. They may explain some of China's dynamism or present-day contradictions, but seldom provide a big picture logic explaining the international ascent of China.

In fact, the challenge of conceptualizing China's transition has led to the proliferation of new conceptual terms. These range from "incomplete state socialism" to "capitalism with Chinese characteristics," "Confucian Leninism," "capital socialism," "bureaupreneurialism," and *"nomenclature capitalism"* (Baum and Shevchenko 1999: 333–334). Since China is a political economy in flux, this proliferation of often paradoxical concepts is a natural phenomenon. Alas, many of these new terms are of little use when trying to synthesize the monumental changes occurring in China and relate them to broader world historical trends.

While the literature on contemporary Chinese affairs has produced a wealth of analysis, it has had considerable difficulties in effectively synthesizing the forces shaping China's transformation. There are therefore few works that have put together the dynamics facing China into a logical and lucid whole while linking them to other well-known historical experiences. Our collaborative effort attempts to accomplish this. We aim to conceptualize the monumental changes taking place in China by recognizing them as part and parcel of a capitalist transition.

China's capitalist transition

While in terms of speed and scale the developments unfolding in China are without parallel in the past, there are intriguing parallels to earlier instances of industrialization and nation-building. China's stunning ascent is associated with the same historical dynamic that catapulted Great Britain, the United States, Germany, and Japan to international prominence – the emergence of a capitalist political economy. The purpose of this book is therefore to offer a new perspective on China's international ascent, conceiving it as the product of a capitalist transition, a term which captures the processes and phenomena associated with the emergence of capitalist political economies.

As noted above, scholars have responded to China's dramatic transformation by producing a variety of works attempting to fathom the logic and nature of China's meteoric rise. Intriguingly, few have directly addressed the nature of China's rapid development while consciously and explicitly applying the terms "capitalism" or "capitalist development." Of course, a number of recent works on China's contemporary political economy use the term capitalism, especially in their titles. However, most focus on particular aspects of this transition and fail to capture the bigger historical picture.

An early and defining work is Gordon Redding's *The Spirit of Chinese Capitalism* (1990). This book constitutes the classic conceptualization of a form of Chinese capitalism. Redding chiefly uses a Weberian notion to develop a detailed psychological and organizational ideal-type of Chinese capitalism. However, his focus rests on the Overseas Chinese in Hong Kong, Taiwan, and Southeast Asia. The contemporary PRC contains elements of this ideal-type, but looks quite different overall.[2] A newer work focusing on the PRC is You-tien Hsing's *Making Capitalism in China* (1998). This book provides a snapshot of China's capitalist transition, focusing on the role that transnational networks of Overseas Chinese entrepreneurs play in transforming local political economies, especially in China's southern coastal regions.

A strong reference to capitalism is made in the title of Doug Guthrie's *Dragon in a Three-Piece Suit: The Emergence of Capitalism in China* (1999). Yet, the author's emphasis rests on micro-social phenomena such as changing labor relations and the growth of rational-legal bureaucracies at the firm level. Little is said about the overall logic of China's emergent capitalism, especially the development of capitalist institutions and interests that shape the national political economy.

Another recent work that deals quite directly with the overall nature of China's transition is Yongnian Zheng's *Globalization and State Transformation in China* (2004). Zheng argues that market reforms and the embrace of global capitalism have necessitated Chinese leaders to undertake far-reaching reforms of the state.[3] Most interestingly, the author consciously engages with the fact that China is undertaking capitalist development. He compares the process briefly to the European experience and argues that although China will follow a different trajectory than Europe's capitalist developers, it will have to establish the rule of law to enable effective governance.[4]

The popular business literature has of course been much more explicit in conceptualizing China as capitalist. From Forbes to Businessweek, the fact that China is a capitalist political economy is taken for granted.[5] Our purpose, though, goes beyond the above-mentioned academic expositions and their more popular counterparts. The term capitalism will not be used in a casual manner. To the best of our abilities, it will be envisaged from a decidedly neutral and objective standpoint.

In other words, this volume will employ a capitalist lens to interpret the massive transformations occurring in the contemporary PRC. The application of a capitalist lens, in turn, requires a definition of capitalism that can effectively assess China's recent transformations. Accordingly, I will build on the large volume of both classical and modern conceptualizations of capitalism, but especially on the works of Robert Heilbroner (1985; 1993). Capitalism will be conceived of as a political economy characterized by three elements or dynamics.

First is the drive to accumulate capital, which can only occur if social and cultural infrastructures enable the relentless accumulation of capital. Second is the emergence of market society, denoting that market forces become the central force guiding the allocation of goods and services. Indeed, markets emerge as the social organizing principle by which most of us make our living, since we must "sell" our labor power on the market or engage in entrepreneurship shaped by market competitive forces. The final defining element of capitalism is the rise of capital-owning social strata to positions of social and political influence. As these new social forces gain in prominence, they attempt to restrain the powers of the state. Ultimately, only a "constitutional" state permits a private property rights system to function effectively.

Chapter 2 of this volume will expand more on how the nature and logic of capitalism relates to China's emergent political economy. In that chapter I will further specify the above definition of capitalism. Then I will use this definition as a conceptual measuring stick and apply it to evaluate the progress of China's capitalist transition.

A logical explanation

Since capitalism originated in Europe in the 16th century, it has been regarded chiefly as an outgrowth of Western civilization. However, while the concept of capitalism is undoubtedly Eurocentric in origin, capitalism has become the dominant mode of social organization in the present global order. It has generated an unparalleled increase in living standards in its core economies. And as it spreads to China and beyond, it appears likely to create similar increases in wealth, while also producing stark manifestations of its dark undersides: inequalities, ecological imbalances, and a disruption of long-held practices, values, and beliefs.

Why then has China's transition only casually or in piecemeal fashion been conceived of as capitalist in nature? Since 1978 the Chinese economy has gradually outgrown state ownership and moved to a mixed economic model. Although state firms and investment remain important, the most dynamic parts of the Chinese economy are now powered by private capital, both domestic and foreign. China has further developed a vibrant market economy in which the vast majority of goods and services are allocated by the price mechanism. And as state institutions have escalated their interaction with markets and private capital, a more conducive environment to capital accumulation has emerged. Evidently, China seems to be progressing towards a form of capitalism.

The problem with conceptualizing China as a capitalist political economy therefore rests less with China's national circumstances. While certainly unique, these are quite straightforward. Rather, the crux of the matter lies with how the term capitalism is understood *and* misunderstood. Capitalism can be used to damn or justify almost any imaginable policy choice or social arrangement. Confusion and disorientation are further amplified because comprehending capitalism involves a diversity of social science perspectives and approaches.

As a result, some perceive capitalism to be a misnomer for our present political economies. Reinert and Daastol (1998), for instance, dislike this term because it emphasizes the role of capital over that of ideas and institutions. Moreover, some of the deepest problems lie in ideological preconceptions. On one hand, capitalism is seen by advocates of socialism and its related ideologies as a system to be superseded. On the other, fervent believers in capitalism tend to gloss over the system's dark underside and advocate the omnipotence of market forces and private enterprise. More fundamentally, capitalism itself can hardly be envisioned as a unified ideological construct. While most modern ideologies are somehow associated with capitalism, such as libertarianism, social democracy, conservatism, and fascism, capitalism does not constitute a distinct ideology in itself.

In the case of China, the Chinese Communist Party's (CCP) own predisposition has aggravated these conceptual and ideological muddles. Modern capitalism is by far more complex than the simple picture of class relations that defines the Marxist image. As capitalism has evolved, class distinctions have become blurred with multiple class roles performed by single individuals and the forming of a whole host of "intermediate" classes. As Adam Przeworski (1985: 393) puts it: "The traditional Marxist theory of the structure of class conflict has been exceedingly crude and, I believe, both logically invalid and empirically false."

Perhaps the underlying problem is that we fail to think of the political economy of capitalism as historically exceptional. We just take many of its contemporary facets for granted, concentrating on subsets of its associated problems, such as the functioning of markets or the consolidation of democratic governance. Much social analysis thus misses one valid window on the big picture. Capitalism constitutes a historically unique system to arrange the human existence that emerged after the 16th century. It shapes our present world in the most fundamental ways and should be up and front in social inquiry.

With the collapse of the Soviet Union there will perhaps emerge a neutral space in which to reconsider the essential nature of capitalism.[6] Unquestionably, communism has lost its luster, while socialist precepts have been successfully incorporated into capitalist political economies from Sweden to Singapore. Any pretense at finding an alternative path to supersede the fundamental nature of capitalism must therefore be questioned, although we will need to think seriously about capitalism's interaction with man and nature.

For lack of a better term, capitalism thus conceptualizes the nature and logic of the predominant political economies of our time. Just like feudalism, capitalism should not be conceived of as an ideology but rather as a social system with both its negative and positive attributes. So, whether we like it or not, ". . . there is in fact no viable alternative to capitalism at this stage in world history" (Lippit 2005: 3).

Following these observations, capitalism will be viewed as a purely analytical concept in our endeavors. We are careful, though, to use the term capitalist transition with respect to China. In this manner, we draw attention to the fact that the structure of China's emergent political economy is being forged by an ongoing process, the outcome of which remains indeterminate. China's capitalist transition could conceivably be arrested by internal political imperatives or external shocks.

Even so, viewing China's dramatic international ascent as generated by the forces of capitalism adds explanatory power. It allows us to use historical and comparative materials about other capitalist developers to inform our analysis. Perhaps most importantly, we can use this analytical lens to indicate certain tendencies in China's political economy, therefore shedding light on what China's international ascent portends for our era.

The premise

The premise of our undertaking is straightforward: to explicitly interpret the enormous transformations taking place in China as associated with the same process of capitalist development that shaped the rise of the world's advanced industrial nations, including Japan, Germany, South Korea, and Taiwan. We explore China's capitalist transition, both as a phenomenon and as it impacts vital aspects of China's domestic and foreign policy.

Perhaps one of the most fascinating aspects of China's capitalist transition is that it is empowering domestic and international capital holders to an extent not seen before. In turn, this is conditioning the *modus operandi* of the Chinese party-state. Since the CCP's legitimacy rests in great measure on its ability to foster economic wealth, the leverage of capital holders has increased. The party-state is now partially dependent on the decisions of capital holders (both foreign and domestic) to manage the economy. In fact, if capital holders decide to take their capital out of the PRC, it could directly undermine China's economic prospects. The CCP has therefore been nudged toward recognizing and guarding private property rights, changing China's social, political, and economic environment.

To capture this underlying dynamic, chapters in this volume cover a wide range of topics, striving to provide a comprehensive overview of China's capitalist transition. Unfortunately, space constraints did not allow for the entirety of phenomena to be covered. The interaction of China's capitalist transition with ideational factors (beliefs, values, and ideology), for instance, is not covered in much detail. In addition, several aspects of the socioeconomic and political phenomena unfolding in China are not dealt with directly, including the role of labor and labor markets, the emerging Non-Governmental Organization (NGO) sector, the massive environmental degradation occurring in China, and the degree to which enhanced economic and technological resources influence China's military capabilities.

Diverse perspectives, common threads

To provide different perspectives on China's capitalist transition, chapter writers were selected from unlike backgrounds. Discussions that shaped this volume are therefore of an international and interdisciplinary character, yet focused on two central questions: if we conceive of China as undergoing a capitalist transition, how can we characterize the political economy of China's emergent capitalism? And second, what are the implications of China's emergent capitalism for the country's domestic development and foreign orientation?

These two questions form the fundament of the volume and permeate all chapters. Before the topical chapters, though, Chapter 2 deals with some conceptual issues. This chapter expands on the definition of capitalism rendered above. It then applies this definition as a conceptual yardstick to evaluate China's recent transformations in the political and economic spheres. Chapter 2 thus builds a conceptual starting point that supports the following chapters.

Each of the nine topical chapters that follow serves as a wedge into the institutional and interest formations that are shaping China's emergent capitalism. Since authors come from different disciplines, a variety of materials, viewpoints, and analyses shape these chapters. Each chapter is therefore somewhat unique.

Conceptually, Chapters 3 through 7 all employ institutional lenses, though analytical emphases differ somewhat. Chapter 6 offers a more detailed treatment of how a capitalist institutional lens can be elaborated. Chapters 6 through 8 also home in on the changing relations among China's sociopolitical interests. Chapter 8 especially focuses on structural political change as shaped by changing class relations. Finally, Chapters 9 through 11 use both economic and foreign policy analyses to map China's emerging role in the global capitalist system.

To facilitate the pooling of diverse perspectives, the process of producing this volume aimed at creating an atmosphere of open and frank academic exchange. Chapters were presented at two workshops in August 2004 and 2005 at the East-West Center in Honolulu. During these workshops intense discussions on the nature and logic of capitalism ensued, especially with respect to China's transition. Chapter authors thus were forced to deal head-on with ideological, cultural, and political preconceptions.

Besides analyzing certain aspects of China's capitalist transition, an additional requirement for authors was to include future-oriented perspectives in their conclusions. Major concerns addressed focus on the emerging shape of China's capitalism, China's integration into the global economic order, and the likely effects of China's international ascent on geopolitical balances.

The central feature integrating the variety of materials, insights, and perspectives presented in this volume is a focus on common threads – the narrative structure of China's capitalist transition. These threads map the forces of change, points of contention, and emerging dynamics that China's capitalist transition is generating.

The first thread is, as Chapter 2 outlines more precisely, the incomplete nature of China's capitalist transition. Most chapters speak in one way or another of the partial nature of market reforms (Chapters 7 and 8) or the blurred borderlines between corporate and government sectors (Chapters 3 through 6). Clearly, China is a political economy in transition, shaped by two fundamental logics that clash: a state dominant logic emphasizing political control and a capitalist logic emphasizing market competition and commercial success.

The interaction of these two logics generates a host of hybrid, intermediary, and often internally contradictory institutions. This is perhaps most clearly expressed in Chapter 7, which analyzes the tensions between political and commercial interests permeating China's media institutions. The fundamental contradictions and dualities characterizing China's emergent political economy also raise several crucial questions. For instance, how can the world's fastest growing economy cope with deteriorating socioeconomic polarization? More fundamentally, how can a burgeoning capitalism be reconciled with China's imperial legacy and more recent Leninist history of state dominance? These issues will be taken up in more detail in the concluding chapter (Chapter 12).

The second thread permeating the narrative of China's capitalist transition is that China is undoubtedly developing a unique form of capitalism. China is blending standard Western features with aspects of its historical and socialist heritage, combining state-led development with bottom-up network capitalism, and harmonizing a highly internationalized export regime with a relatively limiting internal trading system. In this manner, China is contributing to the generation of new capitalist institutions domestically and globally. For example, Chapters 3 through 5 all argue that China is rapidly melding global capitalist practices with China's institutional legacy. The outcome: new modes of Chinese management and new types of Chinese multinationals that are building impressive managerial and technological capabilities.

China has therefore developed specific institutional features and organizational structures that are beginning to constitute a new form of capitalism. Part of the uniqueness of China's emergent capitalism stems from the combination of cutting-edge capitalist practices with the underdeveloped nature of China's domestic economy. Another aspect is the unique nature of China's political economy, combining a dominant Leninist state with vibrant socioeconomic change. Indeed, as Chapter 8 argues, China does not seem to follow any historical model of political development under capitalism. Rather, China's capitalist transition has been initiated, guided, and controlled by an ideologically anticapitalist party-state.

The third thread permeating chapters is an intense concern with how China's unique form of capitalism will impact the globe's economics and geopolitics. Undoubtedly, if China's transition continues to evolve, it will reshape our era. Already China has at a very early stage in its transition produced internationally competitive corporations (Chapter 5). It has also emerged as a formidable trading power, one which is still far from reaching its full potential (Chapter 9). And China's capitalist transition will continue to deepen the country's energy import dependence, necessitating more active Chinese foreign policies to manage the geopolitical environment and avoid conflicts over energy resources (Chapter 10).

Ultimately, all chapters convey some unease about the future of China's capitalist transition and its impact on the international system. As Chapter 11 argues, China's domestic transition must not automatically lead to a liberal polity with a moderate foreign policy orientation. Ironically, China's unrelenting rise is becoming one of China's greatest challenges. As an emerging power, China is starting to "threaten" established geopolitical balances, thus reshaping China's own geopolitical environment.

Therefore, China's incomplete internal transition combined with China's escalating impact on the international environment poses crucial challenges for our world. Chapters 3 through 11 grapple with various facets of this challenge. Each comes from a unique perspective to provide critical insights. The concluding chapter (Chapter 12) will take up these three threads and attempt to shed more light on the future scenarios that might define China's emergent political economy.

Overview of the book

Part 1 of this volume begins with the two introductory chapters and sets the conceptual stage for the remainder of the book. Each of the following three parts constitutes a distinct field of analysis. These are linked by the three narrative threads presented above. Part 2 concentrates on China's corporate sector. After all, capitalist development is first and foremost characterized by the emergence of internationally competitive firms, including institutional infrastructures, such as innovation and financial systems that support these. Part 3 then concentrates on the dynamics unfolding in China's domestic political economy, with a special focus on how new capital-oriented social interests interact with China's dominant state. The final field of analysis directs its attention to China's enmeshment in the global capitalist system, providing three different perspectives and one concluding chapter.

Chapter 3 by Dieter Ernst and Barry Naughton starts with a macro-analysis of China's existing industrial capitalism, distinguishing three tiers of firms: large firms that remain mainly in the hands of the state; medium-sized firms that are hybrids and are starting to form the backbone of China's international competitiveness; and small firms that are mostly private. The chapter proceeds to show how China's information technology firms are upgrading their capabilities while embedded in global production and innovation networks. It ends by concentrating on one of China's foremost technology success stories: the telecommunications equipment maker Huawei.

Chapter 4 by Wei Zhang, Jian Gao, Steven White, and Paul Vega zooms further in on China's new technology firms. It analyzes how these firms are being supported by the remarkably rapid development of a Chinese venture capital system. Although this system follows in process the US model, it is in its practical implementation undergoing major modifications to fit China's transitional circumstances. A dynamic picture of China's evolving financial system emerges that is not reflected in the more common analyses of China's staid state-owned banking system. Perhaps most importantly, the authors hold that the interaction between foreign and domestic management systems, including the influence of the Chinese state, will lead to a period of mutual adaptation and evolution that holds the potential to create a uniquely modern form of Chinese management.

Chapter 5, the final chapter in Part 2, elucidates a key question facing the global economy: will China produce internationally competitive indigenous corporations? Peter Williamson and Ming Zeng clearly answer this question in the affirmative. They note how innovative business strategies have allowed Chinese firms to establish multinational operations that are rapidly approaching world levels of competitiveness. Their analysis also draws attention to the challenges ahead for advanced industrial countries and the multinational corporations domiciled in these. They warn the world to look out for a competitive threat emanating from China that will force existing multinationals to view Chinese competitors as a new breed of partners. They also draw attention to an environment of increased frictions that is emerging as Chinese corporations move up the value-added ladder and directly threaten jobs and profits in the developed world.

Part 2 provides a rather positive outlook for China's corporate sector, noting that China's transition is producing respectable amounts of innovation and international competitiveness. This somewhat rosy picture finds its contrast in Part 3. Analyses here concentrate on how new social interests and institutions are interacting with existing ones to reshape China's emergent political economy.

Chapter 6 starts off with a big picture analysis that delineates the unique institutional contours of China's emergent capitalism. Coming from a historical institutionalist perspective, I argue that China's emergent capitalism is being shaped by three distinct forces: 1,000 years of petty capitalism that has sown the seeds for vibrant networks of small capitalists, many of which are transforming China's political economy bottom-up; the massive influence of the "new global capitalism" that is accelerating China's participation in the world economy; and the role of China's dominant Leninist state in initiating, managing, and sustaining the process of capitalist development from above. The chapter ends by drawing attention to a certain duality in China's emergent political economy that possesses historical antecedents. This duality encompasses a state dominant mode from above juxtaposed with an increasingly globalized and highly networked capitalist mode from below. This raises the question of whether historical tendencies will hamper China's capitalist transition, especially the establishment of the rule of law and a fully fledged private property rights system.

Following this broad treatment of China's emergent political economy, Chapter 7 focuses on a sector that stands at the crossroads of China's polity and economy: the media sector. Maryanne Kivlehan-Wise argues in this chapter that China's media sector provides a fascinating snapshot of how capitalist dynamics and the Leninist nature of China's party-state interact. Her picture is one of continuous cat-and-mouse games. The party and its propaganda arm want to keep tight reigns on media enterprises in terms of content, while editors and managers of newspapers want to maximize revenue in an increasingly competitive market place. Newspapers therefore try to push the limits of what is permissible, since this is the only way to retain the loyalty of readers hungry for new content and information. The party-state, however, has so far kept the upper hand in this game. It has created an atmosphere of self-censorship and used a quintessentially capitalist innovation, the media conglomerate, to further its aim of information control.

In Chapter 8, An Chen pointedly asks "Does Capitalism Push China toward Democracy?" His answer is a resounding no! By analyzing the connection between China's emergent capitalism and the country's prospects for democracy, An Chen argues that China's present form of capitalist development hinders democratic prospects. In fact, the alignment of class interests in China creates a distinct possibility for the polarization of social interests and therefore future political instability. This is because the emerging interests of capital-holders and professionals (the bourgeoisie and middle classes) are aligning themselves closely with the Chinese party-state out of fear that broader democracy could threaten their privileged status and hard-won wealth. China's middle classes are therefore unlikely to become a force for a peaceful democratic transition, perpetuating high degrees of social inequality.

Part 4 takes the reader to China's rapid immersion in the global capitalist system. In Chapter 9, Christopher Edmonds, Sumner LaCroix, and Yao Li provide a pertinent overview analyzing the various aspects of China's stunning ascent to become the world's third largest trading nation. The economic survey they present finds that China trades quite evenly with the world, yet considerably more than would be expected for an economy of its size and level of development. They also distinguish certain parallels between China's rise as an international trading power and the experiences of earlier East Asian capitalist developers, such as South Korea and Japan. Indeed, historical comparisons show that China still has a long way to go in terms of its export boom. This suggests that China's trade performance and policies will exert increasing influence on how the world's trading regime evolves.

Chapter 10 homes in on an aspect of China's capitalist transition that has enormous global repercussions: China's increasing obsession with energy security. Kang Wu and Ian Storey present a comprehensive analysis of China's transformation from an energy exporting nation to a major energy consumer. They elaborate the reasons for why energy security has risen to the top of the Chinese government's agenda, especially the fact that China is faced with ever increasing imports of oil and gas, most of which are likely to come from the Middle East. In terms of the globe's future international relations, the authors note that China's capitalist transition will continue to increase the importance of securing energy supplies for China. At present, though, it is too early to tell whether China's need for energy will entail greater cooperation or competition in the global system. Evidence of both scenarios is apparent. Clearly, the role of energy security in China's foreign relations will remain highly prominent, enmeshing China further with the global system.

Chapter 11 returns to a more expansive perspective. Coming from an insider's viewpoint, Yinhong Shi raises considerable doubts as to whether China's capitalist transition will lead to a more liberal polity and more stable international relations. He points out that the dramatic increase of China's economic strength, diplomatic influence, and military capabilities are likely to bring worries to neighboring states. The United States and Japan, for example, are feeling strategically "threatened" by China and the specter of a huge and dangerous "Japan Problem" is arising. In short, Yinhong Shi provides a level-headed analysis of the foreign policy implications of China's capitalist transition, arguing that changes in China's foreign policy orientation might not be auspicious for the smooth continuation of the country's capitalist development.

The concluding chapter (Chapter 12) rounds out the volume. I ponder here the common threads that tie the chapters together and form the narrative of China's capitalist transition. I then ask what future scenarios might face China's emergent capitalism. Certainly, changes of the magnitude generated by China's international ascent will have considerable repercussions for the rest of the world, including a changed competitive landscape for multinational firms and considerable challenges in the realm of global energy.

Ultimately, though, the most crucial challenges lie in China's domestic political transition. Will capitalism in the dragon's lair create a more liberal Chinese polity? Will China as a result become a moderate and "internationalized" global player? Or will China at some point challenge the global status quo, perhaps triggered by a failure in its domestic evolution? Certainly, China's distinct political, cultural, and historical legacies make the outcome of its capitalist transition indeterminate. Chapter 12 will therefore contemplate both the opportunities and challenges that China's capitalist transition is generating for the future.

Our collaborative endeavor in this book strives to present a big picture analysis of China's massive transformation that is historically and comparatively grounded. Chapters are linked by common threads, grafting a variety of perspectives and materials into a lucid whole. By understanding the fundamental tendencies in and consequences of China's capitalist development, this effort hopes to elucidate "The China Impact" – the tectonic changes in the global firmament that are being generated by China's international ascent. However, before we proceed to the empirical studies, some conceptual thinking is necessary.

So far, the fact that China is capitalist has either been denied, taken for granted, or only indirectly addressed. Drawing out the trends inherent in China's emergent political economy, though, necessitates a detailed treatment of the fundamental nature of capitalism as it relates to China's transition. We must ask: how does the concept of capitalism relate to China's emergent political economy?

Notes

1 For more on these conceptualizations see Chapter 6 in this volume.
2 Another seminal work analyzing the formation of Chinese capitalism, especially among the Overseas Chinese, is the collection by Hamilton (2006).
3 Another recent work putting forward a similar argument is by Yang (2004).
4 There are several other books employing the term capitalism with respect to China in their titles, such as Gallagher (2005). Her work ties into a debate in the field of political science asking why China has developed capitalism but not democracy. See also Tsai (2005) and the contribution by An Chen in this volume.
5 One recent work in the business literature is Woetzel (2003).
6 Very gingerly, such a neutral space is emerging in the social sciences. Analytical work that views capitalism in an objective and neutral manner as the macro-structure shaping the institutions of our era is becoming more common. This literature will be discussed in more detail in Chapter 2.

References

Baum, R. and Shevchenko, A. (1999) "The 'State of the State'," in M. Goldman and R. MacFarquhar (eds.) *The Paradox of China's Post-Mao Reforms*, Cambridge, MA and London: Harvard University Press, pp. 333–360.

Gallagher, M.E. (2005) *Contagious Capitalism: Globalization and the Politics of Labor in China*, Princeton, NJ: Princeton University Press.

Guthrie, D. (1999) *Dragon in a Three-Piece Suit: The Emergence of Capitalism in China*, Princeton, NJ: Princeton University Press.

Hamilton, G.G. (2006) *Commerce and Capitalism in Chinese Societies*, New York: Routledge.

Heilbroner, R.L. (1985) *The Nature and Logic of Capitalism*, New York and London: W.W. Norton.

—— (1993) *21st Century Capitalism*, New York and London: W.W. Norton.

Hsing, Y.T. (1998) *Making Capitalism in China*, New York: Oxford.

Lippit, V.D. (2005) *Capitalism*, London and New York: Routledge.

Przeworski. A. (1985) "Marxism and Rational Choice," *Politics & Society,* 14(4): 379–409.

Redding, S.G. (1990) *The Spirit of Chinese Capitalism*, Berlin: Walter de Gruyter.

Reinert, E.S. and Daastol, A.M. (1998) *Production Capitalism vs. Financial Capitalism – Symbiosis and Parasitism. An Evolutionary Perspective*, Mimeo, Oslo. September 3–4.

Tsai, K.S. (2005) "Capitalists Without a Class: Political Diversity Among Private Entrepreneurs in China," *Comparative Political Studies*, 38(9): 1130–1158.

Woetzel, J.R. (2003) *Capitalist China: Strategies for a Revolutionized Economy*, Singapore: John Wiley & Sons.

Yang, D.L. (2004) *Remaking the Chinese Leviathan: Market Transition and the Politics of Governance in China*, Stanford: Stanford University Press.

Zheng, Y. (2004) *Globalization and State Transformation in China*, Cambridge: Cambridge University Press.

2 Reflections on capitalism and China's emergent political economy

Christopher A. McNally

The first question that springs to mind when analyzing China as a capitalist political economy is whether China can by any means be termed such. In fact, when I recently mentioned to a US government official that China is undergoing a capitalist transition, he retorted that China was hardly capitalist since the state and state-owned enterprises continue to hold a central place in the People's Republic of China's (PRC) economy. The view espoused here was one of "free markets" and "free enterprise" forming the basis of capitalism, a view that would set China apart from how capitalism is purportedly practiced in the West.

A related discussion emerged during the two workshops that led to the production of this volume. One European advisor had strong doubts about the use of the term capitalism, feeling that it carried too much political and ideological baggage. Several Chinese colleagues had even stronger misgivings. As their European colleague, they felt that this term was politically suspect and shied away from using it due to the connotations it carries under Marxist interpretations. More importantly, they feared that they might encounter problems back home in China, where advocating that the contemporary PRC constitutes a capitalist political economy could have repercussions for their professional well-being.

These discussions made clear that the relationship between China's current conditions and the political economy of capitalism needed to be clarified. So far, though, most studies in comparative political economy, especially the varieties of capitalism framework, have concentrated on the institutions of advanced capitalism as practiced in North America, Europe, and Japan.[1] Their applicability to China is thus limited.

In addition, an understanding of capitalism that can be fruitfully applied to China must be as free as possible of ideological precepts. The ruling Chinese Communist Party (CCP) officially holds that China is not developing into a capitalist system. As a result, ideological factors undoubtedly tend to obfuscate the conception of China as a new emerging form of capitalism. In this respect, one advisor suggested that we just replace the term "capitalism" with "market economy," therefore avoiding all discussion about whether China can be termed capitalist or not. However, capitalism encompasses much more than just a market economic system, a point to which I will return shortly.

The purpose of this chapter is to delve deeper into the general nature and logic of capitalism and in this manner provide a benchmark for evaluating China's emergent political economy. Put differently, this chapter will work toward a working definition of capitalism that is both fundamental and precise. This definition can then serve as a measuring stick to judge the progress of China's capitalist transition and elucidate what some of its basic properties are. In the conclusion I will further suggest how applying the capitalist lens can provide new insights on the present and future of China's monumental transformation.

Conceptualizing capitalism

The workshop discussions showed that we must attain a better understanding of capitalist systems before we can effectively apply the capitalist lens to China. Given China's unique national circumstances such a conceptualization of capitalism must be sufficiently encompassing to capture all forms of capitalism across time and space, yet also sufficiently precise to delineate what exactly sets capitalist systems apart from other historical formations. In such a working definition capitalism must also be viewed as a purely analytical concept that eschews ideological emphases.

Over the past 500 years, capitalist systems moved from being minor political economies at the fringes of European civilization to unleashing the most momentous social transformations in human history. Nonetheless, specifying the exact nature of capitalism remains problematic. Definitions of capitalism remain influenced by ideology and generally fall along a spectrum from right to left. On the right or neoliberal side, capitalism represents the "organization of the bulk of economic activity through private enterprise operation in a free market" (Friedman 2002: 4). This conception expresses the notion popular in the United States of the core characteristics of capitalism: private enterprise and "free" markets, while the state only acts as a "night watchman" to enforce economic rules and protect private property.

A more centrist view defines capitalism "as a system in which the means of production, in private hands, are employed to create a profit, some of which is reinvested to increase profit-generating capacity" (McVey 1992: 8). Again private enterprise is up front, but Ruth McVey, a political economist working on Southeast Asia, stresses the expansive nature of capital – private persons must be given opportunities to accumulate capital to reinvest and generate more capital.

On the left, markets and capital accumulation retreat as the central features of capitalism and class relations – the "social relations of production" – emerge instead. Dudley Dillard provides a classical definition of capitalism as inspired from the left: "Fundamental to any system called capitalist are the relations between private owners of nonpersonal means of production (land, mines, industrial plants, etc., collectively known as capital) and free but capital-less workers, who sell their labor services to employers" (Dillard 1992: 85). Dillard's ensuing analysis on the development of capitalism pays attention to a variety of factors, such as the emergence of long distance trade and the monetization of Europe as gold and silver arrived from the new world. Nonetheless, Dillard's definition emphasizes class relations between those with and without capital. It omits market institutions, the pluralization of social forces, and the central role of the state.

All of these three definitions capture popular impressions, but only partially explain the underlying political economy of capitalist systems. Fortunately, over the past years several endeavors have transpired that attempt to shed the ideological baggage surrounding capitalism to arrive at an objective understanding of its properties. Perhaps inspired by the demise of the debate on socialism versus capitalism after the Cold War ended, capitalism in these works is perceived as the underlying socioeconomic system shaping our era. Not unlike the term feudalism, it represents a generic mode of social organization in history.

I will here briefly mention three recent undertakings along these lines, all published in 2005, and then move on to discuss the insightful work of Robert Heilbroner published in the 1980s and 1990s. All of these works attempt to cross ideological battle lines, methodological approaches, and conceptual borders to gain a deeper and more comprehensive understanding of the socioeconomic system we term capitalism. They hopefully herald a future in which capitalism is seen as a type of political economy that can spawn a variety of social arrangements, alternatively incorporating the tenets of socialism, liberalism, conservatism, etc.

In *The Economic Sociology of Capitalism*, Victor Nee and Richard Swedberg (2005a) present a collaborative endeavor to combine insights from institutional economics with those generated by the "new economic sociology." This edited volume constitutes an important attempt at crossing disciplinary boundaries "to advance social science understanding of the distinctive features and dynamics of capitalist economic institutions" (Nee and Swedberg 2005b: xxxv). Capitalism is conceived as a system based on two crucial social mechanisms: "*exchange* and *the feedback of profit into production*" (Swedberg 2005: 7; italics in original) with the market as "*the* central institution in capitalism" (Swedberg 2005: 12; italics in original). While the editors emphasize exploring processes of production, distribution, and consumption, the role of state elites and of conflicts among social interest groups remain largely unexplored.

The edited volume by David Coates (2005a), *Varieties of Capitalism, Varieties of Approaches*, takes the same aim as the Nee and Swedberg volume by attempting to cross disciplinary boundaries. It focuses on mainstream economics, comparative political economy centered on the "new institutionalism," and radical political economy using theoretical frameworks that are predominantly Marxist in origin. Perhaps the most interesting insight is how much deep-seated disciplinary cleavages have hindered a comprehensive understanding of capitalism. Coates notes how each discipline produces its own language and how each of these languages comes, "as languages always do in the social sciences, with considerable theoretical baggage buried inside it" (Coates 2005b: 4). Coates' most fundamental argument is that boundary-crossing creative synthesis will be required to attain a systematic understanding of the contemporary workings of capitalism.

One work that attempts this is Victor D. Lippit's *Capitalism* (2005). Lippit offers an objective and stimulating view of capitalism, especially its dark underside of increasing economic inequalities and environmental degradation. Coming from the tradition of radical political economy, Lippit consciously takes insights from Marxist thought, including an understanding of capitalism's core contradictions and the "grasp of capitalism as a distinctive mode of production and social formation" (Lippit 2005: 15). Nonetheless, he also notes how neither "the labor theory of value nor the falling rate of profit theory is convincing" (Lippit 2005: 16). Perhaps most importantly, Lippit does not succumb to a rigid and deterministic view of class struggle the way many followers of Marx have. In his words:

> Since there is no viable alternative to capitalism, . . ., and since the capitalist system is likely to be with us for several more centuries at least, my analysis of capitalism is intended to promote thinking about the dynamics and contradictions of the system with a view to enhancing its positive features and ameliorate its most destructive and socially reprehensible ones.
>
> (Lippit 2005: 4)

The above just represents a snapshot of new efforts by economists, sociologists, institutional political economists, and radical political economists to grasp the nature of capitalism. In fact, any comprehensive analysis of the fundamental properties of capitalist systems would have to incorporate the works of classical political economy. Space constraints do not allow for this here. Rather, I will build on the insights of the late Robert Heilbroner (1985; 1993). In these works Heilbroner masterfully distilled the insights of Smith, Marx, Schumpeter, and others to arrive at a fundamental, yet precise, conception of capitalism.

Heilbroner emphasizes three central elements that define the nature and logic of capitalism: the drive to accumulate capital; the emergence of market society; and the bifurcation of secular authority. All three of these elements are by nature dynamic and can therefore be applied to assess the character and development of China's political economy. I first introduce these three elements in more detail. In the next section, I apply each of these three elements to the contemporary PRC, thus conceptually "measuring" to what extent China is undergoing a transition to capitalism.

The first defining feature of capitalism is that it unleashes a distinctive drive to extract and accumulate capital by humans. This drive becomes "the major organizing basis for sociopolitical life" (Heilbroner 1985: 143). Since capital is intrinsically dynamic, it can change its form from commodity into money and then back again (cf. Marx's M-C-M'). This dynamic nature of capital engenders a continuous process characterized by the repetitive extraction and reinvestment of capital, a process that unleashes new productive forces or as Heilbroner contends: "Capitalism is a system organized to search for, and to seize on, whatever technological and organizational changes offer profitable chances for expansion" (Heilbroner 1993: 134–135). This in turn fosters social, economic, and political progress, one of capitalism's unique historical properties (see Heilbroner 1993: 30–37).

The second element of capitalism concerns the structuring role of markets. Unmistakably, the first function of markets "is to allocate labor to those tasks that society wants filled" (Heilbroner 1993: 99), a process that cannot take place in a society that controls the flow of labor. Markets are also indispensable to channel other factors of production. Some of the most potent opportunities to accumulate capital result from the establishment of markets for land and financial capital. Most importantly, the market system must dominate the functioning of the economy and be able to create competitive pressures *via* the price mechanism. Markets thus constitute the necessary organizing principle of capitalism, but

> capitalism is a much larger and more complex entity than the market system we use as its equivalent . . . The market system is the principal means of binding and coordinating the whole, but markets are not the source of capitalism's energies nor of its distinctive bifurcation of authority.
>
> (Heilbroner 1993: 96)

The final element of capitalism is seldom explicated, even if it is crucial. Capitalism can only emerge with the rise of a "capital-oriented class . . . from a subordinate position within society to a position of leverage" (Heilbroner 1985: 41). Capitalism thus differs from earlier sociopolitical regimes, such as those based on religious conviction, military force, or a fixed status system.

One cannot overstate this central element of capitalism. Historically, merchant classes existed at the pleasure of state elites. Capitalism could therefore only emerge as state elites saw it in their interest to support the expansion of capital-oriented classes.[2] This in turn entailed some political recognition of capital, such as the freeing of factor markets, the curtailing of predatory government behavior, and ultimately, the defense of private property rights. Capital must therefore arise with the goodwill of state elites, but, as it expands, it "becomes increasingly capable of defying, or of existing 'above,' the state" (Heilbroner 1985: 94). The state comes to rely on capital for the provisioning of revenue and the vibrancy of economic growth within its territory.

The historical reasons for capital's political ascent are complex, involving cultural, social, political, and economic factors. Nonetheless, the underlying logic is quite straightforward. Although the seeds of capitalist production emerged in many world regions, only Europe succeeded. In China, for example, merchants grew rich and could bribe their way to political influence. However, unless they became landed officials, their wealth remained at risk of confiscation by public officials (Jones 2003: xxx). The nature of China's empire made it all but impossible for Chinese merchants to withdraw their capital and move to more accommodating environments. Chinese state elites therefore restrained the power of merchant classes.

Conversely, one of the crucial ingredients for the emergence of capitalism lay in Europe's political fragmentation and growing interstate competition (Jones 2003; North 1981). While Europe possessed long distance market networks and common cultural norms that aided the expansion of market forces, Europe's political decentralization engendered increasing interstate competition. Since this competition took the form of constantly changing and ever more expensive warfare, state elites required escalating amounts of finance. The result: state elites granted a rival social stratum – capital – political space in return for greater tax revenue. Due to Europe's fragmented political order, capitalists could also move capital to territories that offered higher returns and lower risks, engendering institutional competition among and within political units. Two simultaneous dynamics unfolded: the emergence of an economic realm that fostered the expansion of capital accumulation; and the evolution of the modern European nation-state system (Mann 1986; Tilly 1992).

The ascendance of European capital triggered a historically unique arrangement: the bifurcation of secular authority. As commodity flows grew and market forces expanded, entrepreneurs took over the major influencing role in allocating goods and services. The power structures of "the state" and "the economy" became different realms, each with its own logic, yet a need to coexist in the same territory. "What we do not ordinarily bear in mind is that this duality of realms, with its somewhat smudgy boundaries, has no counterpart in noncapitalist societies" (Heilbroner 1993: 69).

In other words, capital survives in a mixed state of independence from and dependence on state power. Views of the capitalist system as being based solely on private capital and markets are therefore misconceived. Although the state's full economic power remains in the background during peacetime, it represents a key force shaping capitalist accumulation. As Douglas North (1998: 13) maintains, ". . . the search for efficient economic organization leads us to political organization, since it is the polity that defines and enforces the economic rules of the game."

Another key point to note is that the bifurcation of secular authority not only benefits capital. The state also experiences an expansion of its authority into new realms. For example, the monetization of the economy creates opportunities for increased taxation, in turn giving the state greater financial resources to expand its authority nationally and internationally. Perhaps most importantly, capital to thrive seeks reconstituted and expanding state power. As Andrew Gamble (1994) has argued, a free economy requires a strong state. Even in the United Kingdom's antistatist Thatcher years the revival of market forces tended to increase state regulation.

To sum up, three central elements distinguish capitalist systems from earlier social systems. First, capital must be able to expand in the continuous process of investment, extraction, reinvestment, and further extraction. The motivating dynamic of capitalism therefore rests on "the driving need to extract wealth from the productive activities of society in the form of capital" (Heilbroner 1985: 33). Second, this condition can only be attained when markets constitute the organizing principle of the economy. The free flow of capital and fierce competition are necessary selection mechanisms, engendering what Schumpeter aptly termed "cycles of creative destruction." Finally, the rise of capitalists to both economic *and* political prominence constitutes the sociopolitical turning point for the emergence of capitalism. With the growth of capital-owning social strata a fairly autonomous, self-directing realm of the economy transpires, bolstered by capitalists' fundamental power to withdraw capital from use if returns are insufficient or risks too high.

In this conception of capitalism, the role of the state and its relation to economic forces play a decisive role. As the productive and financial resources controlled by capital expand, they tend to circumscribe the hitherto absolute authority of the state. Indeed, the relatively autonomous economic realm that characterizes capitalism can only occur with "the recognition of clear 'constitutional' constraints on the power of the state to violate private space of the individual or to commandeer his or her property" (Heilbroner 1985: 89).

Some might see these three elements as omitting what the Marxist tradition views as the central element of capitalism: its unique "social relations of production" centered on the accumulation of the means of production (materials, land, tools, etc.) into the hands of a few capitalists; and the transformation of human labor into wage labor. Individual laborers lose their own means of production, which in turn exposes them to the manipulations of capitalists seeking to maximize profits. Consequently, labor's contribution to production is undervalued, triggering class struggles over the "economic surplus."

While this characterization of the capitalist mode of production expresses one important contradiction inherent in the system, it should be understood as produced by the three fundamental dynamics depicted above. The drive to accumulate capital, the emergence of market society, and the bifurcation of secular authority set in motion a set of social transformations, including the institutionalization of a broad range of social relations and organizations. Yes, wage labor and capital become two major classes under capitalism that are often in conflict, but the plurality of social interests generated by capitalist development is much broader. In fact, as capitalism develops in the 21st century, human capital (the knowledge, skills, and creativity embedded in humans) is gaining increasing currency. Wage labor is thus stratified into an array of classes, ranging from skilled knowledge workers to non-skilled "burger flippers."

China as a capitalist political economy

Capitalism is certainly one of the most difficult and problematic terms in the social sciences, not least because it captures the political economy of modernity that we hope to understand. The three elements of capitalism introduced above might therefore not satisfy all readers. Nonetheless, these elements provide an essential and precise definition of capitalism, reflecting how capitalism's driving force is embedded in human nature (the drive to accumulate capital), acts to intensify and expand market institutions as they become a central part of the human existence (the emergence of market society), and leads to a historically unique power arrangement where two separate yet mutually dependent elites rule (the bifurcation of secular authority).

Due to the dynamic nature of these three elements, they can serve as a conceptual yardstick to assess China's transformation into a capitalist political economy. Each element offers an opportunity to see China's thirty years of reform and opening up through the capitalist lens. Indeed, they allow us to relate what likely constitutes the early 21st century's most important historical phenomenon – China's rapid international ascent – to other instances of capitalist development.

China's drive to accumulate capital

The process of reform and opening up unleashed by Deng Xiaoping after 1978 started a gradual but accelerating process of capital accumulation. Estimates put deposits with financial institutions in China at 34.2 trillion *yuan* by the end of 2006, while foreign exchange reserves with the People's Bank of China were estimated to reach over US$1 trillion at that time (*China Economic Quarterly* 2006: 7). China thus moved from being a country characterized by capital scarcity to one with abundant capital in less than thirty years. How could this happen?

During the first phase of reforms rural households acted as the catalysts in China's drive to accumulate capital. Agricultural reforms triggered a rise in agricultural productivity which allowed farmers to increase their savings. The share of household savings in national income almost tripled between

1978 and 1982 from 4 percent to 11 percent (Naughton 1995: 142). These increased savings provided much needed funds to state financial institutions, allowing entrepreneurial local governments to invest in a manifold of government-guided ventures. In fact, this represents an extraordinary feature in China's development. Local officials did not appropriate or squander newly accumulated capital in conspicuous consumption. Rather, a powerful set of incentives drove local cadres to invest in industrial projects.

Deng's reforms granted greater autonomy to local economic actors, a process that rapidly evolved into economic and political decentralization. Local officials thus attained considerable political space for economic experimentation. At the same time, local government units received decreasing amounts of financial support from higher levels, forcing them to look for new sources of revenue. Finally, local economic performance emerged as the principal yardstick to evaluate local cadre performance under the Communist Party's *nomenklatura* system (Edin 2003; Huang 1996). These three developments prompted local cadres to use the capital accumulated by rural savings to expand and start local industrial ventures. In rural areas many of these ventures were Township and Village Enterprises (TVEs), which became the dynamos of China's light industrial boom in the late 1980s and early 1990s.

Another set of reforms during this period added extra fuel to capital accumulation. China's pricing structure was gradually liberalized; the management of state-owned enterprises (SOEs) given greater autonomy and incentives to maximize profits; and foreign trade and investment allowed to enter sections of the domestic economy. Taken together these reforms set in motion cycles of induced reforms, where each small step at liberalization created pressures for further liberalization.

In fact, as the state's monopoly over industry eased, TVEs were able to enter markets hitherto protected for the benefit of state firms. This at first produced super-profits for TVEs but then gradually intensified competition, hurting both SOE and TVE profitability (Naughton 1992). Especially during the first half of the 1990s, continued industrial expansion created overcapacity and ruthless competition. The profitability of local industries deteriorated and local governments were confronted with fiscal crises. As a result, local governments undertook a range of reforms, most involving some form of partial or full privatization of TVEs and small SOEs (Unger 2002).

During this process the private sector's superior economic contribution and lower draw on financial resources greatly accelerated its development. Capital accumulation moved from state entrepreneurial ventures to private entrepreneurship. As Garnaut and Song (2004: 2) put it, "The success of the private sector in a regulatory environment overwhelmingly geared to the requirements of state-owned enterprises is remarkable."

As private firms grew in economic importance, their regulatory environment improved as well. The introduction of China's first Company Law in 1994 opened new avenues to ascertain private ownership by making the corporate form of a limited liability corporation available. Private firms began to rapidly increase in number and size, while moving into new industrial and commercial sectors.

Changes in China's openness to foreign trade and investment further accelerated the development of private firms. Political decentralization combined with strong incentives to maximize local growth created highly entrepreneurial local leaders that circumvented central rules in feverish efforts to establish global linkages (Zweig 2002). Especially along China's eastern seaboard Overseas Chinese entrepreneurs cooperated with TVEs and other enterprises, using them as convenient low-cost export platforms. Following the gradual privatization of TVEs and small local SOEs in the mid- to late-1990s, a highly internationalized private sector emerged in Chinese seaboard provinces.

Although Chinese government data are sketchy on the contribution of the private sector to Gross Domestic Product (GDP), Xiaolu Wang was able to estimate the contribution of domestic and foreign private firms to Chinese GDP at about 50 percent in 1999 (Wang 2004: 25–26). If including collective enterprises, many of which can be safely assumed to be operating as quasi-private firms, this contribution to GDP rises to two thirds. Overall, privatization has been very widespread in agriculture, industry, construction, retail trade, and road transport. However, it lags in producer goods industries and in the service sector, especially finance.

All told, much of the rapid growth of the Chinese economy during the reform era has been driven by the non-state sector and especially private firms (Wang 2004: 26). The gradual shift from state entrepreneurship to private entrepreneurship corresponds to earlier instances of capitalist development. In Meiji era, for example, the state served during the 1870s as the principal entrepreneur, manager, and financier of modern industry, only to sell most government-established factories to private capitalists during the retrenchment of the 1880s (Duus 1976).

Due to China's large size and developmental gaps, the shift to private entrepreneurship in capital accumulation has emerged quite unevenly, creating widely differing local political economies.[3] For example, many government officials engage in predatory behavior to extract exorbitant fees and fines from the peasantry and small business in China's vast agrarian hinterland and underdeveloped western regions (Bernstein and Lu 2003). Private entrepreneurship is thus stifled. Conversely, along the eastern seaboard and in "suburban" sections bordering China's major cities, some local governments have moved away from direct entrepreneurship to effectively support the private sector. Local officials here employ indirect levers to promote private firms, such as financial incentives and industrial parks tailor-made to the needs of certain industries (Blecher and Shue 2001; Unger and Chan 1999).

Deng Xiaoping's reforms initiated a gradual but accelerating process of capital accumulation. This process is being sustained by the extraordinary vibrancy and dynamism of China's entrepreneurs, even if these are frequently aligned with local officials and/or state firms. And although uneven throughout the country, capital accumulation has transformed the face of China's political economy, nudging it along the path of a capitalist transition.

The emergence of market society

The emergence of a market economy has been perhaps the most widely noted aspect of China's transition. A Chinese study undertaken by Beijing Normal University (2003) reflects how the price mechanism has emerged to allocate the majority of goods and services in China. Government control of prices decreased from 141 items in 1992 to only 13 items in 2001, while the economic value of goods traded with price controls decreased for retail goods from 5.6 percent in 1992 to 2.7 percent in 2001; for agricultural goods from 10.3 percent in 1992 to 2.7 percent in 2001; and for producer goods from 19.8 percent in 1992 to 9.5 percent in 2001. For all matters and purposes, the central planning system has ceased to exist, although the government continues to issue guidance plans for a few select industrial goods (e.g. wood, gold, tobacco, salt, and gas).

Viewed from this perspective, China is a market economy. This fact, though, remains heavily debated. In international trade politics the European Union, the United States, and Japan hold that China's economy cannot be considered a market economy, while countries such as Singapore, Malaysia, and Thailand recognize China as a market economy (*South China Morning Post* 2005b). Certainly, politics plays a central role in the differing assessments of China's economy, but there are empirical reasons too. The most important fact is that China's economy continues to be permeated by state influence. China has so far failed to develop genuine financial capitalism since state firms continue to dominate Chinese financial institutions. Several crucial producer goods also remain almost exclusively in the hands of state firms (e.g. petrochemicals).

The strong influence of the state in producer goods industries and the financial system expresses the legacy of decades of top-down central control that creates a lingering tendency toward government interference. Nonetheless, the trend line of Chinese reforms is clearly in the direction of establishing the rules and institutions that underpin a genuine market economy. China's accession to the World Trade Organization in late 2001 reflects how the government is intent on using the gradual introduction of international competition to force domestic corporations to improve their efficiency. In addition, the central state has consistently worked to set a competition-inducing incentive and policy framework, while yielding substantial autonomy to local governments. This autonomy, though, permits localized government interventions.

As noted before, the CCP's *nomenklatura* system provides powerful incentives that encourage local governments to support local economic growth.

This has tempted local cadres to use a variety of administrative tools to directly guide local economic forces, even if these actions run counter to central government edicts. Systemic ties between local firms and government cadres also tend to create incentives that favor local protectionism. The result is government interference and the uneven application of policies regarding taxation, market openness, intellectual property rights, environmental protection, the rule of law, etc.

The upshot of this state of affairs is the emergence of market forces but in a politicized context. Powers to allocate financial resources and set detailed industrial policies give the central government substantial clout over key economic aspects. Yet, it is the systemic ties between local governments and businesses that tend to produce the most glaring government interventions. While such interventions can achieve local developmental goals, in the long run they slow down the creation of a level playing field and national market.

Just as it took twenty years to shift the locus of capital accumulation to China's private sector, a realm of the "economy" separate and distinct from the "state" is only gradually emerging. Over time, political reforms that institutionalize constraints on government behavior must be implemented to solve deep-seated conflicts of interest in China's political economy. As the next section explains, such efforts are increasingly visible, but so far have not reached their full potential.

The embryonic bifurcation of secular authority

The bifurcation of secular authority, capitalism's unique political materialization, is at best embryonic in the PRC. As a recent study by Bruce Dickson elucidates, most individuals and groups in China do not seek autonomy but "rather closer embeddedness with the state" (Dickson 2003: 159). Indeed, higher levels of economic development in Chinese localities actually create higher levels of shared interest among government and business (Dickson 2003: 160).

This should be viewed as a logical state of affairs. Since the CCP and especially local cadres are highly supportive of the drive to amass capital, the interests of local state leaders and capital often converge in "symbiotic" relations.[4] Consequently, the question of whether China's burgeoning entrepreneurs are a likely catalyst for full democratization is, at least for the time being, premature. The real question is whether capital can prod the Chinese state to restructure and yield substantial autonomy to the realm of the "economy." This would include the building of a relatively impartial legal system, improvements in state administration to diminish potential conflicts of interest and corruption, and greater autonomy and integrity for China's professions. Most importantly, it would entail the establishment of a functioning private property rights system in all its social, political, and economic manifestations.[5]

My interviews revealed that many Chinese entrepreneurs exhibit a strong interest in raising levels of institutional certainty and predictability, especially by improving the efficacy of courts, state agencies, and market institutions.[6] In fact, capital sees itself as a partner of the Chinese state, willing to push for a fairer and less arbitrary system of market norms and rules. It is particularly interested in the recognition of private property rights and the establishment of a less politicized market economy, but remains fearsome of full democratization.[7]

Evidently, China's bifurcation of secular authority is in the process of unfolding. Several major developments have already taken place. First, using a pragmatic approach, the Chinese state gradually eliminated most aspects of the command economy's legacy. Therefore, despite certain idiosyncrasies and a relatively large state sector, the PRC now possesses a bureaucratic structure amenable to that of a developing and globalizing market economy (Zheng 2004).

Linked to state administrative reforms has been the gradual privatization of the professions. Virtually nonexistent prior to 1978, most professions in China started under the sponsorship of government agencies. This lack of independence created strong conflicts of interest and sheltered professionals from litigation and disciplinary action. By the late 1990s efforts got underway to disaffiliate professions from their governmental sponsors, either by forming partnerships or incorporating them. Expanded autonomy improved the integrity of China's professions and created better incentives to provide high-quality, publicly verifiable information. However, major capacity and governance constraints continue to handicap their role, and so far China's professional culture remains riddled with corrupt and unethical practices (Tang and Ward 2003: 144–149).

A second remarkable development has been the gradual writing and codification of China's legal system. Starting virtually from scratch, the Chinese government has passed a series of laws, especially in the economic domain. The judiciary has also been revamped and is undergoing a rapid process of professionalization. Nonetheless, there remain big gaps. Judges continue to be appointed *via* the CCP's *nomenklatura* system, local government interference and corruption is common in Chinese courts, and insufficient avenues for legal recourse exist. In most aspects, China's legal system remains dominated by the CCP.

A third development affecting the bifurcation of secular authority consists of advances in the political recognition of capital. Fundamentally, the CCP realized in the late 1990s that the discrimination of domestic private entrepreneurs was counterproductive. As the most vibrant sector in the economy, producing increasing shares of tax income, employment, and technological innovation, the private sector would have to be supported to assure China's continued economic development and competitiveness. The result has been a gradual process of politically recognizing private capital.

This process began with the explicit recognition of private enterprise as an "important element" of the Chinese economy during the 15th Party Congress in September 1997, followed in March 1999 by a constitutional amendment. Another constitutional amendment in the spring of 2004 redefined private property as "inviolable" and committed the state "to protect lawfully acquired private property." This amendment was backed up by the 2007 ratification of the PRC's first Property Law.

The politically most important move was Jiang Zemin's pronouncement in July 2001 that private entrepreneurs could formally enter the CCP. By 2004 about one out of every three owners of private firms was a card-carrying member of the CCP. This situation was even more pronounced among owners and managers of big private corporations (*South China Morning Post* 2005a). Although the relationship between private entrepreneurs and state officials is still best described as a symbiosis benefiting both sides, within private firms that have CCP representation a rather clear bifurcation of powers has emerged.

A medium-sized Chinese pharmaceutical company is a case in point. The private owner noted that his corporation established a party committee because several CCP members worked within the corporation. One of his two business partners acts as the party secretary, but the owner himself is not a member of the committee. Therefore, unlike in state firms, this party committee does not wield any real power. Its work stays in the background and focuses on building the party's grassroots organization and conducting political study sessions for its members. The party committee also actively supports the establishment of a corporate culture, but management is fully in charge of economic matters. Evidently, the power structure within this private enterprise forces the party organization to be deferential *vis-à-vis* management. A clear division of labor is established that distinguishes the political realm from that of the economy.[8]

Not withstanding these developments, the bifurcation of secular authority is far from complete in China. Private firms continue to face discrimination in financing, market access, and regulatory approvals. Private property rights, although enshrined in the constitution, remain a work in progress. And legal codes are incomplete and ambiguous. The playing field thus remains heavily tilted in favor of state interests or interests closely aligned with the state. This explains why most large private firms in China seek alliances with government and party officials. They remain willing to be co-opted individually, which results in a myriad of clientelistic relations among individual private entrepreneurs and state officials (Wank 1999). Business associations of private firms are in a similar situation. They continue to be closely tied to the party-state's influence *via* corporatist links (Dickson 2003).

In the end, Leninist principles of political organization continue to permeate the Chinese political economy. The CCP jealously defends its monopoly on legitimate political organization, attempting to control and co-opt all social interests possessing resources that could challenge the party's monopoly. Although a private sphere separate and distinct from the public domain has emerged and is eroding the government's coercive abilities, moves toward creating effective constitutional constraints on the party-state have been very timid at best. China is undoubtedly undertaking a form of capitalist development, but the bifurcation of secular authority remains embryonic.

Conclusion

By creating a fundamental yet specific definition of the major dynamics driving capitalist accumulation, I conceptually "measured" whether China's policy of reform and opening up is leading to the emergence of a capitalist political economy. The answer: the process so far clearly indicates that China is generating a form of capitalism.

The best established aspect of capitalism is China's drive to accumulate capital. Almost a thousand years of petty capitalism, although always tempered by a dominant state, has created one of the world's most vibrant business cultures (Gates 1996). It is therefore little wonder that when the door to private capital accumulation was opened after 1978, this process took off.

In terms of China's emergent market society the picture is more mixed. Although the Chinese economy remains permeated by state influence, strides toward a fully fledged market economy are clearly visible, especially after China's entry into the World Trade Organization. The third and most crucial element of capitalism – the bifurcation of secular authority – remains the least evolved. It is therefore in capitalism's political materialization that China's transition faces its biggest challenges.

The bottom-line conclusion is that China is in the midst of a monumental transition, but in and of itself this is not a highly noteworthy finding. A much more important finding is that this transition is being driven by the same fundamental dynamic that catapulted Great Britain, the United States, Germany, and Japan to international prominence – capitalist development. Indeed, as opposed to other conceptual lenses, applying a capitalist lens to China's emergent political economy can provide a comprehensive and historically accurate picture.

First, we can conceptually "measure" the progress of China's transition without falling into black and white categories, such as democracy versus authoritarianism; or market economy versus command economy. It is clear that in coming years the most challenging reforms will be political by nature. In this respect, the most pressing reforms concern the integrity of Chinese courts, professions, and bureaucracies, especially the establishment of a greater sense of professionalism and independence in China's judicial system.

Second, the capitalist lens can provide insights into the political logic and possible futures of China's transition. One of the key distinguishing aspects of capitalist systems is the potential for capital to restrain state action and construct a relatively autonomous realm of the economy. Nonetheless, examples in world history prove that the CCP might not be willing to yield the institutional and political space necessary for Chinese capital to continue its dynamism. As other state elites before it, the CCP seeks a monopoly over political organization. Capital can represent a political competitor, because its possession of wealth can rival the influence of the state. The CCP might therefore opt to keep capital at bay by continuing its direct influence over property rights and exchange systems. This, though, could start to undermine the dynamic economic change experienced by China. In fact, China's political economy could become stuck in a form of "Chinese crony capitalism," a point taken up in Chapter 12.

A final advantage of applying the capitalist lens to China's emergent political economy is that it creates a framework that can weave together disparate perspectives in management studies, economics, and political science. The capitalist lens thus allows us to utilize different viewpoints to map how China's historical legacy, enormous size, and rapid absorption into the world capitalist system are giving rise to a unique variant of capitalism. This distinctly new form of capitalism is especially visible in China's emerging corporate institutions, a subject taken up in Part 2 that follows this chapter. New perspectives on the relationships among the Chinese state, capital, and political interests are provided in part three, while part four focuses on China's emerging role in the global capitalist system. The concluding chapter will then come back to the big questions touched upon here: what are the implications of China's emergent political economy for China's future and that of our world?

Notes

1 See, for example, the volume by Hall and Soskice (2001). One exception in comparative political economy is the literature on the nature and logic of developmental states, which concentrates on the political economies of developing countries as in Evans (1995). I will present a more detailed discussion on the applicability of the varieties of capitalism framework to the case of China in Chapter 6.

2 In the following "capital" will also refer to "capital-holding social strata" or "capital-oriented classes." The term "capital" thus conceptualizes both a tradable stock of assets (e.g. financial capital) and the social influence of capital-oriented classes.

3 Baum and Shevchenko (1999) attempt to conceptualize the large differences in Chinese local political economies. They note four types of local political economies: predatory, clientelistic, state entrepreneurial, and developmental.

4 For examples of "symbiotic" state-business relations under capitalist development see Gerschenkron (1962); Waterbury (1993: chpt. 8); and Laothamatas (1994).

5 See De Soto (2000) on this point.

6 Informants 20–30, 83, 182. See also Dickson (2003: 163). Interviews were undertaken during the summers of 2001, 2002, 2004, 2005, and 2006. All interviews were conducted without the aid of translators in either Mandarin or

Cantonese. Interviewees were assured of utmost confidentiality, and a coding system has been employed to protect their identities.

7 On this point see also Chapter 8 by An Chen.
8 Informants 8 and 28.

References

Baum R. and Shevchenko, A. (1999) "The 'State of the State'," in M. Goldman and R. MacFarquhar (eds) *The Paradox of China's Post-Mao Reforms,* Cambridge, MA and London: Harvard University Press, pp. 333–360.

Beijing Normal University [Economics and Resource Management Institute] (2003) *Zhongguo shichang jingji fazhan baogao* [*China's Market Economy Development Report*]. Online. Available HTTP: past.people.com.cn/GB.jinji/36/20030414/971145. html (accessed April 1, 2005).

Bernstein, T.P. and Lu, X. (2003) *Taxation without Representation in Contemporary Rural China,* Cambridge: Cambridge University Press.

Blecher, M. and Shue, V. (2001) "Into Leather: State-Led Development and the Private Sector in Xinji," *The China Quarterly* (166): 368–393.

China Economic Quarterly (2006) "Major Economic Indices," 10(3): 7.

Coates, D. (ed.) (2005a) *Varieties of Capitalism, Varieties of Approaches,* Basingstoke and New York: Palgrave Macmillan.

——(2005b) "Paradigms of Explanation," in D. Coates (ed.) *Varieties of Capitalism, Varieties of Approaches,* Basingstoke and New York: Palgrave Macmillan, pp. 1–26.

De Soto, H. (2000) *The Mystery of Capital: Why Capitalism Triumphs in the West and Fails Everywhere Else,* New York: Basic Books.

Dickson, B.J. (2003) *Red Capitalists in China,* Cambridge: Cambridge University Press.

Dillard, D. (1992) "Capitalism," in C.K. Wilbur and K.P. Jameson (eds) *The Political Economy of Development and Underdevelopment,* New York: MacGraw-Hill, pp. 69–76.

Duus, P. (1976) *The Rise of Modern Japan,* Boston, MA: Houghton Mifflin Company.

Edin, M. (2003) "State Capacity and Local Agent Control in China: CCP Cadre Management from a Township Perspective," *The China Quarterly* (173): 35–52.

Evans, P. (1995) *Embedded Autonomy: States and Industrial Transformation,* Princeton, NJ: Princeton University Press.

Friedman, M. (2002) *Capitalism and Freedom,* Chicago, IL: University of Chicago Press.

Gamble, A. (1994) *The Free Economy and the Strong State: The Politics of Thatcherism,* Basingstoke: Macmillan.

Garnaut, R. and Song, L. (2004) "Private Enterprise in China: Development, Constraints and Policy Implications," in R. Garnaut and L. Song (eds) *China's Third Economic Transformation,* London and New York: Routledge Curzon, pp. 1–14.

Gates, H. (1996) *China's Motor: A Thousand Years of Petty Capitalism,* Ithaca, NY: Cornell University Press.

Gerschenkron, A. (1962) *Economic Backwardness in Historical Perspective: A Book of Essays,* Cambridge, MA: Harvard University Press.

Hall, P.A. and Soskice, D. (eds) (2001) *Varieties of Capitalism: The Institutional Foundations of Comparative Advantage*, Oxford: Oxford University Press.

Heilbroner, R.L. (1985) *The Nature and Logic of Capitalism*, New York and London: W.W. Norton.

——(1993) *21st Century Capitalism*, New York and London: W.W. Norton.

Huang, Y. (1996) *Inflation and Investment Controls in China: The Political Economy of Central-Local Relations During the Reform Era*, Cambridge: Cambridge University Press.

Jones, E.L. (2003) *The European Miracle: Environments, Economies, and Geopolitics in the History of Europe and Asia*, Cambridge: Cambridge University Press.

Laothamatas, A. (1994) "From Clientelism to Partnership: Business-Government Relations in Thailand," in A. MacIntyre (ed.) *Business and Government in Industrialising Asia*, St. Leonards, NSW: Allen & Unwin, pp. 195–215.

Lippit, V. (2005) *Capitalism*, New York: Routledge.

McVey, R. (1992) "The Materialization of the Southeast Asian Entrepreneur," in R. McVey (ed.) *Southeast Asian Capitalists*, Ithaca, NY: Cornell University Press, pp. 7–34.

Mann, M. (1986) *The Sources of Social Power, vol. I: A History of Power from the Beginning to A.D. 1760*, Cambridge: Cambridge University Press.

Naughton, B. (1992) "Implications of the State Monopoly over Industry and Its Relaxations," *Modern China*, 18(1): 14–41.

——(1995) *Growing Out of the Plan: Chinese Economic Reform, 1978–1993*, New York: Cambridge University Press.

Nee, V. and Swedberg, R. (eds) (2005a) *The Economic Sociology of Capitalism*, Princeton, NJ and Oxford: Princeton University Press.

——(2005b) "Introduction," in V. Nee and R. Swedberg (eds) *The Economic Sociology of Capitalism*, Princeton, NJ and Oxford: Princeton University Press, pp. xxxv–xlvii.

North, D.C. (1981) *Structure and Change in Economic History*, New York: W.W. Norton.

——(1998) "The Rise of the Western World," in P. Bernholz, M. Streit and R. Vaubel (eds) *Political Competition, Innovation and Growth: A Historical Analysis*, Berlin, Heidelberg, and New York: Springer, pp. 13–28.

South China Morning Post (2005a) "China's Capitalists Embrace Communism," February 12, p. B2.

——(2005b) "Howard Stands By Decision on Market Economy," April 20, p. 4.

Swedberg, R. (2005) "The Economic Sociology of Capitalism: An Introduction and Agenda," in V. Nee and R. Swedberg (eds) *The Economic Sociology of Capitalism*, Princeton, NJ and Oxford: Princeton University Press, pp. 3–40.

Tang, J. and Ward, A. (2003) *The Changing Face of Chinese Management*, London and New York: Routledge.

Tilly, C. (1992) *Coercion, Capital, and European States, AD 990–1992*, Cambridge, MA and Oxford: Blackwell.

Unger, J. (2002) *The Transformation of Rural China*, Armonk and London: M.E. Sharpe.

Unger, J. and Chan, A. (1999) "Inheritors of the Boom: Private Enterprise and the Role of Local Government in a Rural South China Township," *The China Journal* (42): 45–74.

Wang, X. (2004) "The Contribution of the Non-State Sector to China's Economic Growth," in R. Garnaut and L. Song (eds) *China's Third Economic Transformation*, London and New York: Routledge Curzon, pp. 15–28.

Wank, D. (1999) *Commodifying Communism: Business, Trust and Politics in a Chinese City*, Cambridge: Cambridge University Press.

Waterbury, J. (1993) *Exposed to Innumerable Delusions: Public Enterprise and State Power in Egypt, India, Mexico, and Turkey*, New York: Cambridge University Press.

Zheng, Y. (2004) *Globalization and State Transformation in China*, Cambridge: Cambridge University Press.

Zweig, D. (2002) *Internationalizing China: Domestic Interests and Global Linkages*, Ithaca, NY and London: Cornell University Press.

Part 2

Firms, finance, innovation, and international competitiveness

3 China's emerging industrial economy

Insights from the IT industry

Dieter Ernst and Barry Naughton

Since the turn of the 21st century, a distinctive Chinese variety of industrial capitalism has taken shape. In this chapter, we trace the contours of China's emergent industrial economy, giving special attention to the role of the information technology (IT) industry. Throughout China's reform era, the IT industry has often been a forerunner of broader trends in the industrial economy, and this continues to be true today. For most of the socialist period, development was equated with large, heavy industrial plants. Even under market transition, the Chinese government at first maintained its faith in guided development and invested resources in large, state-owned firms in the hope of creating "national champions."

However, over the past decade planners have moved away from the "big-is-better" model of industrialization, and instead placed their hopes in science and technology-intensive industry. This focus has recently been formalized in the 11th Five-Year Plan (2006–2010), with its emphasis on human resources, technology development, and a scientific approach to development (Naughton 2005b). The IT industry has thus stepped into the starring role in a long-running drama, that of China's transformation into an industrial economy. We use the IT industry as a wedge to gain entry into the industrial economy as a whole, and to provide insights into the broader development of China's industrial capitalism.

At the same time, we are not just interested in the *context* of IT industry development: we are interested in the changes in business strategy and the building of technological capabilities that are taking place *within* the IT industry. China's industrial economy is already so large and so diverse that it is difficult to make meaningful statements that apply to its entirety. Examining strategy and capabilities – especially innovative capabilities – gives us a crucial benchmark to assess how real the changes in the IT industry have been. What alternative strategies are emerging in China to the now discredited "big-is-better" model? Will China become a leading world technology power? Or will limitations in its economic and innovation system prevent China from moving beyond its current status of a low-cost export-manufacturing platform? In this sense, we assess China's IT industry as an exemplar of China's overall industrial transformation.

From the perspective of the IT sector, we see a fairly successful transition toward a capitalist market economy for China. In the overall industrial economy state ownership is still significant, but it is now concentrated primarily in natural resource sectors and utilities. State-owned firms. while present, play a secondary role in the IT sector, where technical innovation is critical. In fact, China has muddled through to a highly flexible. internationally open, and entrepreneurial solution in sectors such as IT hardware and software.

We therefore disagree with the findings of a pessimistic literature that provides a backward-looking appraisal of weaknesses in China's industrial economy (e.g. Gilboy 2004; Nolan 2002; Rosen 2003; Steinfeld 2004). Rather. we argue that the IT industry has played a crucial role both in transforming China's industrial economy and in forging a peculiar Chinese model of developing a vibrant high-tech industry. A hybrid mixture of ownership and corporate governance patterns has been combined with aggressive policies to foster alliances with global leaders in industry and research. This has enabled Chinese IT firms to accelerate the development of management and innovation capabilities.

The first section of this chapter describes how China's contemporary industrial economy emerged from the state-run economy and introduces our first illustrative case of a Chinese IT company, the computer firm Legend/ Lenovo. The next section describes the emergence of a broader three-tiered industrial system, and indicates where Chinese IT companies fit in. The third section highlights new opportunities and challenges for Chinese IT firms that result from their progressive integration into global production and innovation networks. The fourth section introduces Huawei, China's largest telecommunications and networking equipment manufacturer. our second illustrative case. We examine Huawei's business model and show how the company is seeking to exploit the new international division of labor to foster managerial and innovative capabilities.

Prelude: the IT industry's role in creating a market-driven industrial economy

China's contemporary industrial economy emerged from the state-run economy through a process of gradualist transition and incremental marketization. Early on, hundreds of thousands of small, labor-intensive township and village enterprises (TVEs) sprang up under the auspices of local governments. Yet for a long time, Chinese policy-makers also hoped to improve the performance of existing state-owned enterprises (SOEs) and build up large, state-run industrial corporations as "national champions." Chinese planners expected that state-owned firms would be the main force driving the development of more capital-intensive and technologically sophisticated industry.

Consequently, state firms and foreign investors were forced into what were essentially shotgun marriages, with planners serving as match-makers.

This policy was a recipe for lobbying and rent-seeking by existing large state firms, and absorbed an enormous amount of resources. By the mid-1990s, the policy was already in crisis due to its perceived lack of effectiveness (Naughton and Segal 2002). The program suffered a further blow to its underlying rationale when, with the Asian Financial Crisis of 1997–1998. many of the Korean *chaebol*s that were a source of inspiration for the program ran into serious trouble. It became apparent to Chinese policy-makers, as to Korean policy-makers, that a fundamental restructuring of the biggest firms would be required.

In this environment, the IT industry provided an attractive alternate model. Many of China's early IT successes were so-called *minban* (civilian) firms. These were firms with lineages in the state sector – and often nominal state ownership. However, these firms had grown up independent of the state industrial hierarchy and enjoyed operational autonomy under the direction of high technology entrepreneurs. Beginning in the 1980s. Chinese policy-makers allowed these firms unusual freedom and flexibility for three reasons: they had observed that small, entrepreneurial start-up firms played a key role in the US's technological resurgence in the 1980s and 1990s (the Silicon Valley model); the new firms were started by individuals with unusually impressive skills and especially good contacts with state research organizations; and finally, policy-makers had few, if any, real alternatives, since none of the large state-owned IT companies offered much promise.

All of these factors were exemplified by the success of a single firm, Legend Computer, later known as Lenovo (Ernst 2006b; Ling 2005; Lu 2000; Xie and White 2004). A start-up in the 1980s, it was a spin-off of the Institute of Computer Science in the elite Chinese Academy of Sciences. An impressive number of such firms sprang up in Zhongguancun, the high-tech neighborhood and later development zone in the northwest of Beijing (near the elite Peking and Tsinghua Universities).

In 1998, Legend became a pioneer in another sense – it became what is arguably the first government-sanctioned management buy-out (MBO) of a state firm. Technically, Legend was an SOE, "owned" by the Chinese Academy of Sciences, which provided the initial personnel and modest financing for its creation. Along with other SOEs after the mid-1990s. Legend was to be "corporatized," which involved explicitly demarcating the corporation's formerly vague and ambiguous ownership stakes.

At this point, Legend's managerial group was essentially the same as its founding group. That this management would gain a substantial stake in Legend was completely defensible: they had created the firm from scratch. and they clearly deserved to reap some of the rewards from their entrepreneurial vision. The managerial group initially proposed that a 38 percent stake of the company be distributed to them, but this ran into an existing government policy that no more than 20 percent of the ownership of an SOE should be distributed to existing employees. After intense negotiations,

Legend employees were allowed to purchase, on highly favorable terms, 30 percent of the company. This compromise enabled the Chinese government to nominally hold on to its existing policy and retain the Academy of Sciences as (passive) majority owner, but give effective control to Legend's founders and managers.

Legend became an important precedent. In subsequent years, MBOs became a powerful channel for the transformation of China's industrial structure. Indeed, for TVEs, management buy-outs, or insider privatizations, had already emerged as an important trend during the 1990s. The Legend restructuring signaled that such procedures could be acceptable in the state sector as well. By the early 2000s, MBOs had become the predominant form of transformation for TVEs and an extremely important – and controversial – mechanism for transforming SOEs as well (Naughton 2005a; Naughton 2007: 286–292, 319–325).

As MBOs gained in legitimacy, privatization became an important force reshaping the Chinese industrial economy. China's industrial system thus went through a profound transformation during the early 2000s. At the top of the industrial hierarchy the central government retained the largest, most important state-owned firms. Meanwhile, at the bottom of the industrial hierarchy, the majority of TVEs and many small SOEs were converted to private ownership. Today's industrial economy therefore emerged from the uneven way in which privatization and restructuring were allowed to spread, forming three distinct tiers of corporations that characterize China's present-day industrial capitalism.

China's emerging industrial economy: a three-tier structure

Tier one

The first tier consists of large, central government controlled firms, which are primarily in sectors with some degree of natural monopoly or market power. In 2002, control of these firms was consolidated in a new body, the State-owned Assets Supervision and Administration Commission (SASAC). Initially, SASAC assumed responsibility for 196 firms, a number that was reduced through merger and consolidation to 159 by the end of 2006 (SASAC 2007). Among this number, there are less than 100 industrial corporations. However, many of the corporations are huge, and one corporation may possess many dozens of subordinate industrial enterprises.

At first glance, this tier of large, centrally controlled firms might appear to exemplify the old "big-is-better" model of industrial organization, but in fact there are considerable differences. The sectoral structure of the centrally controlled firms does not replicate the extremely diversified structure of Korean *chaebols*, or Japanese *keiretsu*. Nearly all the firms in the central "portfolio" have a clear business focus on one or two sectors, often in natural resources. Moreover, these firms have been subject to an ongoing process of restructuring that is frequently designed to get them to focus on "core competencies," that is, on specific sectors in which they have a sustainable competitive advantage.

SASAC's mission is to carry out the state's role *as owner* in the industrial economy. The head of SASAC, Li Rongrong, has repeatedly made it clear that he sees SASAC's mission as increasing the value of government assets. While the central government will share ownership stakes with strategic investors and the public by floating some of the companies on stock markets, the government intends to maintain substantial control.

Ironically, SASAC's interpretation of its mandate has increasingly followed a well-known business school logic: focus on core competencies, spin off noncore businesses. Thus, SASAC has adopted the mantra – first mooted by General Electric – that a company should be number one, two, or three in its business. Otherwise, it should get out. The key slogan, then, is "focus," not "big-is-better."

In addition, most of the centrally controlled firms are in sectors where there is a degree of market power. They control the key natural resource, telecom, and trading companies. In 2006, central SASAC's firms produced profit and turned over taxes equaling an enormous 6.8 percent of GDP, evidence of their market power (SASAC 2007). In fact, SASAC's newly important role increases an emphasis on maximizing monopoly rents. Every capitalist would like to have a monopoly position: SASAC is no different. Because SASAC's role is to represent the government *as owner*, it naturally stresses financial returns and puts less emphasis on economic growth, economic reform, and fair competition (roles performed by government regulatory agencies and the National Development and Reform Commission).

The large central government firms that are most important to the IT industry are the telecom operators. As of 2006, four large telecom firms are subordinate to the central government. Three of these were spun off from the old government monopoly service provider: China Telecom (fixed line); China Mobile; and China Netcom (a combine of fixed line and internet backbone services). A new entrant, China Unicom, with a totally different – but still state-owned – background was allowed to provide competing mobile services. All of these firms are predominantly state-owned, and SASAC now "owns" all four. As a result, SASAC seeks to moderate competition among them in order to create a viable combination of healthy firms, tacit collaboration, and high profits.

This objective was particularly in evidence in October 2004 when SASAC shuffled the management of the top three telecom firms, replacing the top manager in each firm with the second or third-rank manager from a competing firm. The message was clear: don't compete too aggressively, for the company you compete with could one day be your own. SASAC's intervention is ongoing: throughout 2005 and 2006, SASAC struggled with different proposals to reorganize the telecom industry, looking for ways to shuffle activities and licenses among operators in order to create stronger, competitive companies that will adopt advanced "third generation" (3G) telecommunications technology.

While SASAC has obviously been looking for ways to support a domestically grown 3G telecom standard (known as TD-SCDMA), it has had trouble finding an effective policy in this market environment. All of the existing telecom firms would like to move into 3G mobile telephony, but none of them wants to be saddled with the unproven domestic standard. In all four cases, the telecom companies have complex corporate structures with minority shareholders inside and outside China, so SASAC is not able to simply redistribute assets (and licenses) among the groups as it could have in the old days.

The dynamics of the telecom industry are very important for China's IT hardware industry, because the service providers are big customers. Choices about technological standards, domestic preferences, and business rules shape the options of the hardware industry. Precisely because the service providers have some market power, they have rich margins that allow them to pay higher costs to support fledgling companies and new initiatives. The telecom firms are not themselves likely to be the cutting edge firms of China's technological future, but they will provide opportunities for other companies that may play dynamic roles.

Several IT hardware companies do show up in SASAC's portfolio, and each has a unique history in the state sector. The first, China Electronics Technology Corporation (CETC), is a grab-bag of forty six research institutes, part of the military industrial complex, but with a number of subordinate profit-making companies as well.[1] The second, China Electronics Corporation (CEC), descended from the firms controlled by the Ministry of Electronics and today groups together sixteen wholly owned subsidiaries and thirty controlled companies. The third, Putian, groups together the telecommunications equipment factories that used to be subordinate to the Ministry of Post and Telecommunications.

Some of the firms subordinate to these three big groups have significant independent capabilities. However, each of these groups is in fact a fairly troubled jumble of companies. The subordinate companies of each seek to establish themselves independently, a feasible objective since ownership of the companies is often shared among state and nonstate groups. Meanwhile, the groups themselves are subject to continuous reorganization. For instance, one formerly independent firm, Great Wall Computer (best known for its joint venture with IBM) was merged into CEC on August 1, 2005 (SASAC 2005).

Two other IT hardware firms show up in SASAC's portfolio. One is a joint venture in Shanghai with Alcatel, "centrally controlled" by historical accident: this is arguably the only successful example of a planner-orchestrated partnership involving foreign multinationals (Mu and Lee 2005; Shen 1999). The final IT firm, IRICO, is a color picture-tube producer near Xi'an, legacy of an earlier stage of China's development.

It is most striking what we do *not* observe in this portfolio of central government IT firms. Unlike the robust, wealthy, and centrally managed large firms in the natural resources, energy, and public utility fields, we do not find in this portfolio a single potential "national champion." SASAC's IT firms are unstable groupings with wildly varying capabilities. With a few exceptions, the most dynamic hardware and software companies are not under SASAC, but rather in China's second tier of companies.

Tier two

The second tier of industrial firms is made up of medium-sized firms operating in competitive markets. Second-tier firms have diverse origins: they may come from the state sector, from foreign investment, or, increasingly, may be domestic Chinese start-ups. Firms that originated in the state sector were usually local government-controlled. Since they were rarely in monopoly sectors, they were exposed to competition and less profitable than central government firms. No strategic rationale thus existed for public ownership and local governments were quite willing to privatize or close down these firms (Li and Lui 2004). As noted above, MBOs have been permitted after 2000 in small- and medium-sized state firms. These firms are now rapidly restructuring and privatizing, creating one of the seedbeds of the new production forces and new interest groups shaping China's emergent capitalism.

As a result of the new flexibility about ownership, hybrid firms are rapidly being created. These firms take on a variety of organizational forms, particularly in the IT sector. There is no single hybrid pattern, but we can identify three characteristics that are often present. First, there is often a dominant manager or managerial group, usually with a significant ownership stake. These firms move quickly because they have personalized decisive leadership; they are not yet bureaucratized companies.

Second, ownership is divided. These firms are usually not 100 percent privately owned. Local governments often hold minority stakes, either directly, or through intermediaries. When these firms are listed on the stock markets, a minority of shares is typically sold. Companies from Hong Kong, Taiwan, and overseas often hold stakes as well. Shared ownership seems to be commonly used to align interests between entrepreneurs and other stakeholders, including local government.

Third, many of these firms are linked to overseas actors through global production and innovation networks. Multiple forms of integration, such as contract manufacturing (in both directions), research partnerships, licensing, equity stakes, and many other means connect domestic with foreign firms (Ernst 2007).

This is the most dynamic part of Chinese industry today. Released from state control, powerful local interest groups are supporting the emergence of new companies, frequently in collaboration with foreign firms. With China's booming economy and its large pool of knowledge workers providing ample opportunities, this segment of industry is undergoing explosive growth and defining the future of Chinese capitalism. Flexibility is the byword, and in many cases it is simply no longer possible to classify firms into the old categories of state-owned, collective, private, or foreign-invested. Some industrial sectors straddle the first and second tiers: for example, steel and automobiles. Large state-owned companies still dominate, but rapidly growing hybrid, mostly private firms with local government backing, are emerging to challenge the leaders.

The steel industry is a good example. State control in this capital-intensive industry was traditionally reinforced by the state's privileged access to financing. But today private firms are growing explosively, especially in Hebei, Jiangsu, and Zhejiang. It is still not entirely clear whether the central government will allow genuine competition between its firms and newly entering private steel companies. In July 2005, the central government promulgated an official industrial policy for the steel industry (National Development and Reform Commission 2005) that clearly intends to shore up the state's position. Foreign companies were forbidden to purchase controlling stakes, but domestic private interests were not. A guess based on China's past trajectory would say that sectors such as steel and automobiles – unlike oil, electricity, and telecom – will within five to ten years be dominated by large hybrid businesses, and fall clearly within the second tier of Chinese industrial firms.

China's IT industry is predominantly in the second tier, since the most important and most dynamic firms are hybrid firms. As we argue in more detail below, the global IT industry is being transformed by an increasing vertical specialization of production – "modularity" of organization is extended across all stages of the value chain, including research and product development. To adjust to the resultant rapid changes in technology and markets, Chinese IT firms require robust innovation and management capabilities and a high degree of flexibility.

Legend/Lenovo Computer demonstrates the importance of strategic flexibility. The company started out primarily as a reseller of foreign computers, and gradually moved into assembly. Its founder espoused a model he dubbed "*mao-gong-ji*," or moving from trade, through manufacturing, to technology development. Contrary to much that has been written, Lenovo never really developed into a manufacturing powerhouse. Instead, it developed a strong domestic brand and good design, distribution, and supply networks. For example, in 2003, Lenovo outsourced 100 percent of its laptops and 40 percent of its motherboards to Taiwan contract manufacturers, thus turning the "international subcontracting" model on its head (Jiang 2004).

Lenovo's subsequent, highly publicized acquisition of IBM's personal computer division built on this foundation to create the ultimate hybrid firm. As part of its acquisition of IBM in late 2004, Lenovo received a

US$350 million private equity commitment from Texas Pacific Group, General Atlantic, and Newbridge. These new investors have reduced IBM's share in Lenovo to 13.4 percent and hold around 12.4 percent of Lenovo's capital. As a result, private equity investors are now involved in much of Lenovo's decision-making (Ernst 2007).

Lenovo's headquarters moved to the US, and the company announced it would adopt English as its official language. In fact, the company hired an American, Bill Amelio, as CEO, an executive who had previously been in charge of Dell Computer's Asia operations. By this choice, Lenovo showed that it believed the ability to manage complex multinational supply networks would be the critical success factor.

Therefore, in the course of its multiple transformations, Lenovo has come to exemplify the "hybrid ownership" that is so distinctive a feature of China's second tier of industry. Like Lenovo, most of the leading Chinese IT firms – Hai'er, TCL, Founder, Huawei, ZTE, Datang, and SMIC – can be accurately characterized as hybrid firms with substantial public and private ownership stakes.

Tier three

The small-scale sector, which forms the third tier, has undergone important changes as well. TVEs have themselves become almost entirely privatized; and their ties with local communities have weakened. The resulting small-scale sector has much more flexible labor markets, and a strong tendency towards industrial clusters and flexible specialization. These industrial clusters – often characterized by hundreds of small firms competing and collaborating – have grown up to serve export markets in sectors of both high and low technology. The town of Zhuji, in Zhejiang, produces 35 percent of world sock output – 8 billion pairs a year – almost entirely from small- and medium-sized enterprises. Another Zhejiang town has hundreds of small electric hand tool component producers and assemblers (Qian 2003; Ross 2004). Thus, openness and flexible specialization is an increasingly important characteristic of China's small-scale sector.

The bulk of the third tier is in relatively low technology, labor-intensive production, but the dividing line between primitive and sophisticated technology is not as clear as it once was. It is no longer the case that small-scale necessarily means low-technology, primitive, backward family firms. Relatively sophisticated industrial sectors now include clusters of small high-tech firms, often linked by subcontracting networks. These can be alternatives to larger firms. When flexible specialization and high technology come together, the result is a cluster like the one around Dongguan, in Guangdong's Pearl River Delta. More than 95 percent of the components of a desktop computer are produced within a 50-mile radius of Dongguan. Most of this production is from foreign-invested firms, but small-scale firms play important roles as suppliers (Huang 2002).

The transformation of the small-scale sector now extends beyond manufacturing, and includes product development and some aspects of applied research. Good examples are Celestial Semiconductor, a start-up company in the Shangdi Information Industrial Base in Beijing's Haidian District that specializes in mixed-signal chip design, as well as Tech-Faith, a firm that recently listed on NASDAQ and specializes in the design of mobile phones. Both are cases of dividing the value chain into increasingly narrow slices that now also include innovation (Ernst 2006a, 2006b).

Opportunities and challenges for Chinese IT firms

Why is flexibility and international openness so important for China's development trajectory? China's opportunities to develop its IT industry differ from those faced earlier by Japan, Taiwan, and South Korea. China has a unique combination of competitive advantages that shape the context in which its IT industry develops. First and foremost, China has a huge and booming market for electronics products and services. Second, China has the world's largest pool of low-cost specialized and easily retrainable labor. Third, deriving from the two previous factors, China has recently seen the emergence of sophisticated lead users and test-bed markets, giving it new opportunities in the area of innovation. Finally, Chinese policymakers can learn from the past achievements and mistakes of their East Asian predecessors to adjust national and local policies.

At the same time, the global environment within which China seeks to develop is dramatically different from that of previous East Asian success stories. Most importantly, China's technological development over the past twenty years has been inseparable from the expansion of global production networks (GPNs) and the relocation of most production stages, including engineering and R&D. China is far more integrated into these networks than were Japan and South Korea earlier.

Incoming foreign direct investment has averaged over 4 percent of GDP in China over the past decade; during Japan and South Korea's high growth period, incoming foreign direct investment was never as much as 0.5 percent of GDP. It is thus about ten times as important in China as in these earlier developers, and nowhere more so than in high technology exporting. In 2005, foreign-invested enterprises produced 58 percent of China's total exports, but fully 88 percent of high-technology exports (Ministry of Commerce 2006). As a result, China's emerging industrial economy in the IT industry cannot be meaningfully assessed except in the context of the GPNs into which Chinese firms are increasingly integrated.

The ability of Chinese manufacturers to participate in GPNs provides valuable opportunities, but also creates new challenges. GPNs are usually organized by global "flagship" firms, who seek to structure them in their own economic interest (Ernst 2002). They have an important element of hierarchy: flagship firms serve as overall architects, and they prefer to define platforms and maintain strategic control to reap rents, while outsourcing as much low cost activity as possible to China. These incentives are at work both in production networks and in innovation networks.

The trend of "innovation offshoring" (Ernst 2006a) has given rise to global innovation networks (GINs) that global corporations are gradually grafting onto their existing GPNs. Both GINs and GPNs are complex and multilayered "networks of networks" that involve both global corporations and "local" companies, that is, East Asian companies that are focused primarily on the region. GINs share two defining characteristics with GPNs: asymmetry, because flagships dominate control over network resources and decision-making; and knowledge diffusion, because the sharing of knowledge is the necessary glue that keeps these networks growing. In fact, the hierarchical nature of flagship-dominated networks appears to facilitate knowledge exchange (Ernst and Kim 2002), and hence provides new opportunities for Chinese IT firms.

Practically all global IT industry leaders, as well as a growing number of second-tier firms, have begun to conduct R&D in China. Increasingly, the focus is shifting from the adjustment of existing technologies to the development of new products and processes dedicated to the Asian market (Armbrecht 2003). In addition, China's "brain drain" has produced transnational skilled migrant communities that can act as highly effective carriers of tacit knowledge about global market and technology trends.

On balance, these global transformations create substantial new opportunities for Chinese IT firms. The cost advantages of China's deep and relatively sophisticated manpower base are well documented (e.g. Banister 2005). Less fully recognized has been the extent to which the Chinese market, in addition to its sheer size, provides many of the advantages of a lead market (Beise 2004). In addition, China's deep integration into GPNs and GINs arguably facilitates knowledge diffusion and exports. The most significant strategies will therefore be those that allow firms to benefit from China's unique combination of competitive advantages: low labor costs for unskilled and some highly skilled workers; large and growing markets for IT products and services; and "openness" to international trade, investment, and technology (Liu 2005).

Pessimistic analysts of Chinese capabilities focus on the limited roles Chinese firms have initially played within GPNs. They argue that integration into GPNs will lead, at most, to gradual improvements of operational and manufacturing capabilities, leaving Chinese firms stuck at the bottom of innovative capabilities. This misses the driving force of creative opportunism which leads Chinese firms to focus on cheaper, simpler products tailored to the Chinese market. These can be profoundly "disruptive" even though initially not seeming to be technologically impressive.

To establish what options are realistic, we draw on two analytic tools: a well-known taxonomy of innovation (see Table 3.1) that distinguishes "incremental," "modular," "architectural," and "radical" innovations (Henderson and Clark 1990); and the concept of "disruptive technologies" (Christensen 1997). "Incremental" innovations take both the dominant component design and architecture for granted, but improve on cost, time-to-market,

Table 3.1 Typology of innovations

changed	<u>architectural</u>	radical
Architecture		
unchanged	<u>incremental</u>	modular
	unchanged	changed

Components

Source: Adapted from Henderson and Clark (1990).

and performance. With "modular" innovation, new component technology is plugged into a system architecture that is fundamentally unchanged. This type of innovation has been a defining characteristic of the personal computer industry; for instance, the multifunctional USB port on the personal computer exemplifies modular innovation.

"Architectural" innovations change the way components are designed to work together, but use existing component technology that is available on the market to implement new designs. Architectural innovations thus introduce substantially new and distinct features to existing system architectures. They also build on a company's familiarity with market demands, as with the development of Chinese-language electronics publishing systems by the Founder Group Company, a spin-off from Peking University (Lu 2000).

Finally, "radical" innovations involve both the use of new component technology and changes in architectural design. They typically involve breakthroughs in both areas, such as the invention of the Internet. These innovations receive the greatest attention, and high margins through premium pricing and strong market entry deterrents. However, radical innovations require an extremely broad base of capabilities, and involve huge risks. They are beyond the reach of most IT companies in China.

Christensen (1993) argues that established, vertically integrated market leaders typically lead in the adoption of new component technology, while successful new entrants rely on architectural innovations. Technological complexity, and hence risk and cost, are lower for architectural innovations than for the development of new components, and architectural innovations lead more immediately to increased sales and profitability. Christensen's (1997) concept of "disruptive technologies" deepens our understanding of these market factors.

Disruptive technologies bring to market very different products: they have features that initially only few new customers value. Products based on disruptive technologies are typically cheaper, simpler, smaller, and, frequently, more convenient to use. Incumbent firms, especially market leaders, generally fail to notice "lower-end" markets that may erode their market leadership. That is because they promise lower margins, their most profitable customers generally do not want products based on disruptive technologies, and the required break from routine requires a different organization from sustaining technologies. Most importantly, developing disruptive technologies requires an organization of innovation with substantially lower overheads.

Chinese IT firms are more likely to produce important innovations that are architectural or incremental, rather than modular or radical. The ability of Chinese IT firms to profit from architectural innovation may seem counter-intuitive, but it follows from their growing integration into GPNs and GINs, and their familiarity with peculiar features of Chinese markets. Chinese firms face relatively low entry barriers for "disruptive" technologies, while they can leverage participation in GPNs and GINs to buy in widely available existing component technology. Chinese IT firms thus will often pursue architectural innovations leading to disruptive technologies.

There is also scope for substantial incremental innovation by Chinese IT firms. To stay in the GPNs, Chinese firms must improve on cost, time-to-market, and performance. Intensifying price competition, especially in the China market, implies that Chinese firms are under tremendous pressure to exploit such incremental innovations across all stages of the value chain. These small incremental innovations gradually add up and may in time shift the rules of global production and innovation activities (Ernst 2007).

By contrast, the focus in much of the current literature on China's technology effort has been on Chinese government attempts to create national champions and mandate technical standards (Linden 2004; Suttmeier and Yao 2004). The Chinese government focuses on core "strategic" technologies ("radical" in the terminology we have used here), while its policies are interventionist, certainly more so than India's. China's ambitious government efforts have caused worries that Chinese firms could successfully create "radical" innovations (US-China Economic and Security Review Commission 2005), while the extremely modest rate of success feeds the technological pessimism described above.

We argue that these areas are simply not likely to be where the action is. Innovative firms trolling through the global knowledge base and opportunistically creating new architectural solutions to new market demands are the more likely seedbeds of technological breakthroughs. As for the Chinese government, it has overall done a reasonably good job of not intervening too much in firm decision-making, while providing a degree of unconditional resource support. It has displayed a healthy respect for the accumulated knowledge base possessed by global corporations, and policy makers have in recent years primarily focused on moving up the value chain within the context of GPN's.

Chinese IT firms responding – the case of Huawei

Incorporated in 1988 and based in Shenzhen, Huawei is China's largest telecommunications and networking equipment manufacturer.[2] Huawei has experienced rapid growth of sales and profits, registering 25 percent annual sales growth since 1998. The company is also a telling example of the hybrid mixture of ownership and corporate governance that is a defining characteristic of China's second-tier industrial companies. In legal terms, Huawei is a "private" company, but it is not listed on any major stock exchange, and hence is not included in the *Fortune* list of "China's 100 Largest Companies."

The real driving force is Ren Zengfei, a People's Liberation Army veteran, who founded the company and who, as the company's president and CEO, exerts strong and idiosyncratic managerial influence throughout the organization. The company has a reputation for secretiveness, somewhat murky corporate governance, and top-down management by command and extensive micro-management. Employees hold the majority of Huawei "inner" shares, which arguably reflects the critical role the company has assigned to its highly skilled workforce – 90 percent of its 30,000 employees worldwide hold bachelor's degrees or higher.

Within a few years, Huawei has been able to establish itself as a serious new competitor in the telecommunications industry. The company's success owes much to its focus on being a "low-cost cloner," seeking to price its products 30 percent lower than global market leaders. In addition, Huawei offers very aggressive sales incentives and exhaustive after-sales services, and it has a good reputation in customizing system engineering to specific requirements of customers who require "no-frill" systems. This business model was well in line with Huawei's initial strategic focus – to penetrate the Chinese market as well as secondary overseas markets in developing Asia, Africa, Latin America, and Eastern Europe.

However, the company is now seeking to expand its geographical presence and to upgrade its product line. It is forced to do so in order to counter aggressive attacks by its main global competitors, who are gaining market share in China.[3] Huawei's aggressive plans for overseas expansion project a fivefold increase in international sales from US$2.28 billion in 2004 to around US$10 billion by 2008. In order to achieve this ambitious goal, the initial focus on secondary markets in developing and transition economies now needs to give way to a substantial expansion in the critical markets of the US, Europe, and Japan. Some initial success stories have been widely quoted in the press. These include British Telecom's decision to include Huawei in its list of eight preferred suppliers for the overhaul of its UK fixed-line phone network; and the decision by Telfort, the Dutch mobile operator, to contract Huawei to build its 3G mobile phone network. In fact, Telfort passed up an offer from Ericsson, its main supplier since 1998.

This is just the beginning of a very long road. To penetrate the world's most sophisticated markets, Huawei now seeks to transform itself from a "low-cost cloner" to a provider of integrated and customized network solutions and services. While fixed-line networks of telecommunications equipment still provide the bulk of revenues, mobile and optical networks are providing the fastest revenue growth. In addition, the company has committed substantial resources to develop value-added communication services and mobile handsets, especially for 3G mobile communication systems. Huawei has continuously invested more than 10 percent of its revenues in R&D. According to the company website (July 29, 2005), Huawei has applied for 6,500 patents, and been granted 1,400 already. After initially earning a bad reputation on intellectual property rights infringement (Einhorn 2004), the company now claims to follow a strategy of stringent protection.

The focus of Huawei's innovation efforts is on a judicious combination of incremental and architectural innovations that provide integrated solutions throughout the life cycle of communications systems. In terms of incremental innovations, Huawei has made a conscious effort to improve on cost, time-to-market, and performance across its product range. This includes, for instance, substantial improvements in the management of product development, quality control, supply chains, and customer relations.

Building on the company's familiarity with market trends and user requirements of operators in developing countries, Huawei has also pursued architectural innovations. It has developed equipment and solution packages that, while under-performing relative to established products in mainstream markets, satisfy the essential needs of operators at much lower cost. An example is "Tel@com," Huawei's patented approach to the alignment of existing fixed networks that allows operators with limited budgets to adjust quickly to and exploit the rapid development of IP (internet protocol) telephony and broadband technologies. Another example is a distributed 3G base station that needs no special equipment room, thus dispensing with costly rental, and which has only two thirds of the average power consumption of similar products in the industry.

Such strategies may now be increasingly effective in the leading telecommunications markets of industrialized countries. After the bursting of the telecommunications bubble in 2000, and the resultant turmoil and wealth destruction, leading telecom operators are much less willing than before to buy the overengineered and very expensive equipment, systems, and services that are on offer from global industry leaders. In short, the overriding objective of Huawei's strategy to upgrade its product portfolio is to provide "integrated communication and network solutions . . . in order to consistently create maximum value for customers," especially those with limited budgets (Huawei Annual Report 2004: 11).

Huawei exemplifies an important characteristic of Chinese IT companies by forging collaborative agreements and alliances with global industry leaders and universities. Huawei, for instance, relied heavily on IBM's consulting arm to develop sophisticated "integrated product development" techniques, and foster Huawei's "integrated supply chain" management. Through its software development affiliate in Bangalore (India), Huawei became familiar with the huge efficiency gains to be reaped from state-of-the-art project management techniques. In cooperation with Carnegie Mellon University, the company's four software development divisions (in Shenzhen, Bangalore, Shanghai, and Nanjing) have all been awarded CMM5 certificates, the highest level of software project management certification.

As for quality control and production flow management, Huawei has heavily relied on Germany's Fraunhofer Gesellschaft, including integrated production line layout and warehouse automation, thus reducing material movement, shortening the production cycle, and improving production efficiency and quality. Global consulting firms (especially KPMG and IBM) have also played an important role in developing key elements for implementing Huawei's move from an equipment supplier to a provider of integrated solutions. Most importantly, Huawei has spent substantial efforts in upgrading its human resource management practices in cooperation with global consulting firms, such as Hay and Mercer. These actions helped the company to improve staff recruitment and development. One positive indicator is that Huawei has been ranked as number five in the July 2005 list of "Best Chinese Students Employer Award," published by ChinaHR.com.[4]

Like other Chinese IT companies, Huawei's initial key competitive advantage was the low cost of its researchers and engineers. Out of its worldwide workforce of about 30,000, over 14,500 (48 percent) work in R&D. More than 6,000 of this R&D workforce are specializing in 3G and related technologies. Most of the R&D personnel are now based in China, where salaries typically are one third to one fifth of US salaries (Ernst 2007). The low cost of R&D personnel explains how Huawei can develop tailor-made solutions that address the specific needs of network operators with tight budgets.

As in other East Asian exporting countries, demographic trends in China will, over the longer-term, slow the growth of the working-age population, creating pressures for wage increases. One of the by-products of the one-child policy in China is that labor force growth will slow dramatically after 2015. Indeed, this is one of the biggest differences between China and India: India is one of the few countries with significant technological capabilities in which the working-age population is poised to grow for the next forty years, keeping wages low.

It will take time before the current huge wage cost differentials between China and industrialized countries will be reduced, but the erosion of labor cost advantages is already a reality for highly skilled labor in the IT industry. In both China and India, IT firms complain about a

Table 3.2 Huawei's global innovation network

Krista/Stockholm, Sweden	Base station architecture and system design; analog-mixed signal design (RF); algorithms
Moscow, Russia	Algorithms; RF design
Bangalore, India	Development of embedded SW and platforms
Plano, Texas (Dallas Telecom Corridor)	Total solutions for CDMA; G3 UMTS; CDMA Mobile Intelligent Networks; mobile data service; optical; voice over Internet protocol

Source: © Dieter Ernst.

severe shortage of experienced engineers and managers, which is driving salaries up and creating a "war for talent" (Ernst 2006a). As jobs become more senior and require greater expertise and experience, pay increases cost proportionately much more in China than in the US. Thus, while China's supply of current engineering graduates exceeds that of any other country, there is a shortage of experienced and highly qualified engineers and scientists.

To overcome this critical shortage of senior and experienced engineers and managers, Huawei has pursued a two-pronged strategy: it is building a variety of linkages and alliances with leading global industry players and universities, while concurrently establishing its own global innovation network. Huawei has thus developed a web of project-specific collaboration arrangements with major suppliers of core components, such as Siemens (as part of China's TD-SCDMA project), 3Com (with a focus on sales and joint product development), as well as Intel and Qualcomm. Huawei's emerging global innovation network now includes, in addition to six R&D centers in China, four major overseas R&D centers (see Table 3.2).

In sum, Huawei displays all the characteristics of a company that is building impressive and genuine technological capabilities. There is no guarantee that Huawei will continue to grow, nor can we predict how many firms like Huawei will ultimately emerge in China. However, this particular case study supports the general picture of openness, flexibility, and technological dynamism which we painted in more general terms in earlier sections.

Conclusion

This chapter presents an optimistic picture of China's industrial development, as seen through the perspective of the IT industry. Both Chinese domestic factors and international economic trends have contributed to the rapid restructuring of the Chinese IT industry into a highly dynamic, flexible, and open structure. The diversity of Chinese industry is its great strength. Equally important are flexibility and international openness that have enabled Chinese IT firms to take advantage of the new opportunities that result from transformations in global production and innovation networks. This has enabled Chinese IT firms to accelerate the development of management and innovation capabilities.

In this context, we should not overestimate the state's role in Chinese industry. Although government policies are pervasive and specific interventions common, the most important activity with respect to the IT industry is not in the government sector at all, but in the second-tier hybrid sector. State ownership is significant in industry overall, and is likely to remain so for the foreseeable future. But state ownership is increasingly circumscribed in areas where it is probably not terribly costly economically, and may even have some justification in providing public goods and social services. The most dynamic sectors are evolving in different directions.

China is developing a multi-centric economy with great local diversity. In a broad sense, we are seeing a shift in the locus of technological dynamism beyond Beijing, and toward the Yangtze Delta (especially), as well as the Pearl River Delta. In the recent wave of technological dynamism, Beijing's Zhongguancun has displayed nowhere near the creativity, or dominance, that it displayed in the earlier, 1990s wave. New centers of semiconductor production and design, software, and new web-based services are growing up outside of Beijing.

In a related fashion, the rapid emergence of industrial clusters, composed primarily of small firms, is reshaping the distribution of both traditional and high-tech industries. This seems to represent the reemergence of a pattern with deep roots in Chinese history and culture. There are many precedents in China for dense networks of competing and cooperating small firms. As this pattern deepens, we expect to see increasing differences in the composition of output across different geographical regions.

We may speculate that this pattern has long-run political implications as well, and may influence the political evolution of China. Firms at both the central and regional levels continue to be characterized by close government-business ties, hybrid ownership, and insider dealing. This characteristic will combine with patterns of regional differentiation to create regional interest groups. It is not far-fetched to expect that region-based interest groups will create the first patterns of open political competition in China. Indeed, perhaps this is already happening, as Beijing politicians seek alliances in the Northeast and West to offset the growing economic clout of the Southeastern provinces.

Our most important conclusion concerns the IT industry itself. Close examination of that industry reveals patterns of organizational and strategic behavior that are likely to foster robust development. Moreover, this is coming at a particular stage in the process of globalization that is enabling new kinds of cross-border cooperation at a deeper level, extending beyond production to design, development, and research. All these activities have economic implications: there is a great deal of successful development of capabilities and transfer of technology as part of these international networks of cooperation and competition. As a result, we expect the IT industry to continue to thrive and provide a powerful impetus to the continuing of China's capitalist transition.

Notes

1 Overall, at least 15 other firms in the SASAC portfolio come from the military industrial complex.
2 This section draws on a detailed case study in Ernst (2006c).
3 These include Alcatel and Lucent for telecom equipment, and Cisco and Juniper for enterprise networking equipment.
4 The survey was conducted among 27,000 recent graduates of 600 Chinese universities. The 2005 ranking is Haier, IBM, P&G, Lenovo, Huawei, China Mobile, Microsoft, Siemens, LG, and GE.

References

Armbrecht, F.M.R. (2003) "Siting Industrial R&D in China: Notes from Pioneers," Arlington, VA: Industrial Research Institute, slide presentation. March 12.

Banister, J. (2005) "Manufacturing Earnings and Compensation in China," *Monthly Labor Review*, August: 22–40.

Beise, M. (2004) "Lead Markets: Country-Specific Drivers of the Global Diffusion of Innovations," *Research Policy*, 33(6–7): 997–1018.

Christensen, C.M. (1993) "The Rigid Disk Drive Industry: A History of Commercial and Technological Turbulence," *Business History Review*, 67(4): 531–588.

——(1997) *The Innovator's Dilemma. When New Technologies Cause Great Firms to Fail*, Boston, MA: Harvard Business School Press.

Einhorn, B. (2004) "Huawei: More Than A Local Hero: The Telecom Gear Maker Aims to be a Player in Global Innovation," *Business Week*, October 11. Online. Available HTTP: www.businessweek.com/magazine/content/04_41/b3903454.htm?chan=search (accessed February 9, 2007).

Ernst, D. (2002) "The Economics of Electronics Industry: Competitive Dynamics and Industrial Organization," in W. Lazonick (ed.) *The International Encyclopedia of Business and Management, Handbook of Economics*, London: International Thomson Business Press, pp. 319–339.

——(2006a) "Innovation Offshoring: Asia's Emerging Role in Global Innovation Networks," East-West Center Special Report, No. 10. Online. Available HTTP: www.eastwestcenter.org/res-rp-publicationdetails.asp?pub_ID=2006 (accessed February 5, 2007).

——(2006b) "Developing Innovative Capabilities in Chip Design: Insights from the US and China," manuscript, Honolulu, HI: East-West Center.

——(2006c) "Building Innovative Capabilities within Global Knowledge Networks: the Case of Huawei," manuscript, Honolulu, HI: East-West Center.

——(2007) "Can Chinese IT Firms Develop Innovative Capabilities Within Global Knowledge Networks?" in M.G. Hancock, H.S. Rowen, and W.F. Miller (eds)

China's Quest for Independent Innovation, Washington, DC: Shorenstein Asia Pacific Research Center and Brookings Institution Press, forthcoming in late 2007.

Ernst, D. and Kim, L. (2002) "Global Production Networks, Knowledge Diffusion and Local Capability Formation," *Research Policy*, 31(8/9): 1417–1429.

Gilboy, G. (2004) "The Myth Behind China's Miracle," *Foreign Affairs*, 83(4): 33–48.

Henderson, R.M. and Clark, K. (1990) "Architectural Innovation: The Reconfiguration of Existing Systems and the Failure of Established Firms," *Administrative Science Quarterly*, 35(1): 9–30.

Huang, G. (2002) "Guangdong 'Sanlai Yibu' chanye shengji [Guangdong's Processing Industry is Upgrading]," *21 Shiji Jingji Baodao* [*21st Century Economic Herald*], September 2, p. 2.

Huawei Annual Report (2004) Shenzhen, People's Republic of China.

Jiang, X. (2004) "2003–2004: Zhongguo liyong waizi de fenxi yu zhanwang [An Analysis and Outlook of China's Use of Foreign Direct Investments]," in G. Liu, L. Wang, and J. Li (eds) *Zhongguo jingji qianjing fenxi 2004 nian chunji baogao* [*Blue Book of China's Economy Spring 2004*], Beijing: Shehui Kexue Wenxian, pp. 202–227.

Li, D. D. and Lui, F. (2004) "Why do Governments Dump State Enterprises? Evidence from China," in T. Ito and A. O. Krueger (eds) *Governance, Regulation, and Privatization in the Asia-Pacific Region*, Chicago, IL: University of Chicago Press, pp. 211–230.

Linden, G. (2004) "China Standard Time: A Study in Strategic Industrial Policy," *Business and Politics*, 6(3). Online. Available HTTP: www.bepress.com/bap/vol6/iss3/art4 (accessed February 9, 2007).

Ling, Z. (2005) *The Lenovo Affair: The Growth of China's Computer Giant and its Takeover of IBM-PC*, Singapore: John Wiley & Sons.

Liu, X. (2005) "China's Development Model: An Alternative Strategy for Technological Catch-Up," Working paper, Institute of Innovation Research, Hitotsubashi University. March 22.

Lu, Q. (2000) *China's Leap into the Information Age: Innovation and Organization in the Computer Industry*, Oxford: Oxford University Press.

Ministry of Commerce (2006) Science and Technology Division, "2005 nian woguo gaoxin jishu chanpin jinchukou an qiye xingzhi fenlei tongji [High Technology Exports for 2005, Divided by Type of Enterprise]," January 26. Online. Available HTTP: kjs.mofcom.gov.cn/aarticle/bn/cbw/200601/20060101434158. html (accessed February 5, 2007).

Mu, Q. and Lee, K. (2005) "Knowledge Diffusion, Market Segmentation and Technological Catch-Up: The Case of the Telecommunication Industry in China," *Research Policy*, 34(6): 759–783.

National Development and Reform Commission (2005) "Gangtie chanye fazhan zhengce [Steel Industry Development Policy]," July 20. Online. Available HTTP: www.ndrc.gov.cn/zwjjbd/hyyw/t20050720_37471.htm (accessed February 5, 2007).

Naughton, B. (2005a) "SASAC Rising," *China Leadership Monitor*, (14). Online. Available HTTP: media.hoover.org/documents/clm14_bn.pdf (accessed February 5, 2007).

——(2005b) "The New Common Economic Program: China's Eleventh Five Year Plan and What It Means," *China Leadership Monitor* (16). Online. Available HTTP: media.hoover.org/documents/clm16_bn.pdf (accessed February 5, 2007).

——(2007) *The Chinese Economy: Transitions and Growth*, Cambridge, MA: MIT Press.

Naughton, B. and Segal, A. (2002) "Technology Development in the New Millennium: China in Search of a Workable Model," in W. Keller and R. Samuels (eds) *Crisis and Innovation: Asian Technology after the Millennium*, New York: Cambridge University Press, pp. 160–186.

Nolan, P. (2002) "China and the Global Business Revolution," *Cambridge Journal of Economics*, 26(1): 119–137.

Qian, P. (2003) "Development of China's Industrial Clusters: Features and Problems," *China Development Review*, 5(4): 44–51.

Rosen, D. (2003) "China Tech," *China Economic Quarterly*, 7(4): 19–40.

Ross, A. (2004) "Sock Hop," *The China Business Review*, 31(1): 54.

SASAC (2005) "Guanyu Zhongguo Dianzi Xinxi Chanye Jituan Gongsi deng 6 hu qiye chongzu de tongbao [Notification on Reorganization of 6 Firms including China Electronic Information Industry Group]," August 1. Online. Available HTTP: www.sasac.gov.cn/gzjg/qygg/200508010197.htm (accessed February 5, 2007).

——(2007) "2006 nian zhongyang qiye fazhan huigu [A Look Back at Central Enterprise Development in 2006]." Online. Available HTTP: sasac.gov.cn/2006rdzt/2006rdzt_0021/zyqy/default.htm (accessed February 9, 2007).

Shen, X. (1999) *The Chinese Road to High Technology*, New York: St. Martin's.

Steinfeld, E. (2004) "Chinese Enterprise Development and the Challenge of Global Integration," in S. Yusuf (ed.) *East Asian Networked Production*, Washington, DC: World Bank.

Suttmeier, P. and Yao, X. (2004) "China's Post-WTO Technology Policy: Standards, Software, and the Changing Nature of Techno-Nationalism," *NBR Special Report*, No. 7. Online. Available HTTP: nbr.org/publications/specialreport/pdf/SR7.pdf (accessed February 5, 2007).

US-China Economic Security Review Commission (2005) *2005 Annual Report*. Online. Available HTTP: uscc.gov/annual_report/2005/annual_report_full_05.pdf (accessed February 16, 2007).

Xie, W. and White, S. (2004) "Sequential Learning in a Chinese Spin-Off: The Case of Lenovo Group Limited," *R&D Management*, 34(4): 407–422.

4 Venture capital and the financing of China's new technology firms[*]

Wei Zhang, Jian Gao, Steven White, and Paul Vega

Introduction

After decades of economic reform, China has finally entered a period in which competitive firm performance is being driven by factors associated with capitalist business systems. Most firms in most industries are already under considerable pressure to address market and customer demands, operate more efficiently, and increase their value. For firms and industries that are linked to international markets and global supply chains, this pressure is even more extreme.

While other chapters in this volume address China's existing industries and firms, we focus our attention on the founding of new technology-based firms and the venture capital system that has emerged to finance them. These high-tech firms and their venture capital backers are perhaps the clearest manifestation of China's transition to an economy in which firms and their owners are able to appropriate returns from proprietary resources, be they organizational, technological, or human. Most of the firms established in the 1990s were able to succeed in commodity industries based on imitative strategies and generic technologies. Today's technology entrepreneurs, however, must start from a basis of competitively valuable proprietary technology and capabilities.

Luckily for these would-be high-tech entrepreneurs, China's investments in its innovation system – universities and research institutes, in particular – have begun to pay off. China's R&D spending is set to surpass Japan's in 2006, amounting to about US$136 billion, and making China the number two R&D spender in the world. China's R&D spending is also tipped to continue its double digit growth in 2006 and sustain a rapid pace in the future, reaching 2 percent of economic output in 2010 and 2.5 percent in 2020 (OECD 2006).

In tandem, the number of Chinese researchers has soared by 77 percent over the past decade to 966,000, ranking second behind the United States' 1.3 million and ahead of Japan's 677,000 (OECD 2006). Chinese researchers are further being joined by large numbers of returnees from programs abroad. No wonder, all measures of codified scientific and technical knowledge outputs have been increasing in China. During the period 1991–2002, the number of invention patents granted to domestic owners increased by 4.4 times to 5,868, and the number of utility patents by 3.3 times to 57,092 (National Bureau of Statistics & Ministry of Science and Technology 2003).

Competitive opportunities provided by increasing technology resources have fueled a boom in new technology start-ups as well as demand for financial support of these ventures. However, China's existing financial system, whose purpose has been to pool financial resources to support state-owned enterprises (SOEs), could not respond to this new demand. After attempting to fill this financing gap through state-directed programs and indirect subsidies, the Chinese government finally allowed more types of organizations to participate in what has come to resemble a venture capital industry. There are already over 200 domestic and foreign venture capital firms operating in China, and in 2004 they invested a combined US$1.27 billion. By the end of 2005, 23 Chinese firms backed by venture capital had listed on NASDAQ and together boast over US$15 billion in market value.[1]

Although representing only a small percentage of China's financial system, the development of venture capital in China has had a disproportionate impact in several areas.[2] First, such funding has greatly accelerated and fostered the development of new industries, including internet-based service businesses, semiconductor manufacturing, integrated circuit design, mobile service design, and new media advertising. These industries would not have received support within the traditional financial system, nor would they have been able to develop so rapidly.

Second, both angel and venture capitalist investors have pushed owners and managers to put mechanisms in place that support good corporate governance and professional management. Venture capital thus supports firms that can serve as examples to other Chinese firms, thereby supporting the Chinese government's objective of raising the standards of domestic corporations *vis-à-vis* global best practices. In contrast, while China's informal financing sector is estimated to represent up to 80 percent of new venture financing (Tsai 2002), participants in that sector usually do not have the experience and capabilities necessary to improve corporate governance and management.

None of these domestic developments – competition based on proprietary knowledge, technology development, financing for new ventures, accelerated development of new technology firms – has taken place in a global vacuum. Rather, they are directly linked to global developments in competition, knowledge, and capital. In this chapter, we describe the dialectic process by which domestic and global forces have interacted and resulted in the trajectory on which we find this segment of China's economic system. Building on the growing literature comparing venture capital systems in diverse national contexts (e.g. Bartzokas and Mani 2004; Jeng and Wells

2000; Kuemmerle 2001), we identify the origins and key developments of China's new venture capital system. We first describe the institutional and policy antecedents to the current system's structure. We then analyze the investment decision-making process that domestic and foreign venture capitalists are implementing. Finally, we note the implications of these features for investors and China's new technology firms, as well as China's broader transition.

System structure

Beginning in the 1980s, the Chinese government's technology and industrial development policies led to a large number of new technology ventures being founded. However, no separate venture capital industry existed at this time.[3] Central government leaders recognized by the mid-1990s that the existing system for establishing new ventures had reached its limit. First, the supply of early stage seed capital was too small, dependent as it was on the very limited resources of research institutes and universities. Banks were also strapped by their non-performing loans, and increasing loans to inherently high-risk ventures was untenable. Indeed, neither the central nor local governments had surplus funds to offer as alternative sources to finance new ventures. Political bias against private ventures compounded these problems.

Second, the government did not recognize venture capital as a legitimate commercial activity, so financing was limited to government-backed incubators or institutes and universities that used their internal resources and/or government subsidies, such as under the Torch Program. Third, the commercial legal code did not provide support for new ventures, since relevant contract law was either inadequate or its enforcement unreliable, and private property rights were not yet formally recognized. Venture capital, defined as high-risk equity investment, is not possible if there is no legal definition and protection of ownership over a new venture's assets.

Gradually, from the mid-1990s, the perception of venture capital shifted from being a type of government funding to being a commercial activity necessary to support the commercialization of new technology. The first venture capital firms (VCs) allowed to operate were government-, university-, and institute-backed. Starting from 1998 these were joined by a wave of corporate-backed VCs, both domestic and foreign owned.[4]

From that point on, venture capital became a rapidly growing segment of China's financial system, evolving in tandem with a new wave of high-tech entrepreneurship. The venture capital industry that has since emerged is depicted in Figure 4.1. The following section describes the institutional trajectory of the primary actors constituting China's venture capital system.[5]

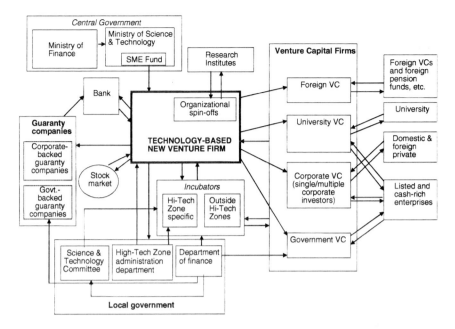

Figure 4.1 China's new technology-based firm financing system structure.

Source: Authors' research and White *et al.* (2005).

Government

The government has played a central role in the development of China's venture capital industry. The Ministry of Science and Technology (MoST; formerly the State Science and Technology Commission) was the primary champion, interpreting venture capital as a key factor behind the success of US high-tech industries. Policymakers came to see venture capital as a means of linking science and technology development with national economic development. During the transition period, MoST was able to garner support from other key central government bodies, including China's State Council, State Planning Commission, and the Chinese Communist Party leadership. This top-level support then opened the way to bring on board other important bureaucratic actors, in particular, the Ministry of Finance and local governments.

We now see a division of labor between central government bureaucracies and local government agencies *vis-à-vis* venture capital. The central government has played three important roles. First, its reform policy of decentralizing responsibility and authority has created the institutional space for lower level actors – local governments, research institutes, and universities – to act entrepreneurially. This "freedom" to be more entrepreneurial is coupled with financial incentives; namely, the central government is providing less budgetary support to lower level actors, so their budgets are increasingly dependent on economic performance. Research institutes and universities, for instance, have spun off sub-units, people, and even whole organizations in the hope of creating profitable ventures.

The second important role has been to provide legitimacy to technological entrepreneurship as a commercial activity and to new ventures as legal entities. For example, the funds provided by central government sources serve as a signal to local governments and banks that the venture is politically legitimate, and therefore a qualified recipient of their support.

Finally, the central government has created an institutional environment that is increasingly conducive to new technology entrepreneurship. For venture capital and new venture firm development, key institutional elements include: corporate law governing investments, contracts, intellectual property, and the status and activities of legal entities; regulation of foreign capital and enterprises; and the stock market and other elements of the capital markets.

Compared to the central government, local governments have played a much more direct role. They are motivated by the same fundamental belief as that of the central government, that is, that greater exploitation of local science and technology resources can support economic and social development objectives, albeit focused on local rather than national benefits. Indeed, local governments face considerable incentives to pay attention to local economic growth, as central government support for both their budgets and local enterprises (especially state firms) has dropped sharply. Local bureaucrats also have individual incentives to support new technology ventures, since their career progress rests on successfully implementing the central government's policy priorities.

Within local governments, finance departments, science and technology committees, and high-tech zone administration departments are key actors providing assistance to new ventures. For example, local departments of finance, in addition to directly supporting new ventures financially, have created government-backed companies to guarantee bank loans to local ventures.

Government-backed high-tech zones and incubators have more generally aided the development of new technology ventures. Through these institutions, governments provide tax incentives, physical space at low rental rates, better social services, greater operational autonomy (especially more flexible personnel policies), and other preferential conditions. After the State Council in 1991 authorized local governments to fund VCs through high-tech zone administrations, their role and activities increased dramatically. By 1992 there were already 52 high-tech zones established throughout China, and 5,569 new technology ventures were registered. By 2002, the number of ventures in these zones reached 28,338, with exports of US$33 billion (Gu 1999: 39).

From the central government's perspective, these zones have generated benefits in two areas. First, they have provided a structure within which local governments act creatively, enabling experimentation in terms of administrative structures, market-oriented operations, and human resource management. Second, the zones have contributed significantly to the commercialization of China's science and technology outputs by non-government technology firms. They also serve as avenues for training and education, thus enhancing the competitiveness of firms by supporting innovation capabilities.

Incubators emerged in force along with the development of science and technology zones in the early 1990s. The first ones were founded within zones as extensions of the initial services provided by zone administrations. The 464 incubators registered nationwide at the end of 2004 are now found both within and outside zones, and include both government-funded and for-profit organizations. Some incubators are even treated as a category of new technology venture firms by their investors. Their collective output has been impressive: by 2002, nearly 38,000 firms had emerged from incubators, including 20 that were listed on stock markets.

Some local governments are providing formal oversight of the incubators within their jurisdictions. Beijing, for example, has the largest number of incubators and has special policies for promoting them, regardless of who backs them and where they are located. In fact, there is a process by which incubators are licensed by the Beijing Science and Technology Commission, including standards of operation and assessments by expert groups. Authorized incubators are re-examined every two years to confirm whether they still meet these requirements.

One weakness of many zone or government-backed incubators is that they are state entities, and many of the managers come from government positions. Performance incentives for these managers are typically inadequate, and most do not have the expertise to provide strong support and value-added services. University-based incubators are better than pure government-backed incubators in terms of both their internal systems and human resources. Corporate-backed incubators are even more strongly focused on creating profit and value, although they are liable to overemphasize short-term profits at the expense of long-term development. Although university, corporate, and purely private incubators may not be under direct government control, most still seek local government support, especially related to physical space, infrastructure, and tax incentives.

VCs and investors

VCs have become one of the main sources of funds for new technology-based ventures in China. The number of VCs operating in China was estimated at 296 in 2002, but decreased to 233 in 2003 (Ministry of Science and Technology 2004). There are, however, four distinct categories of VCs, each with different antecedents, objectives, and operating characteristics. Tables 4.1 and 4.2 present a comparison of these four types, and Table 4.3 a comparison of domestic and foreign VCs.

Table 4.1 Comparison of venture capital firm types in China

	Government VC	Corporate VC	University VC	Foreign VC
Ownership or legal form	SOE and Limited corporation	Limited corporation	Limited corporation	Limited partnership
Initial/primary investor	Local government	Listed companies	University industrial group; other firms	Pension or other funds; corporations
Top manager background	Government bureaucracy and SOE	Securities firm or bank; industry	University's enterprise group or other firms	Foreign VC funds; investment banking
Primary motivation and objectives	Promote local high-tech industry and commercialization	Higher return on investment than alternative investments; related business opportunities	Commercialization of university's science and technology achievements	High return on investment
Investment focus	High-tech	High-tech	High-tech	High growth/potential
Preferred stage	Early	Late, expansion	Early	Growth
Investment time horizon	3–5 years	3–5 years	not clear	3–7 years
Follow-on investment	No	Varies	Varies	Yes
Geographic distribution of investment	Local	Local, regional	Universities and regional	Major metropolitan areas (Shanghai, Beijing, Guangzhou, Shenzhen, etc.)
Internal incentive system	Salary + bonus	Salary + bonus	Salary + bonus	Salary + carried interest

Source: Authors' research and White *et al.* (2005).

Table 4.2 Comparison of venture capital firm types in China (strengths, weaknesses and future issues)

	Government VC	Corporate VC	University VC	Foreign VC
Strengths	Government base provides ready-made channels to government and access to or information about policies and projects.	Strong financial base (proceeds from listing, cash flow from operations) gives them investing flexibility. Industry base gives them management and operational expertise that they can draw on for selecting and monitoring investments, as well as form base for related diversification and pursuing new business opportunities opened up by a new venture.	Strong technology base benefiting from R&D activities and concentration of personnel in university; access to primary source of science and technology in China. University link provides them preferential access to those resources.	Professional experience in financing and managing start-ups and high-growth firms. Can draw on experience in other markets, link Chinese firms to business partners and markets abroad through foreign network of investees and related business activities. Expertise in decision-making and VC cycle, especially exit decision.
Weaknesses	Objectives and incentives are split between financial and social returns to investment; weaker internal incentives than foreign VC. Investments	Short-term investment horizon driven by need (in listed companies) to show annual performance; availability of funds subject to firm's current	Lack of business management experience. Same problems of internal incentives as government VC and corporate VC. Investment opportunities	No strong relationship with major organizations (government, enterprises, universities) in China, so no preferential access to domestic sources

(*Table 4.2 continued*)

Table 4.2 Continued

	Government VC	Corporate VC	University VC	Foreign VC
	influenced by policy objectives. Managers may not be familiar with firm management practices, systems, procedures, etc.	operational performance in core business. Corporations not experienced with managing high-risk investments represented by investee firms. Weaker internal incentives than foreign VC.	limited to those emerging within the university.	of related resources. Must expend time and effort on establishing relationships to access investment opportunities.
Future issues	Local governments will not inject additional capital, so short-term investment capacity depends on ability to find alternative sources of investment funds and, later, returns to investments and financing.	Role in financing tech-based firms will continue to be important, and corporations will continue to be primary source of funds if pension fund, insurance cannot enter venture capital industry.	Lack of key expertise (firm management, VC investment) will drive them closer to corporate VCs and foreign VCs.	Further opening of China and their own good performance will allow them to exploit their VC expertise even more in China. Such expertise and linkages outside China continue to make them attractive to potential investee firms.

Source: Authors' research and White et al. (2005).

The first type to appear in China was the government VC. The earliest of these was established by the central government – State Science and Technology Commission and Ministry of Finance – in 1985. Those that followed, though, were all controlled by local governments. Although initially dependent on local governments for their funding, regulatory changes have allowed these local government-backed VCs to gradually diversify their sources of financing. Many are now increasingly dependent on listed or other cash-rich enterprises.

Government VCs' association with local governments gives them preferential access to information and investment opportunities. Close ties with local government, however, can also be a weakness. VCs can be susceptible to local government pressure to support new ventures whose risk and return prospects are not attractive. They are also not able to attract the most experienced or capable managers.

University VCs emerged in large numbers from 2000. They benefit tremendously from their university ties and privileged access to new venture investment opportunities. Yet, they also suffer from some of the same weaknesses as government VCs. Specifically, their investment opportunities are in practice limited to those that emerge from the university, and they do not have the managerial expertise related to venture capital investing. Moreover, universities are usually not cash-rich, so they depend more and more on other sources of investment capital. As with government VCs, publicly listed and cash-rich enterprises have become their primary backers. Although there are examples of research institutes founding VCs, they are too few to represent a major category of VC. The few that exist share the same advantages and disadvantages of university VCs.

A wave of founding domestic corporate VCs occurred in 1998. Until 2001, when foreign VCs started to dominate, these domestic firms represented the majority of VC firms operating in China. Beijing High-Tech Venture Capital Ltd. and Beijing Venture Capital Ltd. were the first corporate VCs. Founded in October 1998 their government backing was strong, causing many to perceive them as part of the Beijing government's sprawling commercial empire. Then in early 1999 many genuinely corporate-backed VCs were founded, although these still sought local government support. Their managers typically heralded from securities firms, banks, or industry.

Newly listed Chinese firms, who received more cash from their listings than they could use on productive internal investments, became the primary source of funds for domestic corporate VCs. By the end of 2001, 132 publicly listed companies (11 percent of all listed companies) had invested in corporate VCs. Unlisted firms with large cash flows, individual investors, and foreign firms also invested in these.

Quite often, investors are directly involved in the industries in which corporate VCs invest, so they can draw on their industry and managerial capabilities to assist new ventures. In addition to any financial returns to their investment, corporate VCs can help investors identify new business opportunities. At the same time, new ventures benefit from the links of these investors to potential suppliers and customers.

Nonetheless, many corporate VCs and their backers have been disappointed. They invested with the expectation that the new venture would list quickly, and they were not interested in the venture's long-term development. As the government postponed establishing a second board on the Shenzhen exchange for growth stocks, their timeframe for realizing investment returns has become unexpectedly long, and some have suffered heavy losses and gone bankrupt.

Finally, foreign VCs have entered China and become a major source of new venture financing. "Foreign" in this case is defined as a VC originally based outside of China, pooling investment funds from outside of China. In 2004, six of the top ten venture capital investors in China were foreign firms, and fourteen of the top twenty. Like the domestic corporate VCs, most of the foreign VCs are backed by multiple investors, although a few (e.g. Intel Capital) are the investment arms of single firms.

There are also a number of other significant differences between domestic and foreign VCs (see Table 4.3). One fundamental difference is that foreign VCs' focus on high-growth or high-potential investment targets, is not necessarily high-tech. They also have greater expertise in venture capital

Table 4.3 Differences between domestic and foreign venture capital firms in China

	Domestic VCs	*Foreign VCs in China*
Structure and team	Limited company setup, onshore. No general partners, mainly employed investment managers. Some bonus schemes apply.	Limited partnership, offshore. General partners actively manage the investments.
Access to capital	Low: by law, mostly backed by the state or public companies.	High: mainly foreign pension funds, insurance companies.
Experience of team	Limited. Former government officers or SOE managers.	Good deal track record in home markets, highly professional.
Origin of VC team	Domestic team, mostly Chinese.	Senior foreign investors, but localizing with returnees and Overseas Chinese.
Deal size	Typically smaller <$5m.	Considerably larger, often $10–$15m, occasionally even higher.

(*Table 4.3 continued*)

Table 4.3 Continued

	Domestic VCs	Foreign VCs in China
Deal stage	Depends on type: University VCs earlier-stage than other domestic VCs; government VCs were early stage, but a lot of them have moved to later stage/pre-IPO.	Initially focused on later-stage, but now depends on firm; tend to focus on a specific stage.
Market knowledge	Strong relationships, but highly localized.	Focus on industry and sector expertise.
Deal due diligence	Sometimes unstructured process, many inexperienced players in the market. Top-down driven by decisions made by the VC's head.	Tried and tested processes from the home market being adapted for China. Top-down and bottom-up processes.
Emphasis of value added to portfolio	Relationships and introductions; capital.	Formal monitoring, guidance, overseas expansion routes.
Capital convertibility	Not an issue.	Problem in capital repatriation. Offshore domiciling and exit preferred.
Exit route	Domestic trade sale, some local IPOs, rarely overseas.	Overseas IPO. Trade sale (M&A), preferably to Western buyer.
Information access	High, often public disclosure required by regulators. Private information limited to trade secrets and proprietary knowledge.	Limited access, often low quality information. Triangulation and focus on unpublished information.

Source: Research interviews, market research.

management. Zhang and Jiang (2002) found that the managers in domestic VCs averaged 2.1 years of relevant experience, while those of foreign VCs operating in China averaged 11.9 years. Foreign VCs also have better incentive systems to retain managers and manage investments for longer-term gains. Finally, foreign VCs can usually provide linkages to potential customers and partners in foreign markets.

Because of these differences, foreign VCs are able to provide more value-added services to their investment targets. They are also more active in terms of monitoring decision-making. While foreign VCs typically take part in board meetings at least once per quarter, less than half of the domestic VCs participate so frequently. On the other hand, foreign VCs are more politically vulnerable and lack the intimate connections to government bodies, enterprises, and universities that benefit domestic VCs.

Investment decision-making process

Just as the institutional origins of China's venture capital system have evolved in response to both foreign and domestic factors, so has the process by which investment decisions are made and implemented. At a fundamental level, venture capital investors in China have the same objectives as those in the US and other markets. They want to profit from a type of arbitrage, in which a venture capital investor trades off short-term illiquidity by investing in high-risk companies in return for future returns potential (Gorman and Sahlmann 1986). The attitudes, beliefs, and specific practices of venture capitalists, however, may diverge across widely varying national contexts.

One of the fundamental premises of this chapter and volume is to take a historical institutionalist approach to tracing the origins and still-evolving practices of China's capitalist transition. In this section, we use an extensive interview-based study of venture capital investors in China that sought to identify similarities and differences in their investment-making processes.[6] We contrast the practices current in China with the "conventional" practices that have emerged in the US and spread somewhat to Western Europe (see Figure 4.2). We also identify how foreign and domestic investors are reacting to the "same" Chinese environment.

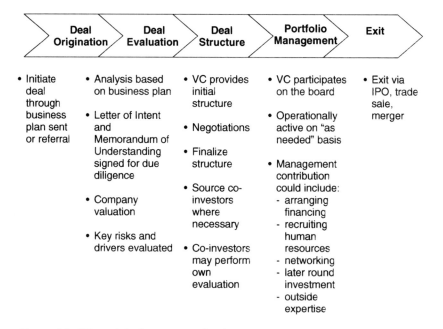

Figure 4.2 US model of venture capital investment process.

Source: Authors' interviews and Bygrave and Timmons (1992), Fried and Hirsch (1994), MacMillan *et al.* (1985), and Wright and Robbie (1998).

Deal origination

Two features of the Chinese environment have had a strong influence on how venture capitalists source deals. First is the importance of personal relationships in sourcing potential investment targets. Strong and long-standing personal relationships (*guanxi*) are considered a critical basis of trust in China, since contracts and other elements of commercial law are still seen as inadequate for governing business relationships (Batjargal and Liu 2002). In practice, relationship cultivation is driven by relatively senior managers in China's VCs. These must have strong connections to the local government, research laboratories, and local entrepreneurs to gain access to inbound deal flows. Although foreign VCs may have strong reputations and sector expertise, they do not benefit from these assets much in China. As a result, most foreign VCs said they spend more effort on outbound deal sourcing, that is, proactively scouting for investment opportunities and undertaking significant primary market research in-house.

Even when venture capitalists do find potential investment opportunities, a second feature of the Chinese environment – the lack of business development skills among entrepreneurs – affects the effort that venture capitalists must expend. Venture capitalists tend to target firms in either emerging technology sectors or rapidly changing industries that have just emerged from state ownership or government protection. Would-be entrepreneurs in such firms tend to have had limited exposure to market-based competition and professional management practices. Venture capitalists must thus help them identify good business opportunities, guide the management team, assist in drafting business plans, and prepare the firm for funding and scale-up. This is less true in the case of start-ups founded by Chinese who have studied and worked abroad ("returnees"), or those with work experience in new Chinese technology-based firms such as Huawei and ZTE. The number of such entrepreneurs, however, is still relatively small compared to the total number of firms being founded.

The Chinese environment thus requires much greater commitments of managerial effort, capital, and time than foreign VCs are accustomed to. For these reasons, more foreign VCs are avoiding early-stage investments and focusing on high-potential later-stage opportunities. Commented one venture capitalist: "I feel more comfortable with later-stage investments. The financials are mostly in order, the management has proven itself, and [we know that] the business can be scaled." In practice, this has resulted in a shift in sourcing criteria to established, rather than leading-edge, technology and high-growth businesses.

A third feature of the Chinese environment is the lack of experience of domestic VCs in developing and adhering to formal deal sourcing guidelines. For example, from the late 1990s when the government began promoting the idea of a second board, many domestic VCs rushed to source investments with the expectation of a quick exit in a domestic listing.

Proposals were passed and investments made that did not meet the domestic VC's own stated investment guidelines, and most of the investments made during this period are now either struggling, have been sold, or have gone into receivership. As a result, domestic VCs, like foreign VCs, now prefer to make later stage investments.

Deal evaluation

Venture capitalists face significant challenges in evaluating both business feasibility and management team quality in the Chinese environment. The lack of reliable information is the first severe limitation on the due diligence process and is an additional reason for why many VCs focus on later-stage investments. Some data are simply not available or are of questionable accuracy. For example, estimates of market size and growth rates, or customer adoption rates tend to be inadequate. This is particularly true for businesses targeting innovative new services or high technology. Similarly, many industries have changed dramatically over the last five to ten years, so even the available historical data is of limited value for benchmarking or extrapolation.

Because regulations and their enforcement are relatively weak, VCs cannot rely on a firm's financial data, nor can they assume that significant company information has been given to investors. Huang and Chin (2003: 1) describe this aspect of China's legal infrastructure as "laden in bureaucracy and uncertainty and lacking the sophisticated tools required by venture capitalists." A Chinese venture capitalist further noted, "It is not uncommon for a Chinese company to have separate sets of financial statements . . . one for the government, another for the investor, and some even for their business partner." This is exacerbated in the case of SOEs, with a legacy of central planning and, as one American venture capitalist commented, a history of building profit and loss statements "top-down."

At the same time, VCs cannot rely on professional service firms – consultants, auditors, law firms, industry research firms – that support VCs in the US. Such firms are relatively few in China, the quality of their analysis is limited, and they have few resources outside of major cities.

The second challenge to evaluating an investment opportunity is the difficulty in assessing management teams. Foreign VCs cited the motives and character of company founders as a more common source of risk in China than in the US, and they have more detailed due diligence and vetting procedures for prospective management teams. Some even interview friends, family, relatives, previous employers and colleagues, suppliers, and potential customers.

To increase the likelihood that entrepreneurs provide more accurate information, venture capitalists also rely on implied or direct threats to reputation and third-party involvement. For example, a Singaporean investor stated, "We make it very clear to the entrepreneur that we would make sure they never raise money again if they try to cheat us." An

American investor added, "We get the government involved at the right level, sometimes as co-investors or as partners. That helps to get things done both internally and externally."

Another source of difficulty in evaluating management teams is China's complex and dynamic business environment. This context places high demands on management teams in terms of business development, networking, and agility across a broader range of management issues compared to that of the US. Even a successful entrepreneurial track record and market expertise do not guarantee success when the environment is changing rapidly and in fundamental ways.

For foreign VCs an additional consideration is cultural compatibility between them and a management team. Although foreign VCs see experience and expertise as important, many of these investors are wary of management teams comprised of only "pure" Chinese who have no foreign experience and limited first-hand knowledge of professional management techniques. As one explained, "Most often, purely domestic Chinese teams don't understand how to work with us and what value we can add to their business as investors. The terminology we use and the concepts we propose are unfamiliar to them. Sometimes, they just see us as a source of dumb money."

As a result, many foreign VCs prefer to work either with returnees or with local Chinese who have worked in first-tier foreign multinationals in China. They see these two groups as sharing with them an understanding of appropriate business practices and also values related to corporate governance and business ethics. Foreign VCs, though, recognize that such similarities do not always lead to commercial success. Even returnees or Overseas Chinese can find it difficult to re-integrate and operate in China's changing and competitive environment. Perhaps to ensure that local knowledge is embedded in the firm, most foreign VCs say that domestic managers are critical, especially in operations and at the mid- and lower-level ranks. Said one foreign venture capitalist, "With sales and operational staff, we found that they have to be local Chinese to be able to work with the local Chinese. Out in the provinces, a Shanghainese manager might have more in common with a New Yorker than the local customer or supplier."

Deal structuring and negotiation

Because of the underdeveloped legal system and contract enforcement mechanisms in China, especially outside the major metropolitan areas, most foreign VCs agree that investment contracts play a less important role than in the US. As one venture capitalist pointed out, "We don't worry about putting too much detail in the term sheet. We would never sue a company in China, especially in their home jurisdiction. If you go to court, you have already lost the battle." While litigation and court action in the US is also a sign of a failed relationship, legal action in that context serves as an implicit and credible threat to both parties against them breaking their contractual agreements.

Both foreign and domestic VCs have responded in several ways. In addition to putting more effort into due diligence to assess the management team's likelihood of acting opportunistically, they structure the deal so that the VCs and entrepreneur's interests are closely aligned. They use a number of additional measures that serve as lock-ins and deterrents, such as using convertible preferred stock or debt, granting stock options with the founders vesting over time, releasing capital in multiple tranches, or setting penalty and bonus systems based on pre-negotiated performance targets. Foreign VCs also use additional means, such as offshore domiciling (in a more predictable legal jurisdiction) and holding some critical resources (such as technical expertise) overseas.

Portfolio management

Portfolio management is much more time and resource-intensive in China than in the US. Foreign VCs use terms such as "proactive management," "closer involvement," "constant supervision," "operational investing," and "frequent interaction" to describe their relationship with investment targets in China. Domestic VCs have also learned that simply holding stakes without actively monitoring them is not tenable. Many of them incurred write-offs during the period between the late 1990s and 2001 when they took small stakes in a large number of new firms, but did not have the time or resources to actively guide companies in their portfolio. Most domestic VCs now realize that they need to become more like foreign VCs, who are much more active in their formal monitoring and participation in strategic decision-making.

Two features of the Chinese environment make it necessary for investors to take a more hands-on approach with their investment targets or portfolio companies. First, an investor cannot rely on the threat of legal sanction to deter opportunistic behavior by an entrepreneur, such as an entrepreneur placing family members on the company payroll or giving procurement and service contracts to close friends in return for kick-backs. Venture capitalists must be geographically close and actively supervise managers to prevent such behavior, since legal redress after the fact is at best uncertain. One foreign venture capitalist noted, "I would not invest in China if I did not have a team that could be with my portfolio company within an hour. Local presence and active monitoring are absolutely critical."

Second, most management teams have little or no experience in growing a new firm. Their challenge is compounded by the rapid and dramatic changes in China's business environment. Venture capitalists can contribute to their investment target's strategic analysis, corporate planning, and execution activities to a greater degree in China than in the US.

Investment exit

While initial public offerings (IPOs) are preferred by VCs in both the US and China, there are considerable barriers to listing a new firm in China. First, China has two IPO markets: the Shanghai and Shenzhen Stock Exchanges, with the latter adding a new board for small and medium-sized enterprises in May 2004. The listing requirements for all of these, however, effectively exclude most new firms. For example, firms are required to show three consecutive years of revenues and three consecutive years of profits. Even if they meet filing requirements, the exchanges have long waiting lists. Because the regulatory body (the China Securities Regulatory Commission) reserves the right to select which companies may tap into the stock market, investors see receiving approval to file an IPO as a political decision. More recently, the formal application criteria have been loosened (for example, geographic quotas have been eliminated). Nonetheless, VCs use the terms "lack of transparency" and "political bias" to discuss the process. Foreign VCs also see regulators as favoring Chinese-backed firms over foreign-backed companies.

VCs have responded to these exit constraints in several ways. First, because trade sales are the primary exit route in China, VCs need to make larger initial investments in order to have a large enough stake to sell later to a trade sale buyer. This leads to another problem: the sale of a controlling stake significantly reduces the motivation of the entrepreneur and management team to continue to build the company, and in many cases they leave the firm following a sale. Second, because there are a relatively small number of potential buyers, the rate of return to the VC is usually considerably lower than from an IPO, and in turn calls into question the US-style VC business model predicated on IPOs being the major source of returns.

In response, foreign VCs push their investment targets to seek listings on exchanges outside of China, such as on NASDAQ, Hong Kong's Growth Enterprise Market (GEM), Hong Kong's main board, or in Singapore. NASDAQ is clearly the preferred exchange, but the total number of Chinese firms that can qualify for a listing there is a very small percentage of the firms that have received venture capital. Listing on GEM, established in November 1999 as an Asian counterpart to NASDAQ, is easier. However, returns to an IPO on it are much lower than on NASDAQ, primarily because of GEM's relatively low liquidity.

Foreign VCs, who must repatriate profits to pay returns to their own investors (usually located outside of China), have the additional concern of inconvertibility for the Chinese *yuan*. As part of their deal selection criteria, they give priority to investments in firms that have a possibility of listing overseas or being sold to a major multinational. They may also help restructure a Chinese firm so that some part of it is domiciled offshore, and then invest in that entity. In these ways they are more likely to generate foreign currency proceeds that can be repatriated.

The evolution of China's venture capital system

The institutional structure of China's venture capital system consists of a particular set of organizational actors, regulations, industry practices, attitudes, and beliefs. Currently, this structure is quite different from that found in the US or other national contexts, and reflects China's institutional legacy.

Within this structure, venture capitalists are creating and implementing a micro-structure: the investment process. Overall, this investment process – from deal origination to exit – converges strongly with that found in the US and other developed venture capital markets. Venture capitalists in China are following a structured decision-making process, albeit heavily modified for the Chinese business environment. For foreign VCs, this has involved "unlearning" some of the processes that they developed in the US environment. For China's much younger and inexperienced domestic VCs, this has involved modifying the practices that they saw in the US venture capital industry while building up their own skills and experience.

China's institutional structure and investment process, however, are starting to co-evolve. Venture capitalists are modifying their behavior in response to feedback from their environment (investment perform-ance, relationships with investees, regulatory enforcement, and normative industry pressures). Concurrently, policymakers are modifying regulations in response to systemic changes and in an attempt to modify the behavior of venture capitalists. Albeit for different reasons, both policymakers and venture capitalists have an interest in the direction and pace of this system's evolution. Based on the current features of both the macro- and micro-structure, we can identify several trends that have clear implications for policymakers, venture capitalists and investees, and, on a broader level, China's transition.

To begin with, the system's structure is more complex than that found in the US in terms of the number and types of actors involved, and this is not likely to change significantly in the short to medium term. In par-ticular, the central and local governments are deeply involved in the system, not only by setting and enforcing regulations, but also as actors; for example, through the incubators and technology zones that they fund and manage.

This environment is reinforced by the central government, which has made the development and commercialization of technology – measured in terms of new technology-based firms and their commercial performance – a yardstick for comparison among locales and one element of a local leader's personal performance assessment. Although this situation is not likely to change, there will be tensions as local government leaders decide how to allocate financial resources. Technology-related projects will have to compete with more immediately pressing social uses, such as physical infrastructure, education, medical care, and environmental protection.

In the near future, we expect the system to become even more complex in terms of the numbers and types of venture capital firms – foreign, corporate, government, and university – operating in China. The existing firms and funds will be joined by new legal forms (e.g. domestic partnerships) and hybrid forms (foreign-domestic co-funding projects and formal joint ventures). Some of this is already underway within the existing regulatory framework (e.g. co-investing), and most observers believe that policymakers are moving toward allowing alternative organizational forms, albeit slowly. The combined effect will be a greater range of options for investors. There will also be more opportunities for pooling the different resources and expertise of different types of VCs.

At present, we find marked differences between foreign and domestic VCs (see Tables 4.1, 4.2, and 4.3). One of the clearest differences is the much shorter-term orientation of domestic VCs, which can be attributed to three factors: their perception of high regulatory, technological, and market uncertainty; pressure to gather new funding that depends on showing returns on prior investments; and short-term horizons for assessing individual venture capitalist performance.

Nonetheless, we see growing convergence between foreign and domestic VCs in their investment decision-making practices. Both are already following the same overall process, from deal origination to exit, although most domestic VCs still lack the experience and technical expertise of foreign VCs. Both types of VCs are also responding in similar ways to the same features of the environment. These features include entrepreneurs without significant management experience, weak or ineffective formal mechanisms for guiding and monitoring investees, mutual suspicion between entrepreneurs and VCs, and constraints on exit options domestically. By nature of their location and backing, foreign VCs now have more options to respond to these features.

Specifically, three forces are accelerating the convergence between different types of VCs. First, the government is gradually putting in place new or revised regulations that are bringing the regulatory framework closer to that of the US and other developed venture capital markets. Second, more and more foreign VCs are entering the Chinese market, reinforcing the institutional norms developed first in the US and permeating the venture capital industry globally. Finally, the flow of skilled people who, largely through their involvement with foreign VCs, have accumulated experience and expertise constitutes perhaps the strongest force for convergence.

Indeed, Chinese who have worked with foreign VCs have been leaving them to set up their own funds, representing a type of spin-off combining Chinese managers with foreign expertise, and often attracting foreign funding. Similarly, more successful Chinese entrepreneurs – the most successful being those who have listed on NASDAQ or other foreign exchanges – are becoming angel investors and venture capitalists themselves. Their transition has the advantage of bringing credibility to VCs in the eyes of entrepreneurs and thus creating enhanced mutual trust.

For most analysts and industry participants, however, the lack of an attractive domestic exit option, that is IPO, constitutes a fundamental impediment to the development of China's venture capital industry. Most adhere to the conclusions of Jeng and Wells (2000) that IPOs are the strongest driver for venture capital investing. For that reason, many domestic and foreign investors are calling for the government to more quickly introduce a growth enterprise market in China, similar to that in Hong Kong. Such a development would make domestic listings (and therefore exits) faster and easier.

The development of China's venture capital system thus hinges on the establishment of an effective domestic IPO exit. Certainly, domestic VCs are increasing their capabilities and professionalism as individual managers gain experience. The supporting institutional infrastructure, in particular the legal system and commercial law, is also being strengthened. And the industry is not starving for funds, since domestic money continues to flow into some (although certainly not all) domestic VCs, and into China *via* foreign VCs. However, the government needs to consider China's institutional infrastructure developed enough to create an attractive domestic exit option. Only then will China's venture capital industry be able to take its next major step forward.

The impact of China's venture capital system

The immediate impact of venture capital has been to provide the capital that facilitates start-ups. As a result, entrepreneurs and nascent firms can focus on developing their core technologies and businesses, rather than having to undertake other activities in order to support themselves financially. This, in turn, increases the likelihood that more of China's new technology ventures are founded and survive the critical early stages of development.

Venture capital is playing a much broader role in China's transition, however, than simply providing an additional source of financing to start-ups. As already described in the introduction to this chapter, it is acting as a catalyst for how firms are founded and managed in China, bringing in management practices and underlying beliefs that in most cases have originated from abroad.

The transfer and adaptation of originally foreign systems, practices, and beliefs is facilitated by the nature of the firms and entrepreneurs in which venture capitalists are investing. In contrast to managers and firms in China's traditional sectors, the segment of Chinese society from which the new technology firms are emerging is usually better educated, younger, tech-savvy, and with foreign work or educational experience. These individuals tend to have a positive attitude towards change and are receptive to external, including foreign, sources of learning.

Even given the relatively greater openness to change that venture capitalists introduce, there will inevitably be a period of adaptation and evolution. This process will to some degree be a contest between foreign and domestic management systems, that is, between alternative and to some degree competing sets of practices and underlying beliefs. Venture capitalists are critical contestants in this process, acting at the microeconomic level to introduce professional management systems. Many of these practices are based on the definition of "professional management" in the US context and, even more specifically, US-based venture capitalists. Founders, managers, and other domestic stakeholders in new ventures represent another set of contestants tied more closely to social norms and beliefs dominant in China. While impossible to predict the precise nature of the outcome, we believe that this interaction will give rise to a uniquely modern form of Chinese management.

China's venture capitalists (both foreign and domestic) are therefore a poignant reflection of China's rapid assimilation of global capitalist norms and practices. Indeed, global capitalism is exerting *via* VCs pressures on China to learn management practices and underlying beliefs originating from abroad. These are then transferred and adapted to Chinese circumstances, thus rapidly introducing cutting-edge management practices, such as notions of effective corporate governance and strategic planning. While the adaptation of these techniques, practices, and beliefs will yield management systems that differ from those currently found either in China or abroad, the emerging institutions will likely constitute an important new competitive force with global ramifications.

Notes

* This research has been supported by the National Science Foundation of China (China NSF Research Project Grant No.70572004), the National Social Science Foundation of China (China NSSF Research Project Grant No.04BJL022), and the Ministry of Education of China (Project Grant No.04JJD630002).
1 Based on authors' calculations and a presentation by Robert Greifeld, CEO of NASDAQ, at Tsinghua University on November 30, 2005.
2 The US$1.27 billion in venture capital invested in 2004, for example, is only 0.5 percent of the new bank loans issued in China that year.
3 For a detailed historical review, see White *et al.* (2005).
4 The main channel for foreign private equity in China before 1992 were China direct investment funds; see Bruton and Ahlstrom (2003).
5 Unless otherwise stated, the following sections, including direct quotes, are based on company data (both Chinese and English sources) and interviews with 40 leading Chinese and non-Chinese VCs active in China and accounting for the majority of VC investments in China during the period of study (2003–2004). Findings are compared to results from additional interviews and literature drawn from the US and Europe. The data gathering and analytic methods used follow those of Eisenhardt (1989), Fried and Hirsch (1994), and Bruton and Ahlstrom (2003). They are described in detail in Vega *et al.* (2005).
6 On historical institutionalism, see Chapter 6 in this volume; on interview methods and the sources of most direct quotations, see Footnote 5 in this chapter.

References

Bartzokas, A. and Mani, S. (2004) *Financial Systems, Corporate Investment in Innovation and Venture Capital*, Cheltenham, UK: Edward Elgar

Batjargal, B. and Liu, M. (2002) "Entrepreneurs' Access to Private Equity in China: The Role of Social Capital," *Organization Science*, 15: 159–172.

Bruton, G.D. and Ahlstrom, D. (2003) "An Institutional View of China's VC Industry: Explaining the Differences between China and the West," *Journal of Business Venturing*, 18(2): 233–259.

Eisenhardt, K. (1989) "Building Theories from Case Study Research," *Academy of Management Review*, 14(4): 532–550.

Fried, V. and Hirsch, R. (1994) "Towards a Model of Venture Capital Investment Decision Making," *Financial Management*, 23(3): 28–37.

Gorman, M. and Sahlmann, W. (1989) "What Do Venture Capitalists Do?" *Journal of Business Venturing*, 4(4): 231–248.

Gu, S. (1999) *China's Industrial Technology: Market Reform and Organizational Change*, London: Routledge.

Huang, J. and Chin, M. (2003) "China Focuses on Venture Capital and M&A: New Rules on Foreign Venture Capital Investments Open Up Easier Access," *Jones Day Commentaries*, August, pp. 1–4.

Jeng, L. and Wells, P. (2000) "The Determinants of Venture Capital Funding: Evidence across Countries," *Journal of Corporate Finance*, 6(3): 241–289.

Kuemmerle, W. (2001) "Comparing Catalysts of Change: Evolution and Institutional Differences in the Venture Capital Industries in the US, Japan and Germany," in R. Burgleman and H. Chesbrough (eds) *Comparative Studies of Technological Evolution*, New York: JAI Press, pp. 219–240.

Ministry of Science and Technology (2004) *Venture Capital Development in China 2004*, Beijing: Economy and Management Publishing House.

National Bureau of Statistics & Ministry of Science and Technology (2003) *China Statistical Yearbook on Science and Technology*, Beijing: China Statistics Press.

OECD (2006) *OECD Science, Technology and Industry Outlook 2006*, Paris: OECD Publishing.

Tsai, K. (2002) *Back-Alley Banking: Private Entrepreneurs in China*, Ithaca, NY: Cornell University Press.

Vega, P., Zhang W., Chong L., and White, S. (2005) "Venture Capital in China: Investment Processes and Decision Making Factors." Paper presented at the 2005 Academy of Management Conference, Honolulu, HI. August 5–10.

White, S., Gao, J., and Zhang, W. (2005) "Financing New Technology Ventures in China: System Antecedents and Institutionalization," *Research Policy*, 34(6): 894–913.

Zhang, W. and Jiang, Y. (2002) "The Relationship between Venture Capitalists' Experience and their Involvement in Venture Capital-Backed Companies." Paper presented at the 9th Global Finance Conference, Beijing University, Beijing, PRC. May 27–29.

5   The global impact of China's emerging multinationals

Peter J. Williamson and Ming Zeng

Introduction

A peculiar, perhaps even unique, feature of the rapid rise of China as an economic power is that it is taking place within the context of an already highly globalized market environment. This is in sharp contrast to the phase of rapid economic development of Great Britain, the United States, Germany, and even Japan and South Korea, that took place in an environment where global flows of capital, resources, products, and information faced much greater impediments and frictions. This opens up new options and strategies for how Chinese development can be achieved. Thus, while China's development is in large part driven by a "capitalist transition" – and one which shares many of the forces that propelled the development of earlier economic powerhouses – the speed, the trajectory, and sometimes even the outcomes of China's rise will be different.

Other commentators have discussed the fact that China's accession to the World Trade Organization (WTO) and large inflows of foreign direct investment (FDI) will have an impact both on the nature of Chinese capitalism and China's foreign policy.[1] However, the results of China's capitalist transition will not only be shaped by the fact that it is occurring within an external market that is highly globalized; they will also be influenced by the fact that Chinese companies are actively globalizing. China's capitalist transition is spawning multinational companies who are fanning out across the globe from a home base that is far from fully developed along many dimensions, including incomplete and highly imperfect markets for capital, resources, labor, property rights, and corporate control. The emergence of global firms from a home base with these characteristics is virtually unprecedented on such a large scale (Child and Rodrigues 2005).

In the past, multinationals generally emerged from a country only after its domestic capitalism was well developed. The fact that China is giving birth to these global firms at such an early stage in the transition cycle will, we argue, have wide-ranging repercussions for China's interactions with other powers in the global economy and, in turn, for Chinese policies on trade, financial flows, intellectual property, and many other aspects of international relations. Thus, the early emergence of Chinese multinationals is not only an aspect of China's capitalist transition worthy of study in its own right; it is also a phenomenon that has implications for China's role in the world (Nolan 2004).

In this chapter we will detail the nature and scale of the emergence and future growth potential of internationally competitive Chinese firms. We will examine the conditions that are giving rise to the international expansion of Chinese firms, their goals of becoming substantial global players. and their strengths, weaknesses, and strategies. We will then turn to explore the likely impacts on global competition in the sectors where Chinese multinationals are expanding.[2] Finally, we will speculate on some of the implications for China's future policy stance and international relations.

The origins of Chinese firms as global players

While there has been much discussion of China's rising export volume and the associated trade imbalances, few have paid much attention to the emergence of Chinese companies as powerful, new actors in the global market.[3] Yet their influence is aptly demonstrated by the US$1.75 billion purchase of an 82 percent interest in IBM's Thinkpad personal computer (PC) business in December 2004 by the Chinese company Lenovo – a transaction which is set to transform competition in the global market for PCs.

Other Chinese companies emerging on the global scene include companies such as Galanz, who now supplies more than one in three of the microwave ovens sold in the global market; China International Marine Containers that now sells 55 percent of shipping containers used in world trade; Pearl River Piano that has won 15 percent of the US market in just five years; and Haier, a US$15 billion company that is now the third largest appliance maker in the world with over US$1 billion sales abroad.[4]

All too often, these new Chinese competitors aren't even on the radar screens of managers, policy-makers, and commentators sitting on the other side of the world. Many Western managers simply dismiss the idea of Chinese companies becoming formidable competitors in the global market. One reason is the belief that most of China's top 100 companies are lumbering and inefficient state-owned dinosaurs. Western companies take further comfort from the fact that China's largest private companies, like the Hope Group, have just a few billions of dollars in sales. It will be decades before Chinese companies become a significant global force, so the argument goes.

These are dangerous illusions. They belie the fact that new breeds of companies are emerging in China: hybrids with the flexibility and profit motive of a private enterprise, but which enjoy the support, albeit often indirect, of one or more arms of the Chinese state. Although hybrid ownership can act as a drag on the global competitiveness of Chinese companies, some firms derive distinct advantages from their ability to combine the benefits of public and private ownership. Paradoxically, hybrid ownership constitutes an unseen benefit of China's incomplete capitalist transition (Lazonick 2004).

Lenovo, the new owner of IBM's Thinkpad product line, is a good example. It battled with multinational giants like IBM, HP, Toshiba, and Acer to become number one in China's PC market with a 29 percent share. Lenovo is listed on the Hong Kong Stock exchange and has been hailed as among Chinese public companies for its exemplary corporate governance. However, Lenovo is a hybrid: it was born as an arm of the Chinese Academy of Sciences, a state agency which remains the largest single shareholder, controlling 30 percent of the equity in this firm of red-blooded entrepreneurs. Similarly, Haier began life as a collective firm, owned by the local administration in its home town of Qingdao. Today it is a joint-stock company with a mix of collective, private investor, and management ownership.

These new Chinese multinationals are in the vanguard of a new wave of competition that is starting to emerge from China. As the Chinese multinationals develop they can be expected to influence Chinese policy-making and international relations both through their own lobbying and as potential arms that can be harnessed, through self-interest, to support government policy goals. In one way or another, they will become a real force in the global competitive arena.

It's true that few are a match for the incumbent global giants today, but they are developing at unparalleled speed. Haier, for example, is less than 20 years old. These multinationals believe that to compete with a new onslaught from foreign competitors after China's WTO entry, they need to succeed abroad; the view that "offense is the best defense." The accelerated learning that successfully operating overseas can provide is also an important motivation. As Haier's CEO, Zhang Ruimin, put it in a recent interview: "A company will never know how strong the competitors are and what rules to follow if it doesn't go out [overseas]." [5]

Finally, there is the issue of national pride. Chinese national prestige is a key driver behind projects, like the Beijing 2008 Olympics, that signal China's resurgence as a world power. The new generation of leaders like Hu Jintao and Wen Jiabao know that to maintain a seat at the top table over the long term, global economic influence is key; and building powerful Chinese multinationals can contribute to this goal.

For its part, the Chinese government is leery of providing too much in the way of direct subsidies to companies' globalization efforts. It believes, probably rightly, that China's global strength will be furthered by having companies who have proved themselves capable of surviving the rigors of global competition, not from those who depend on subsidies. And the government hasn't always kept pace with the kind of support its newly internationalizing companies need. Tight foreign exchange controls, for example, limit the freedom Chinese companies have to invest and make acquisitions abroad. Nonetheless, the many and varied arms of government in China do provide significant indirect, but very practical, support through help with access to bank loans, licenses, and quotas.

The Chinese government has also provided hero's recognition for managers, like Haier's Zhang Ruimin, who succeed. It is therefore not surprising that many Chinese senior managers feel part of the national mission to help China punch its weight globally. This is especially the case in a country where the line between corporate and national interest remains blurred.

The motivations for Chinese companies' entry into the global market are, therefore, both broad and deeply rooted. Understanding the emerging global challenge from China, however, isn't straightforward because it does not necessarily stem from well-known Chinese names like Tsingtao beer (which has substantial exports, but still a tiny share of the global market). This new, global impact coming from China is also difficult to assess because it is not arriving in just one, obvious form. In fact, it is arriving as a quiver of five distinct groups of Chinese competitors in the global market.

Towards a taxonomy of emerging Chinese multinationals

Five groups of emerging Chinese multinationals are discernable, with each group adopting a different strategy: the focused exporters, the globalizing national champions, the networked competitors, the technology leaders, and finally, the resource seekers. Each is worth a brief analysis in turn.

Focused exporters

These companies have attacked the global market by focusing on a particular product or market segment that they then seek to dominate. This was possible either because the established Original Equipment Manufacturers (OEMs) in the West were looking for new, more cost-competitive sources of supply, or because the market was inherently international. Galanz is a prime example. It began as a manufacturer and exporter of clothing. However, it saw only the prospect of cut-throat competition with falling margins as more and more Chinese companies entered its market. In a move reminiscent of Finland's Nokia (which transformed itself from a pulp and paper to TV sets conglomerate into a specialist leader in mobile phones), Galanz decided in 1993 to focus on microwave ovens – a business where it saw huge potential growth in demand that few local competitors had identified.

To overcome its technical inexperience and build international quality into its product, it spent more than US$4 million right in the beginning to purchase the most advanced production line, and signed a five-year technological cooperation agreement with Toshiba of Japan. Its entrepreneurial drive, combined with hard work and fast learning, helped it increase its production to 200,000 units within three years, and overtake Panasonic, Sharp, Samsung, and LG to become the dominant player in China with 35 percent market share.

Leveraging its powerful position in China, Galanz started global expansion. Taking the golden opportunity of European anti-dumping against Korean producers in 1997, Galanz took 10 percent of the world market within three months. Recognizing that its labor cost was less than one twentieth of European levels, Galanz launched a conscious strategy to move the production part of the global value chain to China. Its first offer to a French manufacturer was simple: move the most advanced production lines to us and we will produce for you at 20 percent of your costs.

It was an offer the French couldn't resist. With the same production line that was producing about one million units annually in France, Galanz produced six million units, by working 24/7 shifts, and indeed cut costs by 80 percent. More European OEMs signed on and a number of Japanese microwave oven manufacturers shifted their business to Galanz soon after. This innovative approach helped Galanz to expand its production capacity to a staggering level of 15 million units with minimal investment, and to supply more than 200 brands around the world, accounting for 35 percent of world output.

Initially, Galanz's proposition to the global market was simple: world-class quality at exceptionally low prices (it earned the dubious nickname, "the price butcher," from its competitors in China who were stunned at its ability to slash costs). This was only the first step. As its high throughput propelled it down the learning curve, Galanz moved far beyond simple low-cost assembly to master key technologies and component design and manufacture. It has invested over US$100 million in R&D and holds more than 600 patents. Starting from a low-cost base, it has both broadened and deepened its competitive advantage to become a world leader. Its OEM customers now depend on it not only for manufacturing capacity, but also for technology and engineering.

As with Japanese and Korean companies (such as Sony and Samsung) that came before them, it is only a matter of time before these focused Chinese exporters start building their own brands and controlling their own marketing and distribution. Galanz may be loath to muddy its focus on technology and costs and upset its OEM customers by selling direct through its own brand. However, some focused exporters have already moved down this path.

A good example is Pearl River Piano. Like Galanz, it enlisted the help of Japanese equipment suppliers to help build a basic mass production line in 1992. Once up and running, Pearl River recruited ten experts from around the world to help fine-tune its manufacturing process and help overcome the technological obstacles and quality snags associated with using mass-production techniques to make a product that had traditionally been crafted by artisans. Having mastered the technology it set about scaling up its operations and built the world's largest piano-making plant with the latest equipment.

Rather than acting as a sub-contractor, Pearl River began to explore the US market directly. After speaking with US retailers, Pearl River concluded there was a gap in the market for a good entry-level piano – a gap Pearl felt it could use its low production costs to fill. Starting with a small US sales organization, it began to sign up US distributors and market its brand. Its offering caught the attention of consumers, and in a market that declined 12 percent in 2001, Pearl River's sales jumped 44 percent to win five percent of the market. Today it has 40 percent of the US market in upright pianos and is the number one producer in the world.

Pearl River is now seriously investing in its brand, but rather than the slow and painful process of building a brand from scratch it decided to buy the rights to Ritmiiller – a German brand with roots dating back to 1795. Weighed down by high production costs in Germany, the venerable Ritmiiller had ceased production in 1977. Pearl River brought the brand back to life. It subsequently acquired another respected German brand. Rudisheimer. Having covered the traditional end of the market, Pearl River then entered into an agreement with the maker of trendy modern furniture, Herman Miller, to produce a line of pianos to complement streamlined, modern interiors.

These are just two of China's focused exporters who are changing the shape of the global market for manufactured goods. They thrive in global markets where demand is relatively homogeneous (reducing the need for complex product adaptation to individual markets and differentiated local marketing) and where technology is relatively mature, so that competition centers on manufacturing excellence, cost, and economies of scale. It is true that this is precisely where competition is fiercest. However, this is also the kind of environment where companies can use China's low labor costs, large pool of engineering talent, capability for rapid learning, and willingness to borrow expertise from others.

Initially, China's focused exporters tend to be at a disadvantage in markets where variety, complexity, and local adaptation are high, because the market is fragmented into a multitude of different consumer and geographic segments. In these environments their cost advantage is insufficient and their lack of international market experience is a handicap. Therefore, to become true global leaders they need to build or acquire the technological and marketing skills to enter more specialized, higher value segments, just as Galanz did.

Globalizing national champions

A second group of Chinese companies who are starting to establish themselves as a force in global markets are the "national champions." These have already built strong positions within China's domestic market and are now expanding their horizons. Because these firms historically focused on the Chinese domestic market, they were used to brand building and dealing with retailers. They have now started to replicate and adapt this vertically integrated formula globally.

One might well ask why, when their home market is growing faster than anywhere else in the world, these companies are looking abroad? The answers vary from industry to industry. In many cases the Chinese market is so regionally fragmented, hampered by internal barriers to transport and distribution, and racked with provincial rivalries, that once these national champions get to 20 percent (or in some industries, even 10 percent) market share, further expansion depends on the slow and painful process of industry consolidation. Therefore, even the strongest Chinese player faces constraints on its rate of expansion at home.

However, because China's home market is so huge, national champions have a powerful platform of low costs from which to launch further expansion. They have already passed the volume required for efficient scale production and most have learnt how to successfully wrestle with global players seeking to expand into the Chinese market. Not surprisingly, China's national champions see the global market as a golden opportunity.

Of course, even those who have proven themselves as national champions in China often find their marketing capabilities aren't up to international standards or lack managers experienced in international business. And what sells in China doesn't always satisfy consumers elsewhere. Despite these hurdles, though, some of China's national champions are successfully breaking into global markets.

Perhaps the best know example is Haier. Established just 20 years ago, it is the number one white goods maker in China, with more than 250 models ranging from refrigerators to dishwashers and ovens. It has market shares in some segments of the Chinese market, like premium refrigerators, exceeding 40 percent. And it is used to wrestling daily with global rivals like Whirlpool, Electrolux, Siemens, and Matsushita who have entered China with ambitious goals.

Haier was set up as a collective, "township" enterprise. Realizing that it would need a source of competitive advantage in an environment where hundreds of thousands of other township enterprises were being set up, Haier in 1984 searched the world for a source of superior production technology for refrigerators. It ended up with a license from Germany's Liebherr. Over the next decade it built its market position to become a national champion in the white goods business in China, creating a formidable set of capabilities across quality control, innovation, service, brand building, and continuous organizational change.

It entered the US market in 1994 with a single distributor based in New York. Wishing to avoid a damaging head-to-head battle with local giants like GE and Whirlpool, Haier decided to focus on the small refrigerators that serve as mini-bars in hotel rooms and can be squeezed into student dormitory rooms – segments that were considered "peripheral." This focused strategy worked: today Haier claims a 50 percent share of the market for small refrigerators and a 60 percent share in specialist wine chillers.

In 1999 it began to broaden its product line and set up a manufacturing plant in South Carolina to better learn first hand how to operate in the sophisticated US market (Hu 2005). It has since entered into an innovative deal with Sanyo in which Haier will open its extensive distribution network in China to Sanyo products, in exchange for access to their network of dealers in Japan. Leveraging its dominance in the Chinese market, and the associated scale economies and experience, Haier has determinedly begun to establish an international presence.

Today Haier is the only Chinese company to make Interbrand's top 100 list of the most valuable brands in the world. Although only ranked 95th, Haier has planted the seeds of a global image tailored to the needs of different markets. In the Americas, Haier's positioning is "What the world comes home to" – a cozy image that tries to make a place for the brand in American home life. In Europe, where quality and features are the top priorities among consumers, its tag line is "Haier and higher."

China's other national champions frequently deploy the cost advantages their high-volume operations in the Chinese market confer on them, and target segments where value for money is a key purchase criterion. This strategy tends to work best where there is a clear technical standard set at industry level and available to all. Often such technology is relatively mature and the product only needs to be carefully engineered to meet the particular needs of buyers. The small refrigerator segment where Haier targeted its first assault on the global market, for example, doesn't require particularly new or sophisticated technology. However, a hotel chain buying thousands of fridges to act as mini-bars in its rooms does demand something that is precisely designed, reliable, and competitively priced.

Coming from the intensely competitive, price conscious Chinese market, China's national champions are also experts at ferreting out neglected or under-served segments where incumbents think unit values are too low to make an attractive margin. They have the experience to turn a profit in these segments that others dismiss as unattractive.

Not surprisingly, China's national champions have more difficulty leveraging their domestic market strength where international markets are fragmented, customer buying behaviors differ markedly from China, and distribution is closely tied to local incumbents. Many suffer from a lack of proprietary technology as well as experience in sophisticated marketing and service. Compared with their Western multinational competitors, they also lack experience in managing complex and far-flung international organizations. Like their focused exporter cousins, however, their trump card in overcoming these deficiencies is their capability for rapid learning, a willingness to invest, and openness to trying new ideas in foreign environments.

Networked competitors

This third group of emerging Chinese global competitors is perhaps the most easily missed and the most difficult to properly assess for the simple reason that there is no single company to focus attention on. They are coordinated networks of competitors, something akin to armies of ants, whose collective power is not to be underestimated.

A network of 700 companies in Wenzhou, Zhejiang Province is a prime example. They control an estimated 70 percent of the world market in lighters used by the world's millions of smokers. The industry started in the mid-1980s when locals traveling to Japan brought back lighters as gifts. Entrepreneurial Wenzhouers started disassembling these gadgets and learning to produce replicas. By 1990 there were more than 3,000 families making lighters in the city. The resulting fierce competition led some smaller enterprises to specialize in making particular components, while larger firms began to focus on final assembly. Gradually a cooperative network started to emerge. The increased scale and learning that came with specialization and networking drove down costs: the igniter component that cost over one dollar to make in 1990, costs just 25 cents today.

Seeing the opportunities provided by this low-cost manufacturing network, the leading final product assemblers launched their products in the world market. At first they sold almost exclusively on the basis of low prices. However, as they gained experience, they adapted their designs to world fashion – their flexible supply network making them uniquely well placed for rapid responses to market swings. Market share soared, forcing 85 percent of Japanese and 60 percent of Korean lighter manufacturers to shut down.

The story is repeated in other industries such as men's ties. A network of more than 1,000 tie producers in Shengzhou, located west of Wenzhou in Zhejiang Province, churns out 250 million ties per year and commands 20 percent of the world market. Located far away from the coast in a mountainous area where average income is less than US$1,000 per year, costs are extremely low. This has not stopped the Shengzhou tie network from investing over US$40 million in recent years to hire hundreds of foreign experts to improve technology, quality, and design.

The network now codesigns ties using an Internet platform shared with European fashion houses, creating new designs that can be put into production within the next day. This "virtual alliance," where the Shengzhou network acts as the supply chain for European fashion designers, has allowed network competitors to break into the higher end of the European market. This combination has proven effective in outcompeting vertically integrated competitors who produce in Italy, France, and Spain.

Similar Chinese network competitors have taken global markets by storm in watches, shoes, toys, pens, and Christmas decorations. They tend to thrive in environments that demand high flexibility and fast response, combined with low costs. Due to the small scale of most firms, investments are relatively small and technology easily mastered. As our examples illustrate, the need to plug into the global fashion scene is no barrier: as inveterate net-workers they readily harness the power of foreign consultants, distributors, and fashion houses to fill gaps in their local knowledge base.

The toughest challenge for these putative Chinese global competitors is to get an efficient, coordinated network to coalesce out of a rabble of competing small firms. At first, everybody typically aspires to become an assembler of the final product – the link in the chain that is seen as most prestigious and powerful. Over time, however, participants recognize that they will be better off specializing in the activities that play to their individual strengths: companies start to focus on making particular com-ponents or building scale and efficiency in one process within the chain. Pro-business, local governments in China, seeing the potential economic benefits to their town or region, often help in kicking this process along through incentives and the award of licenses and approvals in ways that encourage specialization and force rationalization to eliminate destructive internal rivalry.

Once an efficient, differentiated network has emerged, usually over decades, the combination of low cost, flexibility, and rapid response it can provide is virtually unbeatable as a supply chain. Its weakness, however, lies in an inability to make the costly and long-term investments required to build a global brand. Therefore, the final step towards building tomorrow's global champions will only come when larger Chinese companies become capable of investing in brands. This would be similar to Benetton's emergence as the standard bearer for Italy's vast network of small- and medium-sized enterprises in the knitting industry.

Technology leaders

Many in the West believe that while industries like lighters or ties are exposed to the rise of Chinese competitors, being in a high-technology sector renders them immune. In reality, there is a deep pool of advanced technology and science in China. Under the old central planning regime, China was successful in concentrating scarce resources to build a comprehensive infrastructure for basic scientific research. Despite the underdevelopment of China's broader economy, sophisticated military-related technologies such as hydrogen bombs and satellites were successfully deployed. However, while the command economy was strong in basic R&D, the commercial potential of technologies remained unexploited.

This situation is changing rapidly, with the increasing pace of reform in the state research system. Entrepreneurial start-ups have begun to harness the unique high technologies lying idle in government research institutes. To exploit the high technologies to which they have access, entrepreneurial start-ups tend to rapidly globalize (Segal 2002).

Lenovo, the Chinese competitor in PCs that we have already mentioned, was a pioneer in this respect. It was started by a group of scientists from the Institute of Computing Technology of the Chinese Academy of Sciences in 1984, when the Chinese government started to shake up what had been an isolated research community. Founder, the Chinese company that dominates the world market for electronic publishing systems capable of handling Chinese characters (a huge market in Taiwan, Hong Kong, and Japan), also drew on technology developed in national research projects. Founder has now gone on to become a global challenger in the area of high-resolution color electronic publishing systems that combine the Roman alphabet with digital images. In this case, the basic science and technology came from state-funded research projects at Beijing University (Lu 2000).

More recently, Vimicro Corporation has established itself as a leading semiconductor company developing chips for multimedia applications. John Deng established Vimicro in 1999 at the invitation of Li Lanqing, a vice-premier of the State Council, and in cooperation with the Ministry of Information Industries, which invested several million US dollars into the venture. Deng is a graduate of the University of Science and Technology of China and later received a PhD in electrical engineering and dual master degrees in both industrial economic management and physics from the University of California at Berkeley. After graduation, Deng worked as a high-level researcher at IBM, obtained five patents, and received numerous awards for his research.

Vimicro achieved sales of US$10 million in 2001. By 2005 its total sales were valued at US$950 million, a surge of 89 percent over 2004. It is now promoting its role as a worldwide industry leader in the multimedia chip industry. Clients include Microsoft, HP, Samsung, Philips, and Fujitsu.

Another example is Innova Superconductor Technology, acknowledged as a global leader in high temperature superconductor production and applications. Its chairman, Dr. Han, worked for ten years on cutting edge superconductor research in Europe and now divides his time between the company and his directorship of the superconductor research centre at Tsinghua University. Founded in 2000, Innova has successfully produced the world's longest high temperature superconductor wire and ranks number two in global market share.

China also has potential gold mines of latent science in a string of institutes specializing in biotechnology and broadband mobile telephony. Da Tang Telecom, for example, developed its competing third-generation mobile broadband standard, dubbed TD-SCDMA, drawing on research done by the State Telecommunication Research Institute. One of its subsidiaries, Datang Micro-electronic Technology, is also becoming a major player in chip set design and manufacturing.

One of the key advantages these emerging technology leaders have is an ability to access science from China's state-funded research institutes cheaply. The reasons are simple: the costs of the research have already been fully funded by the Chinese state, and research organizations have few alternative channels through which they can commercialize technologies. The technology leaders' key challenge, meanwhile, is to build a global sales and service organization given their limited resources and international experience.

In some cases, technology leaders are overcoming these limitations by enlisting the support of Overseas Chinese. This is not primarily the old Chinese Diaspora on which trading companies and the Chinese government typically relied in the past. Instead, the emerging technology leaders are tapping into the large number of new emigrants who have left China to study and work overseas since 1978. Sometimes this is referred to as the "reverse brain drain." It is not unusual to find start-ups in China with a local CEO, a CTO groomed in Silicon Valley, and a CFO from Hong Kong or Taiwan.

Resource seekers

One plank of China's reform program has sought to transform state-owned enterprises (SOEs) into the leaders of highly regulated industries or those considered to be important for national security. In industries such as oil, steel, mining, telecommunications, shipping, and banking the state has thus actively pushed industry consolidation to create a few mammoth SOEs. Part of the rationale is to help companies become globally competitive, both in terms of their final products and their ability to access the resources necessary for China's continued development. Rather than relying on uncertain and volatile spot markets for commodities, the Chinese resource seekers are investing directly in overseas mining and transport infrastructure to secure supplies.

The Shanghai Baosteel Group is a good example. Baosteel was established in 1985, as one of the most important projects to foster the modernization and upgrading of China's industry in the early days of economic reform. After 20 years of focused effort, Baosteel has become one of the most competitive steel companies in the world. In 2004, its annual sales reached US$19.5 billion, earning US$2.7 billion in profits. Originally reliant on imported technology and equipment, Baosteel is developing its own R&D aggressively: it applied for 400 patents in 2004. It has been equally active in seeking to secure global supplies of key resources.

As China becomes the world's largest steel producer, its imports of iron ore are growing 20 percent every year, so Baosteel is joining forces with foreign firms with extensive iron ore reserves. In 2004, Baosteel's joint venture with Hamersley Iron from Australia began production. It will export 10 million tons of iron ore to Baosteel annually over the next 20 years. In the same year, Baosteel started to build a massive steel plant in Brazil, giving it secure access to rich supplies of iron ore and opening new markets in the Americas. Baosteel now has eleven foreign subsidiaries along with several strategic alliances or joint ventures with global leaders, including Arcelor and Nippon Steel, for high-end products. Its stated aim is to become the world's third-largest steel company within the next decade.

Sinopec, meanwhile, is the largest integrated petrochemical company in China with 2004 sales of US$75 billion (ranked 31 in the global Fortune 500). It is now aggressively expanding its international reach and participates in oil and gas projects in six countries. Its smaller cousin, the China National Offshore Oil Corporation (CNOOC), is responsible for offshore oil and gas exploration and production in China. It hit the headlines in 2005 with its attempted hostile takeover of America's Unocal. Bidding against Chevron, its ultimately unsuccessful acquisition effort became a political "hot potato" in the US Congress.

As the resource seekers continue their globalization drive, more controversial equity stakes and takeover bids are sure to follow. Since the CNOOC retreat, for example, China Minmetals Corporation (a US$15 billion metals trader operating in 44 countries) made a US$5 billion bid for the nickel and copper miner Noranda Inc. of Canada. As Chinese SOEs step up their international drive to control resources, their close alignment with national goals is sure to exert some influence on China's international relations. Indeed, they may well act as instruments through which China's ambitions for global integration can be forwarded.

In sum, more and more well-equipped Chinese companies have global markets in their sights. In the next decade, Chinese global competitors are likely to emerge in additional industries like steel, oil, chemicals, and machinery. Their starting point is usually their cost advantage, be it in manufacturing, an ability to tap into a large pool of low-cost engineers, or access to state-funded high technology. Building on this powerful platform of cost competitiveness, the five different groups we have identified are building new layers of competitive advantage in different ways.

The focused exporters are exploiting the advantages of scale, focus, and learning that accrue with their low costs to become the world's dominant players in particular market segments. China's established national champions, in turn, are leveraging the volume base that they enjoy in China. Indeed, they are adept at finding the weak points of incumbents, like the under-served segment for small refrigerators.

Networks that bring together hundreds of small, specialized Chinese companies are conquering global markets with a powerful combination of low costs and extreme flexibility. Building on this base, they are not afraid to rope in foreign consultants or established brand names to fill gaps in their networks and move up-market. While it may take years before China's emerging technology leaders create revolutionary breakthroughs, they are building their knowledge of international markets by serving specialist, high technology niches that span the globe. Finally, the state-backed resource seekers are expanding globally to secure China's access to raw materials needed to sustain growth and development.

Future strategies of emerging Chinese multinationals

In some ways the emergence of Chinese multinationals represents a classic competitive challenge to incumbent global companies based on accessing low costs. In leveraging this basic advantage into international markets, initial indications suggest that Chinese companies will increasingly emphasize three, in some ways rather novel, strategies.

First is a strategy of moving into higher value activities and technologically sophisticated industries and market segments at an early stage in their development cycle. Many in the West now accept that China is becoming "the factory of the world." However, they do not expect Chinese companies to challenge them in activities like R&D, engineering and design, or branding. As we see from the examples above, many Chinese companies are moving into more advanced industries and activities. Taking advantage of more open global markets for technology, international acquisitions, and knowledge-based services such as marketing expertise and design, Chinese companies are accessing and building a range of sophisticated capabilities even as their home economy remains at an early stage of its capitalist transition (Warner *et al.* 2004).

Such strategies allow China's emerging multinationals to target "high-end" businesses that Western nations and Japan have hitherto considered their sole preserve. This implies that in the not-too-distant future high value added jobs, which were thought to be immune from Chinese competition, will start to come under pressure in developed nations.

A second strategy is what might be termed "outside-in" geographic expansion. When competing with foreign multinationals in China, local companies frequently employed a strategy of building low-end volume in rural areas as their foundation. Following Chairman Mao's rule of guerrilla warfare – "surround the cities from the rural areas" – they leveraged their existing rural volume and market share to attack urban markets.

Chinese companies are now deploying the same strategy as they venture abroad: they attack the global market where western multinationals are weakest and concentrate resources on building volume and experience in these markets. After having built an international platform, they challenge their global competitors in the core markets of the US and Europe. This "outside-in" strategy also suggests that Chinese companies, often with the help of their government, intend to build strong relationships with countries in Latin America, the Middle East, Africa, and developing Asia to smooth their path of becoming globally competitive.

One good example of the "outside-in" strategy is Huawei, analyzed in more detail in Chapter 3. It started to enter global markets in 1996, but hardly made any progress. The first contracts it won were in Vietnam and Laos during 1999. Huawei then made good progress in Russia and Africa. In 2001, it started to move into Europe, becoming the only Chinese telecommunications equipment supplier to penetrate this market. Its European sales were US$30 million in 2003, US$100 million in 2004, and on track to achieve US$500 million in 2005.

A third, and equally far-reaching, strategy is Chinese companies' use of international expansion for the purpose of knowledge seeking. By going overseas they not only expand their sales and increase scale economies, they also gain access to new technologies, know-how, and understanding of customers and markets. In fact, the emphasis of Chinese competitors as they globalize is to build effective international networks, rather than traditional corporate hierarchies. They thus aim to enhance global competitiveness by assembling the most effective network of capabilities and knowledge. For example, Cellon, one of the largest independent mobile phone design houses, has its headquarters in the US, major R&D centers in China and France, and most of its market in China. In 2001, the company bought the R&D division of Philips Consumer Communications in Le Mans, France, and turned it into a major design, prototyping, and certification center. The facility employs 350 engineers and houses a comprehensive prototype manufacturing center that includes in-house testing and certification.

When successful, these knowledge-seeking strategies set up a virtuous spiral. As firms expand overseas, they learn more, allowing them to capture and absorb more of the world's knowledge, thus increasing their base of competencies. The resource seekers are also benefiting from this "learning effect." Although their initial aim was to secure stable flows of resources, their participation in international joint ventures and acquisitions is helping them to improve their knowledge and capabilities.

Chinese companies clearly are moving into higher value activities and technologically sophisticated industries at an early stage in their development cycle. Indeed, they are building international knowledge networks that enable them to achieve high levels of integration into the global economy even while much of the Chinese domestic economy remains underdeveloped. The emergence of Chinese multinationals is likely to have important implications for the process of China's integration into the global economy, including China's foreign policy and international relations.

Implications for China's future policy stance and international relations

As it has gathered pace over the past 30 years, China's capitalist transition was almost universally welcomed around the world. To many commentators it was viewed as a windfall: leading to the "opening up" of the potentially huge Chinese market and promoting a more predictable and transparent set of economic relationships within China. Today, however, there is evidence that some outside China are becoming reluctant to accept the unanticipated consequences of China's capitalist transition. That reluctance is perhaps best illustrated by the reaction of some American politicians and policy makers to the attempted takeover of Unocal by CNOOC in July 2005.

US companies have been massive investors in China. They have also been in the vanguard of acquiring Chinese companies after China's market for corporate control was opened. Yet, the idea of a Chinese company taking over a mid-sized energy company in America was treated as an anathema by influential politicians and some media commentators. Dubious arguments ranging from national security concerns about Chinese control of "strategic energy resources" (the majority of which comprise gas in the ground in Asia) through to the "unfair competition" from a Chinese state-backed company and consequent lack of a "level playing field" were trotted out.

CNOOC eventually dropped its offer in August 2005 after the US Congress decided to delay the review of its bid. A similar fate might have awaited Haier's bid for the struggling icon of the American appliance industry, Maytag. The poor economics of the deal, though, led Haier to withdraw first.

This recent experience suggests that important sectors of the public in the developed world may be poorly prepared for the international repercussions of China's capitalist transition. In particular, they might be rankled by the expansion of Chinese companies abroad aided by a globalizing world economy with falling trade barriers and more open international markets for technology and corporate control. These concerns and the risks of protectionist or potentially retaliatory policies are aggravated by the fact that the key driver of overseas expansion by Chinese companies, China's capitalist transition, remains far from complete.

This incompleteness, in turn, is associated with often opaque policy-making, underdevelopment of the economy's "soft" infrastructure, and significant distortions to market-driven resource allocation. Consequently, we can expect increasing frictions as the emergence of Chinese multinationals collides with the economic and political interests (spiced with the prejudices) of the developed world.

Despite these probable frictions, the global expansion of Chinese companies is likely to continue apace. In October 2003, Vice Premier Wu Yi said simply: "We will actively foster our own multinationals" (Embassy 2003). This has led to important changes in government policy toward China's internationalizing firms. Twenty-two major companies have already been earmarked for government support in becoming global champions. The leadership has also eliminated some red tape. For instance, a rule requiring firms investing abroad to give the government a deposit to guarantee 100 percent repatriation of profits from overseas operations has been abolished. Furthermore, the State Administration of Foreign Exchange has launched a trial in 14 provinces to allow its branches greater power in authorizing foreign exchange for use in international investments.

More broadly, the emergence and active support for building Chinese multinationals is likely to have implications for China's policy toward both its Asian neighbors and other countries around the world. China is moving decisively from seeing itself solely as a recipient of foreign investment toward a position of full integration with the global economy. China is thus likely to take on a role that befits its size, resources, and heritage (Shenkar 2005).

The impacts on international relations will be far-reaching. Economic considerations, and in particular the need to smooth the path for China's internationally expanding corporations, will rise in importance as drivers of Chinese foreign policy. On the defensive side, policies will increasingly emphasize keeping markets open for Chinese companies, protecting overseas investments, and securing resources to improve the competitiveness of China's emerging multinationals. A particularly interesting point here is that, so far, the resources China needed to secure economic development have mainly been raw materials and energy. As the shift toward higher value-added segments gathers steam, the focus will shift to securing access to global technology, knowledge, and intellectual property rights.

These developments will be accompanied by more proactive Chinese policies to promote the overseas expansion of China's emerging multinationals. An interesting reflection of this trend is the fact that virtually every overseas trip by a senior Chinese official now includes a visit to the local Huawei subsidiary. Meanwhile, within China, budding multinationals complain that Chinese policy is failing to take sufficient account of their concerns and that Chinese officials lack experience in managing international relations for the benefit of home-grown companies. Given the need to maintain economic growth and international integration, these calls for a shift in policy, and an upgrading of capabilities, are likely to be heeded.

The heightened importance of these economic considerations in China's international relations will require deft handling both by China and other world powers. Frictions are likely to increase as Chinese companies expand into "higher-value" activities and the jobs associated with these activities in the developed world. The world's established powers will also need to develop a response to China's increased influence in the developing world. Both the "outside-in" strategy of emerging Chinese multinationals and China's need to secure supplies of natural resources are increasing the intensity of China's policy focus and influence in Latin America, Africa, Russia, and among neighbors in developing Asia.

Despite these potential frictions, the emergence of Chinese multinationals is likely to play a significant role in deepening global economic integration. Faced with the competitive challenge emanating from China's emerging multinationals, the global corporate sector is beginning to shift its focus to harnessing the unique capabilities and economics of China. This is leading incumbent multinationals to explore a strategic alternative to slugging it out with their rising Chinese competitors: to ally with them.

Given the fact that the competence bases of global multinationals may be the mirror images of Chinese firms, alliances have obvious attractions. However, these alliances would be very different from the kinds of joint ventures that have characterized the China scene to date. Rather than the Chinese partner simply providing dubious *guanxi* or government access, new-style alliances would be fully fledged partnerships and networks between a foreign firm and a Chinese company, where each brings competencies of its own.

This next stage of global economic integration, in which Chinese firms act as partners who enhance the global competitiveness of existing multinationals, opens the way to a new set of benefits from China's capitalist transition. In an environment of increased frictions and global unease with China's international ascent, however, a key question remains: is the world prepared to make the adjustments necessary to capture this upside potential?

Notes

1 See, for example, China (Hainan) Institute of Reform and Development (2002); Fishman (2005); and Studwell (2003).
2 In Chapter 3, Dieter Ernst and Barry Naughton focused on how globalized supply chains are influencing the process of China's capitalist transition. In this chapter we focus on the other side of this coin: the implications of China as the home base of a new breed of multinationals.
3 Notable exceptions are Yeung and Olds (2000) and De Trenck (1998).
4 All the materials on Chinese companies appearing in the following sections, except where cited, are derived from interviews, personal communications, and internal company materials. These were collected over the period from 2002 until August 2006 within China.
5 TV interview with Mr. Zhang Ruimin, CCTV-2 Dialogue, December 15, 2003.

References

Child, J. and Rodrigues, S.B. (2005) "The Internationalization of Chinese Firms: A Case for Theoretical Extension," *Management and Organization Review,* 1(3): 381–410.

China (Hainan) Institute of Reform and Development (2002) *China's Accession to the WTO and Infrastructure Reform,* Beijing: Foreign Language Press.

De Trenck, C. (1998) *Red Chips and the Globalisation of China's Enterprises,* Hong Kong: Asia 2000.

Embassy of the People's Republic of China in the United States of America (2003) "China to Speed Up Breeding Multinational Corporations," November 7. Online. Available HTTP: www.china-embassy.org/eng/jjmy/b/t40352.htm (accessed December 22, 2006).

Fishman, T. (2005) *China, Inc.: How the Rise of the Next Superpower Challenges America and the World,* New York: Scribner.

Hu, Y. (2005) "20 years: Haier Textbook," *China Entrepreneur Magazine,* May 20. Online. Available HTTP: www.blogchina.com/new/display/75427.html (accessed January 5, 2007).

Lazonick, W. (2004) "Indigenous Innovation and Economic Development: Lessons from China's Leap into the Information Age," *Industry and Innovation,* 11(4): 273–298.

Lu, Q. (2000) *China's Leap into the Information Age: Innovation and Organization in the Computer Industry,* Oxford: Oxford University Press.

Nolan, P. (2004) *Transforming China: Globalization, Transition and Development*, London: Anthem.

Segal, A. (2002) *Digital Dragon: High-Technology Enterprises in China*, Ithaca, NY: Cornell University Press.

Shenkar, O. (2005) *The Chinese Century: The Rising Chinese Economy and its Impact on the Global Economy, Balance of Power and Your Job*, Upper Saddle River, NJ: Wharton School Publishing.

Studwell, J. (2003) *The China Dream: The Quest for the Last Great Untapped Market in the World*, New York: Grove Press.

Warner, M., Ng, S.H., and Xu, X. (2004) "'Late Development' Experiences and the Evolution of Transnational Firms in the People's Republic of China," *Asia Pacific Business Review*, 10(3): 324–345.

Yeung, H.W.C. and Olds, K. (2000) *Globalization of Chinese Business Firms*, London: Macmillan Press.

Part 3

State, capital, and political interests

6 The institutional contours of China's emergent capitalism

Christopher A. McNally

The purpose of this volume as laid out in Chapters 1 and 2 is to apply the capitalist lens to China's emergent political economy and thereby create a comparatively accurate understanding of China's international ascent. Chapters 3 through 5 focused on how Chinese business institutions are transforming China into one of the most formidable capitalist competitors of our era. This chapter will undertake a more expansive analysis. It will map the unique institutional arrangements permeating China's budding capitalism. The focus will rest particularly on how state and capital institutionally interact and shape China's political economy.

The next section will briefly introduce the conceptual approach taken in this chapter – the capitalist institutional lens. I will then elucidate what I hold are the three most salient institutional contours of China's emergent capitalism: "network capitalism"; the rapid absorption of China into the "new global capitalism"; and the distinctive role of state institutions in China's capitalist development. In the concluding remarks I will comment on China's long historical trajectory and argue that contemporary state-capital relations possess certain parallels to those characterizing China's imperial political economy over the past 1,000 years. However, due to the contemporary international environment this historical trajectory is likely to be broken.

The capitalist institutional lens

Over the past two decades, several conceptual lenses have been used to analyze China's political economy. Most of these are grounded in recent world historical events and are of a less general nature than the capitalist lens applied in this volume. The most important interpretations are associated with the experiences of the East Asian "developmental state," the postsocialist transitions in Eastern Europe and the successor states to the Soviet Union, as well as pure crony capitalism.

First, there have been numerous attempts to apply the concept of a capitalist developmental state, especially as practiced in Japan, South Korea, and Taiwan, to China. Yet, these efforts either stretch the concept unduly or find that the case for China as a developmental state is not tenable (Howell 2006). Certainly, the unitary image of a developmental state guiding the economy from low-value added to high-value added production processes hardly holds up in the face of Chinese reality. Intense rivalries among the Chinese state's various agencies and jurisdictional levels put considerable implementation constraints on central policies. In fact, overlapping and incongruous features often characterize the Chinese state apparatus, including amalgamations of regulatory, entrepreneurial, clientelist, developmental, and predatory state formations (Howell 2006).

Similarly, the view of China as a postsocialist transition economy finds only one comparable world historical occurrence: Vietnam.[1] All of the other postsocialist transitions experienced a sequencing of political and economic reforms that, unlike China, at first prioritized political reforms. For instance, market economic reforms happened alongside the development of democratic politics in Eastern Europe and under the framework of potential integration with the European Union. Consequently, these cases faced political parameters highly unlike those present in the People's Republic of China (PRC).

Finally, an understanding of China as primarily shaped by crony capitalism fails to account for the enormous vibrancy of the PRC's political economy.[2] Crony capitalism is a system in which capitalists are in cahoots with state officials, using their influence over government to create an anti-competitive environment in which only their firms can prosper. While rent-seeking, corruption, and, more generally, a politicized market economy are hallmarks of China's reform era, there are other factors at work that make China's political economy much more dynamic and multifaceted than pure crony capitalism.

Applying the capitalist lens to China raises the question of whether analytical frameworks used in the literature on comparative studies of capitalism, generally termed the varieties of capitalism (VoC) approach, can be applied. To date this literature has not incorporated a comparative analysis of China. As Jonas Pontusson (2005) notes, the VoC approach forms an important fundament on which the comparative study of capitalist political economies can build, yet this literature focuses "exclusively on the nature and sources of variation among advanced capitalist political economies" (Pontusson 2005: 164). It pays less attention to how advanced capitalisms differ from those in the developing world.

To effectively capture the case of China, the VoC approach would therefore need to move beyond existing classifications to incorporate the dynamics unfolding in transitional, developing, and evolving cases of capitalism. As Pontussen (2005: 164) succinctly observes: "The VoC literature has a great deal to say about 'varieties,' but surprisingly little to say about 'capitalism.'" Despite these shortcomings, the VoC approach can serve well to inspire an exploration of the institutional contours of China's capitalism.

Accordingly, my analysis will build on the VoC approach and, in particular, its use of insights contained in the "new institutionalism." This conceptual prism understands institutions as "building-blocks of social order" (Streeck and Thelen 2005: 9). Specifically, I employ a historical interpretation of institutions, while also borrowing insights from related schools (see Thelen 1999). I see institutions as "humanly devised constraints that shape human interactions" (North 1990: 3), forming "durable lock-ins or amalgamations of interests and social relations" (Swedberg 2005: 6).

A historical view of institutions captures their "stickiness" or substantial inertia to change. Any social system is embedded in its historically formed political, social, and cultural background. The origins of a social system thus form a key influence on how it is constituted and where it is going, creating degrees of path dependency. I must, however, stress that institutions are endlessly reshaped by the ideas and interests of social actors embedded in institutional settings. An iterative view of institutional change along the lines of continuously recurring feedback loops can perhaps serve our understanding of social change best.

This chapter will apply a capitalist institutional lens to map the unique features of China's emergent political economy. As the VoC framework and approaches in radical political economy (see Lippit 2005) elucidate, capitalism evolves over time and space into distinct institutional, ideational, and distribution of power arrangements. Different institutional structures of capitalism can be distinguished across both temporal and geographical axes. Most works in the VoC literature, for example, include some sort of matrix to map institutional variations, especially among national forms of capitalism.

China's capitalist institutions, though, are in the process of forming and differ in important respects from those found in advanced capitalist systems. I will therefore consciously eschew a comparative mapping of China's capitalist institutions. Rather, I will stress certain analytical features and note their historical parallels to other forms of capitalism.

Mapping the institutional contours of China's emergent capitalism

Although in terms of speed and scale the developments unfolding in China are without parallel in the past, there is congruence with the processes that catapulted Great Britain, the United States, Germany, and Japan to international prominence. All of these experienced the emergence of a capitalist political economy, manifested first and foremost by the twin processes of urbanization and industrialization. These processes in turn triggered the establishment of nation-wide infrastructures, the rapid expansion of wage labor, and the formation of professional classes.

Despite these parallels, the historical, geographical, and external conditions facing China's emergent capitalism are producing unique institutional features, three of which I will outline here: first, the constitution of capital, particularly China's mushrooming "network capitalism"; second, the role of external factors, above all the influence of the "new global capitalism" on China's development; and finally, the Chinese state's role in initiating, enabling, and sustaining China's capitalist transition.

Bottom-up: network capitalism

Analyses of East Asia's stunning economic development have distinguished between two broad categories of capitalism, although considerable variations are found within these two categories. Asia's pioneer in capitalist development was undoubtedly Japan. Although Japan has undergone structural economic changes since the 1990s, it generated a unique form of "coordinated capitalism" during the heyday of its capitalist development. Central to coordinated capitalism is a strong state that can effectively coordinate investment behavior throughout the economy by forging close cooperative relations with private business. Ronald Dore (1997) sees Japan's form of coordinated capitalism as representative of an Asian model of capitalism in general. However, only the political economy of South Korea bears a compelling resemblance to Japan's coordinated capitalism.

The other form of capitalism distinguished in Asia is "network capitalism." It is prevalent in those regions where Overseas Chinese businesses dominate, including Taiwan, Hong Kong, and the Overseas Chinese communities of several Southeast Asian nations. Asia's network capitalism is generally associated with a generic model of Chinese capitalism and therefore sometimes termed "Sino-capitalism" or "*guanxi* capitalism" (Hamilton 1996; Redding 1990).

Network capitalism is built from the ground up and does not tend to overly rely on legal contracts and the supervisory role of the state. Rather, it depends on a myriad of small-scale (often family-based) businesses. In comparison to coordinated capitalism, these businesses do not tend to expand into large bureaucratic structures, but rather achieve wealth accumulation through the multiplication of small ventures (Lever-Tracy 2002). To overcome the disadvantages of small size, large numbers of firms coalesce into sizeable clusters of related businesses.

Naturally, all forms of capitalism are to some extent based on networks, but the Chinese variant is especially pronounced and quite open to new members. It relies on two institutions in particular: the family, especially in the form of family firms, and *guanxi*. *Guanxi* denotes the establishment of long-term informal reciprocal personal relationships. It is a form of social capital that acts as a binding agent among social actors. *Guanxi* ties can therefore create enduring trust which facilitates collaborations among firms and aids them in adjusting to changing circumstances.

Coordinated capitalism and network capitalism have both deeply affected the shape of Asia's capitalist development. Japan's coordinated capitalism has had important practical and ideational influences on the second (starting in the 1950s) and third (starting in the 1970s) wave of capitalist development in East Asia. Central to Japan's coordinated capitalism has been the notion of a developmental state, a type of state that is conceived to have perfected methods of state intervention in the economy while heeding market forces and cooperating with private enterprise. Such state interventions, in turn, depended on the existence of small, inexpensive, but elite bureaucracies which possessed sufficient scope to take initiative and operate effectively.

One of the economies heavily influenced by Japan's coordinated capitalism was Taiwan. Taiwan is often grouped with South Korea and Japan to constitute a generic model of Asian capitalism, yet its political economy differs from its two northern counterparts. Despite remarkable policy-making and implementation capacities, the Taiwanese state's influence over private industry has been more indirect than in Japan and South Korea (Gold 1986; Wade 1990). In fact, the Taiwanese state has relied for direct economic control on a large state sector, unusual in size and reach for a nonsocialist country (Gereffi 1990). Taiwan's capitalism thus combined top-down planning focused on state firms with a vibrant private sector structured by network capitalism.

This raises distinct parallels between Taiwan and the PRC. As on Taiwan, state firms and research institutes dominate most direct developmental interventions in China, such as in the aeronautic, automobile, and heavy machinery industries (Nolan 2001). And as on Taiwan, China's private sector was at first discriminated against or faced indifference by the agents of the state. This initial disregard of private sector activities by government triggered in both Taiwan and the PRC entrepreneurial responses based on family firms and *guanxi* networks (see McNally and Chu 2006). Jon Unger (2002), for instance, argues that both Taiwan and certain areas of China exhibit a common pattern of "Chinese" entrepreneurship based on family firms, informal financing, and major roles for the wives of entrepreneurs in managing internal operations. Even more significantly, large segments of the private sectors in Taiwan and the PRC have coalesced into vibrant business networks.

The fact that Taiwanese family firms and partnerships have tended to cluster into business groups based on *guanxi* ties has been widely reported (Gates 1996; Hamilton and Biggart 1997; Shieh 1992). Similar to Taiwan, networks of small-scale firms have emerged in China. These networks often boast thousands of small businesses working in similar product markets and exhibiting fine divisions of labor. They rely on reciprocity and mutuality in firm relations to take advantage of economies of agglomeration. Some of these networks even dominate their respective product categories in world markets.

However, given China's vast geographical expanse, a plethora of locally embedded networks has emerged. One prominent example is located in the western Pearl River Delta.[3] Situated along state route 105 in the jurisdiction of Zhongshan City are a variety of townships and villages, each of which specializes in one or sometimes two types of products. These "specialized towns and villages" (Eng 1997) include: Dachong (mahogany furniture; textiles); Xiaolan (metal products; home appliances); Shaxi (jeans); and Guzhen (lighting products).

The origins of these specialized towns and their production clusters are quite varied. Some enjoy long traditions of working in certain product categories. These traditions either survived the Cultural Revolution or were reinvigorated by returning emigrants at the beginning of the reform era. Some clusters were initiated by foreign investors, chiefly from Hong Kong and Macau, while others were started by small private workshops at the beginning of the reform era. A final set of clusters can trace their origins back to one or several state or collective firms. Over time these firms expanded, privatized, and created collaborative relations with other firms, gradually giving rise to networks of firms working in related product categories.

Regardless of their origins, these networks have over time created specialized clusters, thus locking in advantages of agglomeration. Small firms embedded in these networks can access market information, upgrade product quality and technology, and reach economies of scale that drive down manufacturing costs (Zeng and Williamson 2003). Although at the outset there was generally little government planning or initiative involved, in recent years many of these networks have been supported by both local and provincial governments. For example, the Department of Science and Technology under the Guangdong Provincial Government initiated in 2002 a program aimed at creating centers for innovation and technology development within the confines of specialized production clusters (Bellandi and Di Tommaso 2005: 713–714).

Government efforts have also focused on building industrial parks tailor-made for certain production processes, and exhibition centers used to showcase a jurisdiction's specialized products. The town of Guzhen, for instance, has built a gigantic Lighting Plaza that hosts an annual exposition called the "China (Guzhen) Lighting Fair." In fact, Guzhen has been officially recognized by the China Federation of Light Industry as the "Lighting Capital" of China. The city boasts about 3,000 registered lighting manufacturers employing over 50,000 workers.

Guzhen's lighting cluster grew out of the skills of two collective enterprises. During the reform era, the technological expertise of these two firms was combined with an active commercial tradition. This led to the gradual emergence of perhaps the largest industrial cluster in the world dedicated to lighting goods. The specialization of the town is palpable when traveling down its 10-km long "Lamp Street," which is lined with large exhibition spaces displaying a dazzling array of indoor lighting systems, chandeliers, street lamps, outdoor LED displays, and other lighting goods.

Guzhen and the other specialized towns in Zhongshan City have benefited enormously from their proximity to Hong Kong and Macau. The increased autonomy of local governments during the reform era allowed Overseas Chinese capital to either initiate or link up with emerging production clusters. Low-level Chinese officials driven both by their personal and career interests further facilitated these linkages. Over time, the influx of Overseas Chinese capital strengthened these localities' bargaining power *vis-à-vis* higher levels of government (Hsing 1998: 144). Alliances among Overseas Chinese investors, local officials, and local firms expanded, creating direct linkages to world markets.

The agglomeration of large numbers of often small firms in elaborate production clusters is not only confined to China's eastern seaboard in provinces such as Guangdong and Zhejiang. It is also becoming more prevalent in China's landlocked interior. One example of a tightly networked cluster of textile firms is located in Yiyang City, Hunan Province (Guiheux 2003). Yiyang is far removed from China's coastline and therefore proves that network capitalism is spreading into regions where private sector development is a recent phenomenon.

As in all economies with strong ethnic Chinese influences, the reliance of entrepreneurs on family firms and *guanxi* networks contains a clear functional aspect. Chinese government agencies and state banks tend to lend little support to private firms, especially smaller firms. Private entrepreneurs therefore rely on family, *guanxi* networks, and hybrid forms of ownership to access finance, overcome government indifference, compensate for institutional uncertainty, and create profit-making opportunities (International Financial Corporation 2000: 20–34; Wank 1999).

The changing structure of China's political economy, though, is inducing Chinese local governments to increase their support for private sector activities (Blecher and Shue 2001; Unger and Chan 1999). Privatization has made enterprises independent of local governments, since private entrepreneurs can move across administrative boundaries to seek the best investment climate. At the same time, the yielding of substantial autonomies to local governments opened the door to strong interjurisdictional competition, with each local authority seeking to attract private enterprises with better investment conditions. The macro-outcome has been a rapidly improving investment climate for private firms and the conscious support by local governments of China's network capitalism, especially by establishing designated industrial parks.

The highly networked structure of China's private sector is also enabling the emergence of a plethora of hybrid ownership forms. On one hand, the initial discrimination of private firms and private property rights made the use of *guanxi* networks to hook up with government officials paramount for creating a modicum of institutional certainty. On the other, many former state managers have become private entrepreneurs (sometimes while keeping their official positions), a situation that creates incentives to leave the ownership of assets in China vague. In both cases, *guanxi* networks have created the conditions for a variety of joint private-state ventures to flourish, such as when private entrepreneurs invite government officials to sit on their boards or act as silent investors. The hybridization of ownership forms in China and the emergence of network capitalism are thus closely linked.

In conclusion, China exhibits a distinct prevalence of network capitalism in its domestic private sector. This implies that China's emergent political economy resembles to some extent the political economies of Taiwan, Hong Kong, and Southeast Asia. Perhaps the closest analogies are to the case of Taiwan. Capitalist development in Taiwan and the PRC is characterized by a certain duality. A large state sector dominates the commanding heights of the economy and is the direct counterpart to the central government's industrial policies. However, this state sector coexists, and in the case of China, melds with a private sector characterized by a myriad of small- and medium-sized firms structured by networks based on *guanxi* relations. Put differently, while producer goods sectors, transportation, and finance are in the state's hands, the vibrancy of the domestic economy is being driven in large part by Chinese network capitalism.

Outside-in: development under the new global capitalism

Chapters 3 through 5 provided the reader with pertinent insights on aspects of China's globalization. For example, Wei Zhang *et al.* analyzed an outside-in dynamic of China's integration into the global capitalist system by exploring the unique melding of foreign (chiefly North American) and home-grown institutional arrangements in the evolution of China's venture capital sector. In contrast, Zeng and Williamson focused on an inside-out dynamic. They traced how the rapid emergence of multinationals (MNCs) domiciled in China is changing the global competitive landscape.

This section will employ a wider perspective. I will trace how the timing of China's entry into the world capitalist system at the end of the 20th century is influencing the institutions of its emergent capitalism. As noted in the paragraphs introducing the capitalist institutional lens, capitalism as a socioeconomic system is not cast in stone. It evolved in world historical time, moving from humble beginnings to a system encompassing most of the globe (Braudel 1982–1984; Heilbroner 1985; Wallerstein 1974–1989).

Somewhat ironically, capitalism's earliest origins lay in an alliance of state and capital, namely in the form of merchant capitalism. Internationally, this was a highly competitive system, but nationally merchant houses possessed the privilege of monopoly. "The secret of making high profits was to secure monopolies by one means or another, exclude competitors, and control markets in every possible way" (Fulcher 2004: 4).

Merchant capitalism was gradually replaced by a more market-driven system in the 19th century. This phase came to an end in the first half of the 20th century as the industrial strife and human dislocations resulting from the Great Depression and the Second World War triggered a reconstitution of the basic institutions of capitalism. A form of managed capitalism (Fulcher 2004: 41–47) transpired, which was characterized by large corporations run by professional managers, corporatist class organizations, and extensive state intervention.

The combination of low economic growth, high inflation, and greater global competitive pressures in the 1970s ushered in the gradual demise of managed capitalism. Our current era dawned, characterized by a drastic reduction in union power, deregulation and privatization, and the ascent of free-market ideology, especially in the United States and Great Britain. I will term this contemporary period the "new global capitalism."

Two remarkable facets of the new global capitalism must be noted here as they both affect China's transition. Although globalization has been part of the capitalist accumulation process from its very inception, this new era of capitalism involves more people than ever before. The collapse of the Soviet bloc and the opening of India, China, Latin America, and parts of Africa to global trade and investment have created a truly global dynamic of capital accumulation. This is most succinctly expressed by the expanding reach of global production and innovation networks noted in Chapter 3. Equally significant, the high-tech boom in the United States and beyond fuelled a massive increase in new ventures, new knowledge, and new business models. The individual entrepreneur stands once again at the center of capital accumulation, aided by increasingly sophisticated communication technologies and financial mechanisms.

The effects of the new global capitalism on the contours of China's emergent capitalism become clear when comparing the PRC to earlier developers in East Asia. Japan, South Korea, and Taiwan during their period of rapid industrialization in the 1950s, 1960s, and 1970s opted to keep foreign investment and imports tightly under control while building up indigenous corporate institutions to compete internationally (Amsden 2001; Johnson 1982; Wade 1990). Only the much smaller economies of Singapore and Hong Kong possessed open economic environments, mainly due to their roles as trading and (later) financial hubs.

The PRC entered the world capitalist system in the 1980s and 1990s. Chinese policy makers thus faced different pressures and opportunities than earlier developers in East Asia. Even though China constitutes a continental sized economy, it is surfacing as a comparatively open system. China possesses a very high GDP to trade ratio and its export sector is highly internationalized.[4] Indeed, China has developed one of the highest "absorption capacities" for the forces of globalization among developing economies.

Much of China's openness did not result from central design. For sure, the Chinese leadership initiated the open door policy and established during the early 1980s four Special Economic Zones. The aim of these zones was to aid political efforts to reintegrate Hong Kong, Macau, and

Taiwan with the PRC, and to foster limited and controllable contacts with the world capitalist system. They succeeded in this latter respect and attracted the first waves of Overseas Chinese investment with their more liberal environments.

Despite these early policy initiatives, large segments of Beijing's political establishment continued to oppose strong internationalization during the 1980s and 1990s (Zweig 2002). Over time, though, these forces were run over by the many unintended consequences flowing from China's open door policy. The success of the Special Economic Zones generated further momentum for internationalization. Driven by cultural affinity and China's comparative advantage in cheap labor, Overseas Chinese moved beyond the zones to set up vast production networks. In particular, they cooperated with small-scale rural industries, which "swapped access to China's domestic markets in return for international capital and access to international markets" (Zweig 2002: 160).

In this manner, Overseas Chinese capital worked wonders. It won over cadres who, rather than enforcing restrictive central regulations, opted to use their grassroots regulatory power to facilitate international exchanges. A domestic hunger for global linkages was unleashed that generated economic gains for China's local officials and, more importantly, linked coastal communities with the global market, paving the way for them to become the "workshop of the world."

Evidently, the melding of Overseas Chinese network capital with China's own played a crucial role in opening China to the world. Between 1982 and 1994, more than 70 percent of all foreign investment in China came from Overseas Chinese sources (Hsing 1998: 147). China's opening, though, was also driven by the rampant competition among Chinese local governments for investment capital. As with the rapid growth of China's indigenous network capitalism, interjurisdictional competition triggered local adjustments to the demands of investors. The central state, seeing increased capital flows from abroad, reacted to this situation by gradually constructing a more market-friendly macro-regulatory environment.

In the 1990s these improvements began to attract the first major batch of MNC investments. Lured by China's potentially huge consumer market and its cheap and increasingly skilled labor force, these MNCs exerted further pressures to improve the investment climate. In 2001 these developments took a final leap forward with China's entry into the World Trade Organization (WTO).

The terms of China's WTO accession are onerous and exceed in most respects those of earlier developing country entrants (Lardy 2002). China's decision to join under these conditions reflects the leadership's eagerness to secure access to major export markets in the developed world. It also reflects former Chinese Prime Minister Zhu Rongji's intention to use the WTO agreement as a means to force reluctant domestic interest groups to accept greater economic liberalization (Fewsmith 2001).

Due to its WTO accession, China is now opening significant parts of its domestic market to foreign investment and trade. Even more importantly, WTO-required reforms are prodding China to establish an investor-friendly institutional infrastructure. China's accession to the WTO is thus locking the country into "international norms" of trade (Breslin 2004). These changes are also aiding China's private sector by creating greater institutional certainty and loosening restrictions on private operators' scope of business.

Both domestic and international factors have therefore interacted to accelerate China's participation in the world capitalist system. In hindsight, the increasing permeability of national barriers to world trade, the rising flows of capital and information, and the growing ability of manufacturers to move swiftly to regions with favorable endowments have all created enormous costs to any nation seeking to insulate itself from globalization. Due to the timing of China's capitalist transition, the new global capitalism opened China as much as China opened to the world.

The process of China's opening has in large part been driven by greater competition for investment capital and export markets, not only within China, but also between China and other export-oriented economies. These competitive pressures are exerting a disciplining influence, since governments must heed the desires of international investors in order to attract and retain capital. The result has been the construction of a remarkably liberal and internationalized export regime in China that favors foreign investment.

This liberal export regime, though, sits alongside a relatively closed and protected domestic trading regime (Lardy 2002). The restrictions of China's internal trading regime apply especially to key sectors dominated by state firms (petrochemicals, telecoms, airlines, etc.), agricultural goods, and the domestic financial system. Although international competitive forces are increasing after WTO entry, the duality of a liberal export regime juxtaposed with a restrictive internal trading regime is likely to continue. The closed financial system, for instance, has served as an insurance against speculative attacks on China's currency, a situation that China's leadership is unlikely to alter until the whole financial system is on a stable and internationally competitive footing.

This duality is also expressed in another institutional facet of China's emergent capitalism. Economic spaces that are divorced from China's domestic economy but highly integrated into global production networks have been created in some Chinese localities. The industrial parks in Suzhou and Kunshan adjacent to Shanghai in Jiangsu Province are examples of how certain jurisdictions are adopting a "Singapore model" – they rely on MNC capital for domestic economic development. Industrial parks in these jurisdictions are segregated from the domestic economy at large and provide excellent hard and soft infrastructures. Separate governance systems have therefore been created for the sole purpose of accommodating MNC capital.

To conclude, China's development under the new global capitalism has shaped the institutions of its emergent political economy. After the initiation of the open door policy, ethnic Chinese investors built bridges linking China to world markets. In the process, the network capitalism of Overseas Chinese melded with networks of Chinese domestic producers. Gradually, the investment climate improved to the extent that global production networks incorporating MNCs made China their base for assembly operations. After WTO accession, China's integration into the new global capitalism further accelerated, starting to spawn the first generation of Chinese MNCs and bringing increasingly sophisticated ideas and technologies to China, as with the rapid growth of China's venture capital sector.

At this point, it still is unclear how successful China will be in moving away from its role as a low-cost assembly site in the international division of labor to more value-added production processes. As Chapter 3 argues, MNCs and Chinese domestic corporations are already upgrading their operations and undertaking intensive research and development efforts. One thing is for sure: China's insertion into the global capitalist system is highly unlikely to be reversed. As in the past, external economic actors will continue to interact with domestic forces to shape the institutional contours of China's emergent capitalism.

Top-down: the role of the Chinese state

In Chapter 3, Dieter Ernst and Barry Naughton elucidate how the central state continues to control the top tier of Chinese industrial firms and thus the commanding heights of the Chinese economy. In addition, internationally competitive mid-tier firms are often privately run, but remain closely linked to state agencies or continue to be partially owned by local governments. Unmistakably, China's industrial capitalism remains heavily shaped by the hand of the state.

This is little wonder. China's reform era did not start from a clean slate but rather originated from a state socialist system in which the state owned the vast majority of productive assets. After the establishment of the PRC in 1949, the Chinese Communist Party (CCP) undertook a gradual, but ultimately highly thorough process of nationalizing most industrial, commercial, and agricultural assets that were in private hands. This process reached a peak with the collectivization movement in the late 1950s, ebbed during the early 1960s, and was then driven to new extremes during the Cultural Revolution (1966–1976). Only in the late 1970s emerged the will to leave the state socialist legacy behind and fundamentally restructure China's economy.

Why would the CCP leadership desire to change a state socialist system which facilitated its political control? Internally, the chaos of the Cultural Revolution created a pressing need to regain legitimacy for the CCP. Externally, CCP rulers noticed the rapid wealth accumulation taking place in Asia's capitalist developers. The realization dawned that increased economic wealth could translate into internal legitimacy and international power. A reform process gingerly exploring capitalist development began.

The factors prodding China's reform leadership are actually not much unlike those prompting the leaders of other nations to explore capitalist development: the existence of perceived or real threats to national and/or regime survival (Stubbs 1999; Tilly 1975). Throughout the reform era the Chinese leadership perceived industrialization and technological upgrading as a means to buttress CCP legitimacy and China's national greatness. This mindset continues to the present and provides ample incentives to continue China's reform process.

In essence, China's leadership jettisoned communist ideological limits and displayed a strong "will to develop." A dual aim of ensuring socio-political stability *and* rapid economic growth emerged, generating a unique melding of polices. The party retained the power of its personnel appointment process – the *nomenklatura* system – to control the career tracks of China's economic, political, and social leaders. Simultaneously, party leaders encouraged economic decentralization and experimentation to encourage rapid economic growth.

The *nomenklatura* system constitutes the backbone of the Chinese polity. It functions like mucilage, the main source of systemic coherence that strengthens central authority by creating incentives for party members to adhere to central edicts. The CCP's *nomenklatura* system, with its counterpart in the government's administrative hierarchy, thus persists in guiding the behavior of local cadres (Edin 2003; Huang 1996). Since 1978 this system has evaluated CCP leaders primarily in terms of local economic performance, creating strong incentives for local cadres to ensure high paced economic growth in their jurisdictions.

At the same time, reforms granted greater autonomy to local governments, leading rapidly to the decentralization of economic decision-making. Local autonomy was reinforced by the central state's fiscal disengagement. Higher government levels granted fewer and fewer financial resources to local government units, forcing these to rely on local economic prospects for increased revenue flows.

The result of combining strong incentives for maximizing economic growth with local autonomy was that local governments became ever bolder in undertaking economic experiments. Local initiatives often circumvented restrictive central policies. Especially along China's coastline, local governments engaged in feverish attempts to attract foreign capital. This introduced foreign knowledge, technology, and ideas to China's vanguard of reform. It also opened up political space for the recognition of domestic private entrepreneurs, giving rise to China's vibrant network capitalism noted above.

The central state often tried to clamp down on local autonomies, though with limited success. Ebbs and flows of permitting, restricting, and again permitting economic liberalization have therefore come to characterize the initial reform process. For example, in the aftermath of the 1989 Tiananmen Incident the central government put a halt to economic liberalization measures, especially the sway of nascent private entrepreneurs. However, by 1992, Deng Xiaoping's *nan xun* (Southern Tour) reinvigorated the reform process and opened up spaces for bolder reform initiatives. In the end, the CCP's desire to ensure regime stability and enhance China's international power forced it to facilitate grassroots liberalization efforts, thus enabling ever more expansive processes of capital accumulation.

Overall, the Chinese state remains a central force, but its reach is not absolute. CCP incentives have generated a "growth-above-all-else" mentality among local cadres, prodding them to see restrictive central policies as running counter to local growth prospects. The result: local cadres often stifle the effective implementation of central policies and foster resource misuse in terms of industrial duplication and environmental degradation. In view of this situation, we might best understand China's state as constituting a "diffuse developmental state" (McNally and Chu 2006). Due to their "growth-above-all-else" mentality, local leaders stand at the forefront of establishing symbiotic interactions with private firms and undertaking direct developmental interventions. The central state, in contrast, sets the overall incentive and policy framework, although local autonomies tend to limit the reach of many central policies.

The Chinese state has therefore played a crucial role in initiating, managing, and sustaining the process of capitalist development. However, it would be a stretch to conceive of it as an internally coherent actor along the lines of the developmental states which have characterized the coordinated capitalisms of Japan and South Korea. Rather, the Chinese state constitutes a bizarre and often contradictory system. It might display enormous "developmentalism," but institutionally it is not a homogenous actor that can effectively coordinate private economic activities in the interests of the nation.

In other respects, though, there are some compelling resemblances between China and Asia's earlier capitalist developers. Like these earlier developers, China boasts a very high savings rate enabling high levels of investment in fixed assets (infrastructure, real estate, factories, etc.). Jonathan Anderson (2006: 12), for example, argues that from a macroeconomic perspective the PRC "looks almost exactly like its Asian predecessors." Growth relies heavily on fixed asset investment and export-oriented industrialization, while domestic consumption demand lags behind.

Macroeconomic parallels are only part of the resemblance. Savings have to be effectively converted into investments *via* financial intermediaries. Accordingly, the states of most late capitalist developers have harnessed financial institutions to intimately support the rapid development of industrial firms in cutting-edge industries (Gerschenkron 1962). This is reflected in how the state exerted direct influence over financial institutions in South Korea and Taiwan to guide investments into higher value-added industries (Wade 1990; Woo 1991).

In parallel, state control over finance has allowed Chinese policy makers to keep interest rates low, thus unleashing waves of credit expansion. When these expansions get out of control, the Chinese state tends to use administrative measures, especially the sanctions and rewards the CCP can hand out *via* its *nomenklatura* system, to squeeze credit growth (Huang 1996). The Chinese state has in this manner been able to maintain a considerable degree of macro-economic stability while facilitating vast investments in education, industry, and physical infrastructure.

As in other state-guided financial systems, the Chinese system has its dark underside. This is reflected in the amassing of nonperforming loans and inefficiencies in the allocation of capital (Lardy 1998). Local government leaders, for example, can influence the branch managers of local state banks to finance projects for political or social reasons without regard to commercial profitability, a further reflection of the downsides of local government autonomy.

Another cause of financial sector inefficiencies is that Chinese state banks extend large amounts of credit to state firms. This, though, encumbers economic efficiency, since the corporate governance systems of Chinese state firms tend to provide dysfunctional incentives to their managers (McNally 2002). Much of China's large stock of nonperforming loans can be traced back to the inefficiencies of state firms.

The importance of state firms reflects another institutional feature that differentiates China's emergent capitalism from its East Asian counterparts. For sure, the Taiwanese and Singaporean governments have made extensive use of state firms for industrial policy purposes. China, though, had to face head-on the legacy of a state socialist system. As a result, the Chinese state had to consciously focus resources on the construction of market institutions during the reform era. This included a fundamental restructuring of the state apparatus and the building from scratch of financial and enterprise institutions necessary to run a successful market economy. Clearly, the PRC differs strongly from its East Asian predecessors in terms of its institutional legacy.

An equally fundamental difference to Asia's earlier capitalist developers lies in size. China's landmass is vast and introduces considerable complexities to governance. As noted above, the central government's interests and viewpoints differ from those of local governments, creating substantial problems of policy coordination and implementation. China's large size also introduces starkly differing local conditions, creating an image of many local forms of capitalism coexisting within China. In some areas, local governments cooperate with private entrepreneurs in symbiotic relations to foster capital accumulation, while in others, local government officials engage in predatory behavior, creating political economies that contain "the worst of feudalism, capitalism, and socialism all in one."[5]

The above was merely meant to sketch the role of the state in China's emergent capitalism. It is certainly not possible to reflect the totality of institutional arrangements characterizing the Chinese state's interaction with economy and society. This would have to be the subject of a book-length exposition.[6]

Nonetheless, the foregoing shows that there should be little doubt as to the state's contribution to China's capitalist development. There should also be little doubt that due to China's large size, state socialist legacy, timing of entry into the world capitalist system, and other factors, conceptions of the Chinese state must differ from those of the Asian developmental state. The Chinese state exhibits strong developmental impulses, but ultimately constitutes a multifaceted entity in which "a complex mix of local state formations, policies and economies" (Howell 2006: 292) coexist.

Concluding remarks: a historical perspective

China is in the process of creating a unique form of capitalism, incorporating aspects of network capitalism, the new global capitalism, and state-led capitalist development. One of the central characteristics of China's emergent capitalism is a marked duality, reflected, for instance, in the coexistence of an internationalized export regime alongside a relatively limiting internal trading system. More fundamentally, this duality is manifested in the Chinese state's continued dominance over crucial aspects of the economy, tempered by the dynamism of China's small-scale capitalist producers.

The two processes of state-led development from above and network-based development from below meet at the local level, where local officials and private economic actors have played a crucial role in initiating, enabling, and sustaining capitalist accumulation. As a consequence of this dynamic, state-capital relations have been localized and engendered considerable variation. Some local political economies resemble Singapore by their dependence on MNC capital. Others rely heavily on Overseas Chinese capital that melds with China's indigenous network capitalism. And yet others are anchored in the lasting importance of China's state sector.

Perhaps the best means to comprehend the marked duality of China's emergent capitalism is to employ a historical perspective. In particular, there is a striking resemblance between China's contemporary political economy and the political economies of the Song to late Qing dynasties. Hill Gates' (1996) work elucidates this point:

> The Chinese people have lived for at least a thousand years within the reach of two different political-economic patterns that offered them different and partially contradictory possibilities and limitations. One is the state-managed tributary mode of production for state use, the

other the petty-capitalist mode, a system of commodity production by kin corporations.

Gates (1996: 7)

These two modes of production displayed a tendency to grow more sophisticated and complex over the course of history, although the duality of a state dominant mode juxtaposed with petty capitalist production remained intact. For instance, during the late Qing dynasty petty capital gradually gained in force, especially in commercial centers such as Hangzhou, where more completely privatized channels of production and commerce took hold (Rowe 1984). Moreover, as Western capitalists began to encroach on China, the state dominant mode resisted these developments. Petty capitalists, in contrast, embraced new opportunities for profit, "often in flagrant contravention of ruling-class wishes" (Gates 1996: 8).

The dominant imperial state thus attempted to control both capital and markets for its own purposes. A reliance on personalized ties to undertake business dealings was strongly reinforced by state officials, since these viewed impersonal business dealings that could lead to the amassing of large fortunes as a potential threat to state dominance (Gates 1996: 32). Ultimately, the driving force of Chinese history was "the petty-capitalist tendency toward accumulation unrelentingly harnessed by tributary might, turned to tributary rather than capitalist purposes" (Gates 1996: 8).

In this sense, real capitalist accumulation could never progress.[7] The dominant state attempted to check any challenge, setting social limits on the private accumulation of resources. Sizeable wealth that could not be effectively hidden within the realm of family and kin was often converted into political power (*via* investing in the education of offspring to pass examinations for public office). "The rich had to find a public role to safeguard private property" (Gates 1996: 38). The state dominant mode put political control over commercial efficiency.

This historical legacy has left a deep imprint on China's emergent political economy and raises the question of whether a similar dynamic is playing out at present. The state's dominance over crucial industrial and commercial interests means that much capital accumulation remains driven by the state. Moreover, many private firms, despite their cumulative importance, remain small in scale. Only in the last five years have more powerful private corporations emerged in such sectors as real estate, electronics, foodstuffs, etc.

China thus exhibits an emergent political economy characterized by two opposite forces: state-led development from above; and development from below that is activated by Chinese network capitalism and the forces of the new global capitalism. Both of these interact and drive the growing importance of markets in China's political economy. The result: a gradual strengthening of private capital and its associated social interests.

Nonetheless, these interests remain politically weak, reflecting how both China's imperial history and Leninist state structure shape its emergent political economy. An Chen hones in on this point in Chapter 8 and argues that China's capitalists are inherently state-subservient, middle and professional classes are just emerging, and the lowest rungs of society are politically powerless. Therefore, despite almost thirty years of rigorous capitalist development, no social force beyond the state possesses the political clout to challenge the CCP. State dominance remains intact, making a transition toward democracy quite remote.

How long state dominance can remain intact, though, is unclear. China's emergent political economy creates a dynamic that pits a state-led logic emphasizing political control against a capitalist logic emphasizing efficiency and capital accumulation. Maryanne Kivlehan's chapter (Chapter 7) on the Chinese media sector captures these tensions pertinently. In her view, prospects for material gain will continue to drive media professionals to produce news that meets consumer demands, thus pushing the envelope of press freedom and reducing state dominance.

Logically, a state-led logic harnessing capital accumulation for the purposes of CCP legitimacy must at some point exhaust itself. Certainly, we do not live in a static world. There are enormous competitive pressures emanating from the global capitalist system. Rapid capital accumulation within national borders can serve a state to repel these pressures. Consequently, CCP hegemony does not stand above any perceived need for economic expansion. Rather, the two are intricately linked. The CCP must ensure continued economic growth to retain its own internal political legitimacy while ensuring China's standing in the world.

Competitive pressures emanating from the international system could therefore prompt Chinese state and party in the direction of continued economic liberalization, fostering increased political prominence for private capital. Whether this will ultimately result in the bifurcation of secular authority and the emergence of a "constitutional" state, as mentioned in Chapter 2, remains to be seen. I will come back to this problem in the concluding chapter (Chapter 12) when I attempt to highlight the most likely future scenarios facing China's emergent political economy.

Notes

1 For comparative attempts along these lines see the contributions in Nee and Stark (1989); and McCormick and Unger (1996).
2 See Wedeman (2003) and He (1998) for crony capitalist interpretations of China's developmental dynamics.
3 The following information on Zhongshan City's production clusters builds on various interviews undertaken during the summers of 2005 and 2006. See Footnote 5 in Chapter 2 for information on interviews conducted in China.
4 See Chapter 9 on these points.
5 Interview, summer 2004, Chengdu.

6 See, for instance, the excellent recent works on this topic by Zheng (2004) and Yang (2004).
7 There has been some debate on this point, reflected by the substantial literature on whether indigenous commercialization and the resulting "sprouts of capitalism" during imperial times represented capitalism in China. For a brief overview of this literature see Gates (1996: 18; 38–41).

References

Amsden, A. (2001) *The Rise of the Rest*, New York: Oxford.

Anderson, J. (2006) "China's True Growth: No Myth or Miracle," *Far Eastern Economic Review*, 169(7): 9–16.

Bellandi, M. and Di Tommaso, M.R. (2005) "The Case of Specialized Towns in Guangdong, China," *European Planning Studies*, 13(5): 707–729.

Blecher, M. and Shue, V. (2001) "Into Leather: State-led Development and the Private Sector in Xinji," *The China Quarterly*, (166): 368–393.

Braudel, F. (1982–1984) *Civilization and Capitalism 15th – 18th Century*, New York: Harper and Row.

Breslin, S. (2004) "Capitalism with Chinese Characteristics: The Public, the Private and the International," Asia Research Centre Working Paper No. 104, Perth: Murdoch University.

Dore, R. (1997) "The Asian Form of Capitalism," in P.H. Admiraal (ed.) *The Corporate Triangle*, Malden: Blackwell.

Edin, M. (2003) "State Capacity and Local Agent Control in China: CCP Cadre Management from a Township Perspective," *The China Quarterly*, (173): 35–52.

Eng, I. (1997) "The Rise of Manufacturing Towns: Externally Driven Industrialisation and Urban Development in the Pearl River Delta of China," *International Journal of Urban and Regional Research*, 21(4): 554–568.

Fewsmith, J. (2001) "The Political and Social Implications of China's Accession to the WTO," *The China Quarterly*, (167): 573–591.

Fulcher, J. (2004) *Capitalism: A Very Short Introduction*, New York: Oxford University Press.

Gates, H. (1996) *China's Motor: A Thousand Years of Petty Capitalism*, Ithaca, NY: Cornell University Press.

Gereffi, G. (1990) "Big Business and the State," in G. Gereffi and D. Wyman (eds) *Manufacturing Miracles*, Princeton, NJ: Princeton University Press, pp. 90–109.

Gerschenkron, A. (1962) *Economic Backwardness in Historical Perspective: A Book of Essays*, Cambridge, MA: Harvard University Press.

Gold, T. (1986) *State and Society in the Taiwan Miracle*, Armonk, NY: M.E. Sharpe.

Guiheux, G. (2003) "The Transformation of an Urban Economic Area in Hunan Province: From State Enterprise to a Specialised Market," *China Perspectives*, 49: 4–16.

Hamilton, G.G. (1996) "Overseas Chinese Capitalism," in W. Tu (ed.) *Confucian Traditions in East Asian Modernity: Moral Education and Economic Culture in Japan and the Four Mini-Dragons*, Cambridge, MA: Harvard University Press, pp. 328–344.

Hamilton, G.G. and Biggart, N.W. (1997) "Market, Culture, and Authority: A Comparative Analysis of Management and Organization in the Far East," in

124   *Christopher A. McNally*

M. Orru, N.W. Biggart, and G.G. Hamilton (eds) *The Economic Organization of East Asian Capitalism*, Thousand Oaks, CA: Sage Publishing, pp. 52–94.

He, Q. (1998) *Xiandaihua de xianjing – dangdai Zhongguo de jingji shehui wenti [The Pitfalls of Modernization – China's Present Economic and Social Problems]*, Beijing: Jinri Zhongguo chubanshe.

Heilbroner, R.L. (1985) *The Nature and Logic of Capitalism*, New York and London: W.W. Norton.

Howell, J. (2006) "Reflections on the Chinese State," *Development and Change*, 37(2): 273–297.

Hsing, Y. (1998) *Making Capitalism in China*, New York: Oxford University Press.

Huang, Y. (1996) *Inflation and Investment Controls in China: The Political Economy of Central-Local Relations during the Reform Era*, Cambridge: Cambridge University Press.

International Financial Corporation (2000) *China's Emerging Private Enterprises: Prospects for the New Century*, Washington, DC: International Financial Corporation.

Johnson, C. (1982) *MITI and the Japanese Miracle*, Stanford: Stanford University Press.

Lardy, N.R. (1998) *China's Unfinished Economic Revolution*, Washington, DC: Brookings Institution Press.

——(2002) *Integrating China into the Global Economy*, Washington, DC: Brookings Institution.

Lever-Tracy, C. (2002) "The Impact of the Asian Crisis on Diaspora Chinese Tycoons," *Geoforum*, 33(4): 509–523.

Lippit, V.D. (2005) *Capitalism*, New York: Routledge.

McCormick, B.L. and Unger, J. (eds) (1996) *China after Socialism: In the Footsteps of Eastern Europe or East Asia?*, Armonk, NY and London: M.E. Sharpe.

McNally, C.A. (2002) "Strange Bedfellows: Communist Party Institutions and New Governance Mechanisms in Chinese State Holding Corporations," *Business and Politics*, 4(1): 91–115.

McNally, C.A. and Chu, Y. (2006) "Exploring Capitalist Development in Greater China: A Synthesis," *Asian Perspective*, 30(2): 31–64.

Nee, V. and Stark, D. (eds) (1989) *Remaking the Economic Institutions of Socialism: China and Eastern Europe*, Stanford, CA: Stanford University Press.

Nolan, P. (2001) *China and the Global Economy: National Champions, Industrial Policy and the Big Business Revolution*, Basingstoke: Palgrave.

North, D. (1990) *Institutions, Institutional Change and Economic Performance*, New York: Cambridge University Press.

Pontusson, J. (2005) "Varieties and Commonalities of Capitalism," in D. Coates (ed.) *Varieties of Capitalism, Varieties of Approaches*, Basingstoke and New York: Palgrave Macmillan, pp. 163–188.

Redding, S.G. (1990) *The Spirit of Chinese Capitalism*, Berlin: Walter de Gruyter.

Rowe, W.T. (1984) *Hankow: Commerce and Society in a Chinese City, 1796-1889*, Stanford, CA: Stanford University Press.

Shieh, G. (1992) *Boss Island*, New York: Peter Lang.

Streeck, W. and Thelen, K. (2005) "Introduction: Institutional Change in Advanced Political Economies," in W. Streeck and K. Thelen (eds) *Beyond Continuity: Institutional Change in Advanced Political Economies*, Oxford: Oxford University Press, pp. 1–39.

Stubbs, R. (1999) "War and Economic Development: Export-Oriented Industrialization in East and Southeast Asia," *Comparative Politics*, 31(3): 337–355.

Swedberg, R. (2005) "The Economic Sociology of Capitalism: An Introduction and Agenda," in V. Nee and R. Swedberg (eds) *The Economic Sociology of Capitalism*, Princeton, NJ and Oxford: Princeton University Press, pp. 3–40.

Thelen, K. (1999) "Historical Institutionalism in Comparative Politics," *Annual Review of Political Science*, 2(1): 369–404.

Tilly, C. (1975) "Reflections on the History of European State Making," in C. Tilly (ed.) *The Formation of National States in Western Europe*, Princeton, NJ: Princeton University Press, pp. 3–84.

Unger, J. (2002) *The Transformation of Rural China*, Armonk, NY and London: M.E. Sharpe.

Unger, J. and Chan, A. (1999) "Inheritors of the Boom: Private Enterprise and the Role of Local Government in a Rural South China Township," *The China Journal*, (42): 45–74.

Wade, R. (1990) *Governing the Market: Economic Theory and the Role of Government in East Asian Industrialization*, Princeton, NJ: Princeton University Press.

Wallerstein, I.M. (1974–1989) *The Modern World-System*, New York: Academic Press.

Wank, D. (1999) *Commodifying Communism: Business, Trust and Politics in a Chinese City*, Cambridge: Cambridge University Press.

Wedeman, A. (2003) *From Mao to Market: Rent Seeking, Local Protectionism, and Marketization in China*, New York: Cambridge University Press.

Woo, J.E. (1991) *Race to the Swift: State and Finance in Korean Industrialization*, New York: Columbia University Press.

Yang, D.L. (2004) *Remaking the Chinese Leviathan: Market Transition and the Politics of Governance in China*, Stanford, CA: Stanford University Press.

Zeng, M. and Williamson, P.J. (2003) "The Hidden Dragons," *Harvard Business Review*, 81(10): 92–99.

Zheng, Y. (2004) *Globalization and State Transformation in China*, Cambridge: Cambridge University Press.

Zweig, D. (2002) *Internationalizing China: Domestic Interests and Global Linkages*, Ithaca, NY and London: Cornell University Press.

7 China's media in an age of capitalist transition

Maryanne Kivlehan-Wise

This chapter examines the effects of China's capitalist transition on the country's media system since the end of the Cultural Revolution. It discusses the content of the People's Republic of China's (PRC) news media and describes four broad trends that are shaping the media's development. It then looks at the tensions China's move to a more capitalistic system unleashed, specifically the conflicting demands of the market and the party to determine news media content. Finally, it describes some of the new professional practices and institutions that have arisen in response to these tensions and discusses the role they are playing in China's media evolution.

Content control in the PRC news media

Discussing how China's capitalist transition is affecting the content of China's media is difficult. While most recognize that extraordinary change has taken place during the reform era, there is little consensus among scholars as to what these changes actually signify.

Some scholars detect dramatic growth in China's media. They see advances in information technology and a rapidly changing society that seeks out news from an ever-growing network of potential sources. Consequently, they are optimistic about the prospects of real press freedoms developing in China. There is, indeed, reason for such optimism. It cannot be questioned that in the past 25 years the PRC media has begun publishing on countless topics that would previously have been considered taboo. Innovative and cutting edge reporting in PRC media has resulted in some tangible changes to government policies. A series of corruption scandals has given local and provincial-level officials good reasons to fear investigative journalists. Moreover, at times, central government leaders have publicly reversed themselves in response to PRC reporting. Examples include the reporting on SARS in 2003 and a scandal involving an explosion linked to the manufacture of fireworks in school grounds that took place in rural Fanglin Village, Jiangxi Province, in March 2001. These events appear to be indicators of deeper change in the relationship between the press, the PRC government, and China's society.

Other analysts take a more cautious view of change. These scholars point to the seemingly arbitrary crackdowns on media outlets seeking to expand the area of acceptable reporting and increasingly common incidents of self-censorship, where editors and reporters themselves choose to repress certain stories rather than incite government reprisal. While acknowledging that the numbers and types of topics the PRC press is now permitted to report have increased, they couch these changes in terms of the expansion of a cage rather than the emergence of any meaningful freedom. There is compelling evidence for both arguments.

China has a tradition of conducting ideological indoctrination or "thought work" (*sixiang gongzuo*) that predates the founding of the PRC. The concept of imparting to the populace a "correct" understanding of political ideas and the relationship between the central authorities and society in order to more efficiently render political control was present in dynastic and republican China.[1] Its current form, however, bears the clear stamp of Mao Zedong and the Chinese Communist Party (CCP).

The central concept that underlies the CCP's domination over the media is the "party principle" (*dangxing yuanze*). This principle is often described as comprising three obligations that the news media must meet (Zhao 1998): first, to accept the CCP's ideology as its own; second, to accept the CCP's programs, policies, and directives; and finally, to accept the CCP's leadership and adhere to the CCP's organizational principles and press policies. Two and a half decades of reform have spurred important innovations in China's approach to governance, yet these three obligations remain unchanged.

Three types of content

When examining the PRC news media, single explanations or rules of thumb for why news content is selected for publication are elusive. PRC news media content selection can best be understood when considering the three separate phenomena outlined in Figure 7.1. Some news content is selected to appear in Chinese news media despite a significant lack of consumer interest or preference; some news content is repressed despite a significant level of consumer interest or preference; and some news content appears to be driven almost solely by consumer interest and preference. For this reason, PRC news media content can be divided into three categories: obligatory content; discretionary content; and forbidden content.

Obligatory content

In the Chinese media, there are certain stories or types of information that consistently show up, regardless of whether a media outlet's target audience

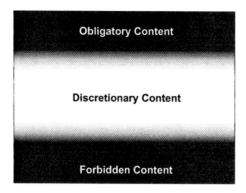

Figure 7.1 Three types of media content.

is interested. This type of reporting can be referred to as obligatory content. Examples include the text of certain speeches, detailed reports about the travel and meeting schedules of China's central leaders, or the arrival and departure of foreign delegations. Key events, such as CCP congresses often bring out a coordinated release of these types of stories throughout China.

Media outlets are required to publish obligatory content. Therefore, the incentives for including it are defined by the state. Refusing to comply with such guidance could result in closure of the media outlet or other disciplinary actions.

Discretionary content

Not all content in the PRC media is obligatory. There are also a host of stories and types of information that a Chinese news media outlet is permitted to include if it chooses to do so. This can be referred to as discretionary content.

Incentives for publishing discretionary content vary. Editors and reporters may derive satisfaction from reporting on issues of personal importance. Corrupt practices, such as bribes for publishing on individuals or business entities also play a role. In other instances, media professionals may seek personal advancement or institutional support by designing a story to win plaudits from party officials. Finally, discretionary content is often selected because it appeals to an outlet's target audience and thus has the potential to increase advertising and subscription revenue.

Forbidden content

At the same time, there are a host of topics and types of information that cannot be reported on regardless of how interested a media outlet's target audience would be. These topics can be referred to as forbidden content.

When the CCP determines that reporting on an issue would violate a core party interest, it retains the ability to clamp down and completely stop reporting. The media's handling of the SARS epidemic in 2003 is testimony to this sobering reality. Identifying the absence of forbidden content from afar is difficult. Observers are often reduced to tracking crackdowns and listening for silence.

China's leadership sometimes reverses a decision and allows reporting on what was once forbidden content. In some cases these changes are marked by a clear announcement. For example, on September 12, 2005, Shen Yongshe, a spokesman for China's National Administration for the Protection of State Secrets announced that information pertaining to the death toll for natural disasters would no longer be considered a state secret (*People's Daily* 2005). In other cases the change in rules can only be surmised from an upsurge in reporting on previously risky topics. For example, reporting on corruption in China was once considered taboo. Today, though, reporting on these topics is permissible, albeit subject to special constraints.[2]

Despite the all too frequent occurrence of crackdowns on wayward media professionals and institutions, some publication of forbidden content continues to occur. The incentives for publishing forbidden content are not straightforward. Media professionals may feel strongly about an issue and be willing to risk the consequences of a crackdown. Alternatively, these professionals might derive some material benefit from including such content by increasing sales or other revenue. Finally, media professionals might simply be uncertain of where the boundary between forbidden and discretionary content lies.

China's changing media landscape

As with most spheres of reform in the PRC, a central event in the development of China's media system was the redirection of the nation's development strategy following the Third Plenum of the 11th Central Committee in December 1978. At this meeting, the CCP decided to shift away from class struggle and toward modernization. This began a period of economic reform and rapid development, in which dramatic growth in the number of PRC media organs occurred and the types of topics considered acceptable for publication increased. At the same time, the reintroduction of market forces into China's media complex and a decline in state subsidies triggered a partial corrosion of the state's capacity to supervise media content.

During the early reform period, government restrictions on the establishment of media outlets were relaxed, allowing for unencumbered expansion. Disbanded publications were revived, and new ones sprang up rapidly. According to one scholar, media expansion was so rapid that during the high growth period from 1983 to 1986 a new newspaper opened in China once every four days (Stevenson-Yang 2003: 225).

This increase was remarkable. At the lowest point of the Cultural Revolution, China may have had as few as 46 newspapers (Polumbaum 1990). During the mid 1980s, it had over 3,000, though this number decreased to about 2,000 by December 2003 (Cambreleng 2003; Stevenson-Yang 2003: 225). A similar trend is in place for PRC magazines: between December 1978 and December 2003, their numbers grew from a few hundred to a reported 9,000 (Cambreleng 2003).

To encourage growth in this sector, the PRC government demonstrated a new openness to publicizing information. Topics once considered taboo because they were devoid of political merit became tolerated in the Chinese media. Editors and journalists received guidance indicating that, while clear limits remained, some reporting on negative issues could be permitted. For example, in April 1985, then-CCP General Secretary Hu Yaobang stated that 20 percent of all news content could be negative, but that approximately 80 percent should be positive (Polumbaum 1990: 41).

The implications of these changes are worthy of some reflection. Within a span of 25 years, the administrative structure that had been put in place to oversee a couple of hundred newspapers and magazines needed to adapt to the existence of several thousand. At the same time, a Chinese populace accustomed to an extremely limited variety of news outlets was given an opportunity to select from a vast expanse of news media, all of which were disseminating a volume and variety of information unprecedented in the history of the PRC.

At times, the Chinese government expressed concern over this combination of a stressed administrative structure and a possibly overstimulated population of media consumers. Overall growth in China's media sector was therefore punctuated by several periods of contraction, reflecting the larger debates taking place in China's rapidly transforming polity. Examples include the anti-spiritual pollution campaign of 1983, the antibourgeois liberalization campaign of early 1987, and the post-Tiananmen crackdown in 1989. Although not similarly spurred by a single political event, many would argue that China's media system is currently in a period of significant contraction.

Mechanisms of control over media content

Faced with an exponentially larger number of outlets, the CCP was faced with the challenge of adapting the existing administrative structure to enforce rules and guidelines for media content. What mechanisms were (and are) available to control the ideological content of media? In general, the PRC government employs prepublication review, written and verbal guidance, post-publication reviews, and control over the administrative rights of media businesses.

Prepublication review

All media outlets are subject to some form of prepublication review by the CCP. At a minimum, the editor-in-chief of a media organ is responsible for reviewing all material prior to public release. In China, media organs are government institutions. As such, the job of editor-in-chief is a civil service position. Those appointed to this position are almost always party members and are selected, either directly or indirectly, by party committees. Therefore, the person who holds this position wears two hats, fulfilling both duties to the media enterprise and the CCP.[3]

In some cases, higher-level CCP oversight of news media content can be required. When this occurs, the CCP Central Propaganda Department or an appropriate-level provincial or municipal propaganda department exercises direct supervision over the news content of certain media outlets and reviews news content prior to publication or broadcast. The process by which this is done varies. In some cases, key sections of a newspaper edition or television program may be selected for prepublication review; in other cases, a specific newspaper or television program may undergo prescreening prior to release.

Despite the attention that it sometimes receives in the West, prepublication review by officials outside of a media outlet's editorial department is comparatively rare. The ratio of censorship staff to media organs makes large-scale prepublication review prohibitively difficult. To most efficiently use their small staffs, CCP propaganda departments usually focus their direct supervision on party papers and other media organs with close ties to the CCP.

Formal lists of specific media outlets subject to prepublication review are simply not available. At the national-level the Central Propaganda Department is rumored to exercise some level of prepublication control over the news content of at least Xinhua News Agency, *People's Daily, Seek Truth Magazine, Guangming Daily, Economic Daily, China Daily*, CCTV, China National Radio, and China Radio International.

Written and verbal guidance

Regardless of whether they receive prepublication supervision beyond what they receive from the editor, members of the Chinese propaganda system receive regular guidance on the content of their news stories and broadcasts. Guidance can be passed through official documents, formal meetings, or verbal directives.

The CCP propaganda departments and party committees at the central, provincial, and municipal levels regularly issue guidance on how the media should (or should not) report particular issues. General rules and parameters for news operations are issued through party resolutions, directives, announcements, and internal bulletins.

Therefore, members of the PRC media system are the recipients of regularly produced documents. One of these is *Propaganda Trend (Xuanchuan Dongtai)*, which is issued by the Central Propaganda Department once a week to provide general editorial guidance on domestic news reporting

(Zhao 1998: 20). General guidance on propaganda work is also disseminated in professional journals targeted at members of China's media complex, such as reporters and editors. Examples of journals that provide this type of guidance include: *China Reporter* (*Zhongguo Jizhe*), *Military Correspondent* (*Junshi Jizhe*), *Media Observer* (*Chuanmei Guangcha*), and *News Front* (*Xinwen Qianshao*).

In addition to written guidance, several knowledgeable observers of the Chinese media system note that verbal guidance is passed on through regularly scheduled meetings, ad hoc meetings, and informal conversations. In fact, much of the Chinese propaganda system is guided and governed by meetings. Some take place annually at specific times of the year, while others are driven by events. As in any professional field in China, national-level meetings for propaganda professionals are significant events. They provide an opportunity for propaganda professionals to gather and discuss pressing issues. Careful examination of media reporting at the conclusion of such meetings can provide insights into the near-term priorities and directions of the PRC propaganda system.[4]

Post-publication review

More widespread than prepublication review and more directly relevant for the contents of specific articles or broadcasts than written and verbal guidance is the process of post-publication review. Within the Central Propaganda Department is a group of censors who are responsible for reviewing finished media products and determining whether they have violated propaganda guidance. Provincial-level propaganda departments also have offices that concentrate on reviewing media products produced within their province.

Many individuals engaged in such work are not full-time government employees; they tend to be retirees experienced in editing and propaganda work.[5] If individuals charged with post-publication review identify a news report that appears to counter core party principles or contravene party guidance on media content (i.e. news reports that contain forbidden content), they report it to the proper authority, such as the appropriate-level General Administration of Press and Publications (GAPP) or State Administration of Radio, Film, and Television (SARFT) office. These agencies will then contact the media outlet's editor and determine appropriate actions, punishments, or sanctions (Stevenson-Yang 2003: 225; Zhao 1998: 20–22).

A common observation heard among Chinese media professionals is that, at all levels of government, the number of censors engaged in post-publication review is small compared to the number of media outlets under examination. As a result, enforcement of media guidance often appears haphazard, with no clear demarcation as to what actions will catch the attention of censors or bring about punishments. When punishments are meted out, it is rare for the instigating event to be made clear to other members of the media. Instead, observers are left to suppose the widest possible definition of the individual's offense, generating the assumption that similar actions taken by other media professionals could result in more punishments.

Punishments resulting from unfavorable post-publication review can range from reprimands and self-criticism to detainment, arrest, and jail time. The arbitrary nature of post-publication review and the potential repercussions of negative findings by censors are yielding a regime of self-censorship among China's media professionals. In such a system, explicit prohibitions to report on certain topics or issues are not usually necessary. Most reporters and editors seek to fly beneath the radar of post-publication reviewers and therefore avoid including news content that they themselves deem to be too risky or controversial.[6]

Controlling the administrative rights of media establishments

The final means of maintaining control over media outlets occurs *via* personnel appointments and the strategic granting and revocation of administrative rights over business establishments. The Chinese government, through GAPP and SARFT, maintains control over all media broadcasting and publishing companies in the country. Licenses to publish or broadcast are not granted capriciously; obtaining such a license is an expensive and convoluted process.[7] These licenses can be revoked at any time without public explanation or prior notice. When this occurs, it is often the result of negative post-publication reviews.

Such events are not uncommon. For example, in August 2003 the popular journal *Strategy and Management* (*Zhanlue yu Guanli*) was closed down in apparent retribution for publishing an article highly critical of then current PRC policy toward North Korea. Another example is the controversial closing and then reopening of the Beijing-based journal *Freezing Point* (*Bingdian*) in early 2006.

As previously mentioned, editors of most newspapers and radio and television programs are both government and party officials. As such, they are selected with great care and can be removed without notice. As with the closing of media outlets, no public explanation needs to be offered for these personnel decisions.

The advent of market competitive pressures and challenges to CCP control

The mechanisms for control listed above have been available since the founding of the PRC. The dramatic expansion in the number of media outlets and topics considered suitable for publication brought about by the introduction of market forces, however, have stretched the CCP's ability to oversee media content. Maintaining a level of control on par with the pre-1978 period would have entailed either a vast expansion of press freedoms or a dramatic increase in the resources applied to media oversight.

Dramatic increases in the resources applied to media oversight do not appear to have been treated as a viable option. The number of officials at the national level charged with supervising media content stayed constant and then dropped during the reform era. In fact, according to one scholar, during the 1998 government-restructuring campaign the already-diminished staff at the State Press and Publications Administration was further cut in half, to about 150 (Stevenson-Yang 2003: 231–234).

The CCP, it appears, determined that it was willing neither to accept relinquishing control over media content nor to apply the needed financial resources to maintain control in the manner it had in the past. Instead, it opted to first allow expansion of the media sector to support China's reform policies and then cull the types of media institutions that it deemed undesirable. Put differently, the CCP strategically applied media regulations to combat the most potentially damaging reports and criticisms while accepting that total and consistent application of its guidelines was impossible.

As the CCP was struggling to maintain adequate oversight over media content, China's media system experienced a crucial development: the decline of state subsidies and the reintroduction of market forces. These two trends pivoted on two related policy decisions: the PRC decided to make media outlets responsible for their own profits and losses; and all media units were allowed to sell advertising.

Funding generated through advertising increased steadily in the 1980s. According to one source, the total amount of revenue derived from advertising in China increased by a minimum of 50 percent every year since 1980 (Stevenson-Yang 2003: 231–234). As the Chinese media complex began generating massive advertising revenues, the government instituted cutbacks in state subsidies. Media outlets thus became ever more dependent on advertising to cover operating costs. For example, as early as 1995, 80 percent of China National Radio's operating costs were covered by advertising revenue (Stevenson-Yang 2003: 231–234).

This change in revenue source had far-reaching implications. In order to remain viable, Chinese media outlets had to ensure that they had a strong base of loyal readers, listeners, or viewers. Without this base, a media outlet not only failed to receive adequate subscription revenue, it also left itself poorly positioned to sell advertising. Media enterprises thus needed to meet the expectations of their target audience if they wanted to survive.

Besides financial viability, editors and media managers knew that growing a loyal audience could be the key to personal wealth through increased bonuses and fringe benefits. This was a critical development. Without making individuals and institutions invested in identifying and growing an audience, there was really no incentive to take advantage of the CCP's efforts to (slightly) loosen controls over media content.

As media outlets became dependent on their respective consumer bases, they began to differentiate themselves from one another and target specific audiences. Some media, for instance, sought out intellectuals, producing reports asking tough questions about China's reforms. Others targeted the business community by creating reliable sources for information on commercial and economic issues. And yet others targeted the broader community, producing elements of traditional news with a heavy emphasis on human-interest stories or investigative reporting. Sensationalist coverage also increased, as some Chinese media sought out the lowest common denominator.

Differentiation by media outlets helped create a more informed Chinese public, though competition and fear of being "scooped" resulted in pandering to some baser instincts and mistakes. Sometimes the results were comic. For example, on June 7, 2002 *Reuters* reported that the *Beijing Evening News,* which claims a daily circulation of 1.25 million, republished as fact a tongue-in-cheek article from the satirical US newspaper *The Onion.* The article noted that the US Congress was threatening to move to a new city unless it received better facilities, a tactic common to US professional sports teams. It took a few days, but the newspaper eventually issued a correction.

Emerging dilemma: party line or bottom line?

As China's media system is maturing, media professionals are faced with a dilemma that reflects in many ways a key contradiction shaping China's capitalist transition: the tensions between continued party control and mounting capitalist competition. In fact, how can a media outlet meet an increasingly sophisticated audience's desire for unfettered information, while at the same time satisfying the CCP's intent to control the content and tone of news reporting? In other words, how does one succeed in a business when facing conflicting commercial and political pressures?

The Chinese media complex cannot afford to totally ignore either of the two masters it serves: commercial demands, and the demands of the CCP. Media outlets that specialize in promulgating party policies must also include information that is of general interest to their target audience. Otherwise few would consume that product, the media outlet would not remain commercially viable, and party propaganda would not reach its intended audience.

Conversely, media outlets that specialize in catering to public tastes cannot afford to ignore CCP policies. Publicizing too much information that is considered taboo or failing to sufficiently meet requirements to "support the party" would invite closure and personal punishment. As one PRC journalist stated: "As a journalist, my job should be focused on writing a good report. But half of my effort is spent on considering how to get a story past the censors and the likelihood of punishment" (Watts 2005).

Consequently, China's media professionals remain trapped "between the party line and the bottom line" (Zhao 1998). This does not mean that PRC media professionals have been passive bystanders. They have attempted to navigate their difficult environment by circumventing media policies and creating a host of new institutions.

Circumventing media policies

As China's media system faces escalating material incentives to give the public the information it desires, media outlets have become more aggressive in circumventing government policy and avoiding party guidance. Reporters fear not only that they will be scooped by commercial competitors, but also that CCP or government officials will find out about a story that would have popular appeal and intervene before it is published. This is a particularly common concern for stories regarding corruption.

For some reporters and editors, the discovery of a hot story marks the beginning of a complicated game of cat and mouse with their local party committee. If they think a topic is sensitive and sense that unwanted guidance might be coming, they refuse to answer their phones. Plans to report on that topic are kept quiet until the evening, when government officials have left for the day.

Stories describing such efforts are common in the Western press (Cody 2004). Most share a common thread. When presented with information that is deemed to be of high interest to a media organ's target audience but also deemed potentially sensitive, some media professionals take a passive-aggressive approach. While not defying any rules or directives, they go to great lengths to avoid party guidance. Items with forbidden content are not published or broadcast, but editors and reporters try to take advantage of the blurred lines between the discretionary and forbidden realm. They seek to be as forward-leaning as possible while still escaping the attention of party officials. In many cases individuals are successful in this approach; in some cases, however, miscalculation can lead to prompt official sanction, including job loss, fines, or imprisonment.

By maximizing opportunities to circumvent restrictive policies, Chinese media professionals have over time created pressures that challenge CCP rules governing media content. As noted above, rising commercial pressures have generated strong incentives for each media outlet to differentiate itself from competitors. Since audiences could choose among different media outlets, they began to demonstrate a deep interest in sensitive topics. This led to the inclusion of more and more discretionary content. In fact, discretionary content emerged as a key to commercial success and with that the definition of what could be considered discretionary gradually expanded.

At the same time, media outlets became more responsible for their operating costs, which made the inclusion of obligatory content financially burdensome. Exploring risky topics also became less dangerous since the consequences for being singled out for discipline, while still disturbing, are now less severe than during the Cultural Revolution.

Opposing these trends, the CCP continues to view control of the media as an essential tool to reign in or redirect potentially dangerous social trends. Although enforcing these control mechanisms can be costly and unwieldy, efforts to maintain control over the scope of discretionary content continue.

The result has been a constant push and pull along the boundaries of forbidden and discretionary content as depicted in Figure 7.2. Party forces push down, attempting to shrink the scope of acceptable content to what are considered more manageable levels. Pushing upward in the opposite direction, commercial forces constantly strive to expand the area of discretionary content in order to appeal to a wider audience.

This dynamic has allowed some media outlets to rise to popularity by challenging the formal and informal rules that bound Chinese news content. The result is often commercial success coupled with high-profile disciplinary action. For example, the highly profitable Nanfang Daily Media Group published in Guangdong Province has built itself a reputation for reporting on topics that would normally be considered taboo and engaging in often daring criticism of party officials. Three newspapers in this group have been singled out for special attention: *Southern Weekend, Southern Metropolis Daily,* and *21st Century World Herald.* Examples of increasingly provocative reporting by these publications include repeated attempts to undermine PRC prohibitions on reporting on SARS; reports on corruption and police brutality, such as a 2003 incident where college student Sun Zhigang was beaten to death while in the custody of the Guangzhou police; and an interview with Mao Zedong's former secretary, Li Rui, who called for reforms and was highly critical of current CCP policies.

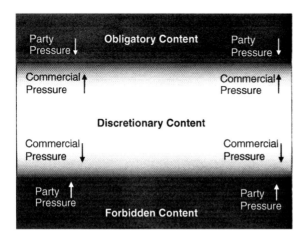

Figure 7.2 Pressures at work in China's media evolution.

These reporting efforts were met with a strong response. *21st Century World Herald* was forced to suspend its operations in March 2003. *Southern Weekend* fared little better and was the subject of a series of crackdowns beginning in 2001. Finally, several editors of *Southern Metropolis Daily* were investigated for financial impropriety during early 2004. Then-current editor Cheng Yizhong was arrested, while then-current deputy editor Yu Huafeng and former editor Li Minying were sentenced to 12 and 11 years in prison respectively. Many viewed these investigations as an act of retribution, intended to silence an often-vocal critic of China's status quo.

Although singled out for punishment and subjected to special scrutiny on numerous occasions, the Nanfang Daily Group remains a commercial success. Most observers of PRC media would assert that Nanfang Daily's repeated challenges to government regulation of news content have served to expand the scope of discretionary content. As Liu Aimin, a media insider, stated, "I think the group has greatly influenced journalism. ... they have moved away from control by the party and the government, and towards the market. This has changed the way they produce news" (Watts 2005).

Creating new institutions: tabloids and the decline of party papers

As individuals experimented with circumventing and challenging party policies, new institutions emerged that enabled members of the PRC media complex to more efficiently balance the conflicting needs to satisfy consumer interests and promulgate CCP messages. This was especially true in the area of print media.

PRC journalists now often make reference to tabloids, major newspapers, and party papers. The Chinese use the word "tabloid" (literally "small newspaper"; *xiaobao*) as a description of the physical characteristics of the newspaper. That is, newspapers with small pages that turn like a book, such as the *New York Post*, or the "compact edition" of the *Times of London*, are considered "tabloids." Broadsheet newspapers that fold over, such as the *Washington Post,* are considered "major newspapers" (literally "big news-paper"; *dabao*). Major newspapers are generally older, while tabloids tend to be subsidiaries of a major newspaper.

In China, the word "tabloid" does not have negative connotations. There are some highly credible, widely circulated newspapers that fall into this category. For example, several of the newspapers of the Nanfang Daily Group, such as *Southern Metropolis Daily*, are tabloids. In general, tabloids have been the format in which most of the innovative, forward-leaning journalism emerged in the PRC. Some tabloid advances, such as investigative journalism highlighting official corruption, have been the subjects of inter-national praise. Other developments, such as populist appeals to xenophobic nationalism, have been criticized as being irresponsible. However, both are essential elements of China's "new media."

It is important to note that the terms for "major newspaper," which would literally translate as "big newspaper," and tabloid, which would literally translate as "small newspaper," are not representative of subscription base or capacity for revenue generation. A successful tabloid can easily generate a wider circulation and thus more revenue than the major newspaper to which it is a subsidiary.

Some newspapers are considered mouthpieces (*houshe*) for the institutions to which they are affiliated. These newspapers are faced with commercial pressures, but are also obligated to express the viewpoint of their affiliated institution. For instance, *Anhui Daily* (*Anhui Ribao*) is affiliated with the Anhui Provincial Party Committee, and serves as its mouthpiece.

Among the newspapers that serve as mouthpieces for an affiliated institution, there are some that fall into a special category. These newspapers have a closer relationship with local CCP party committees, receive some sort of government funding, and are more likely to be subject to some sort of prepublication review. These newspapers are called "party papers" (*dangbao*).

Party papers are subject to some of the commercial pressures of regular Chinese newspapers. However, they receive government funding to defray a portion of their operating costs. Therefore, they are the ones most likely to adhere to party guidance and to be entrusted with expressing CCP policies and messages.

The PRC had many party newspapers in the past. These were supported by direct state subsidies and through a policy of mandatory subscription – officials and work units were required to pay for a subscription to these special newspapers and magazines regardless of whether they wanted to read them. In July 2003, the PRC passed a series of media regulations, which abolished the practice of mandatory subscriptions. Provinces and municipalities were told that they needed to limit the number of "party papers." Party committees at the provincial-level were permitted one newspaper and one magazine, while party committees at the municipal-level were permitted only one newspaper. Other institutions, such as trade unions, associations, and research institutes at or below the provincial-level were told that they could not provide funding to their own personal mouthpieces. Their newspapers and magazines had to become commercially viable or shut down (*Beijing Review* 2003: 11–17).

It is uncertain whether these new regulations are being uniformly implemented throughout the country. In the past, two of Shanghai's most prestigious papers, *Liberation Daily* (*Jiefang Ribao*) and *Wenhui Bao* were both considered party papers. However, once the 2003 regulations were passed, *Liberation Daily* became Shanghai's official party paper, and *Wenhui Bao* lost this status.

Creating new institutions: media conglomerates

With all of these new types of media outlets, each appealing to different population segments and forced to cover operating costs, it is not surprising to learn that editors would begin to seek economies of scale and simplify CCP oversight by grouping together. These collections of media enterprises are known as media conglomerates or media groups. They generally possess a similar structure.

Each group has a major newspaper that acts as the leader of the group.[8] Often, this lead newspaper is a party paper.[9] Moreover, the name of this newspaper tends to be incorporated into the name of the media group. For example, the *Anhui Daily* media group is lead by *Anhui Daily*, the party newspaper for the Anhui Provincial Party Committee. The administrative headquarters of a media group are generally collocated at the headquarters of its lead newspaper. Below the lead newspaper is a collection of subsidiaries. Some are also major newspapers; some are tabloids; some are magazines or weekly papers.

To maximize revenue potential, the media group is structured so as to appeal to the widest total audience possible. At the same time, the group performs an important political task. In an era of increasing competition for limited government resources, securing adequate funding to promulgate CCP messages is becoming increasingly difficult. Formulating propaganda messages that resonate adequately with all members of Chinese society is particularly tricky due to the diversification of societal interests triggered by China's capitalist transition. In fact, social changes have resulted in a disparity of receptiveness to propaganda messages among the general populace. The establishment of media groups makes it possible for propaganda committees at all levels to more efficiently reach the modern Chinese populace.

Media groups therefore ensure that the CCP has an active and diverse readership that is willing to consume at least some of its propaganda. For example, according to one member of the PRC media complex, the Shanghai-based Jiefang (Liberation) Daily Media Group has nine newspapers that target different segments of the population.[10] *Jiefang Daily* has a circulation of 400,000, the *Morning Post* has a circulation of 500,000, and the *Shenjiang Fuwubao* has a circulation of more than 400,000. The total circulation for all nine papers is over one million, which is even higher than *Jiefang Daily*'s was during the height of the Cultural Revolution, when media was much more tightly regulated and there was little competition.

Anecdotal evidence suggests that each media group has its own party committee, known as the *jituan dangwei* and consisting of around five members. The members of this group are appointed by the appropriate-level party propaganda department. For a provincial-level media group this would be a provincial-level propaganda department, while for a municipal-level media group this would be a municipal-level propaganda department.

Moreover, certain newspapers are singled out for special attention; in these cases, the entire municipal or provincial-level party committee may get a vote in the media group's party committee's selection.[11]

Within a media group, each individual newspaper also has its own party committee. Membership in these committees is determined by the media group's party committee as depicted in Figure 7.3.[12] When considering a media group's structure, it is worth noting that all positions of authority are in some way linked to party appointments. Even for lower-ranking newspapers, appointments of editors-in-chief are made by a party committee.

Although media groups are useful means of creating economies of scale, in some ways, their present administration makes more sense politically than economically. Observers of the PRC media will note that the lead newspaper in a media group is generally not the most profitable. In fact, more profitable tabloids often provide revenue to support money-losing ventures. Moreover, in some cases media groups have been forced to take on media outlets that are not commercially viable because the outlet is deemed to perform an essential aspect of CCP propaganda.

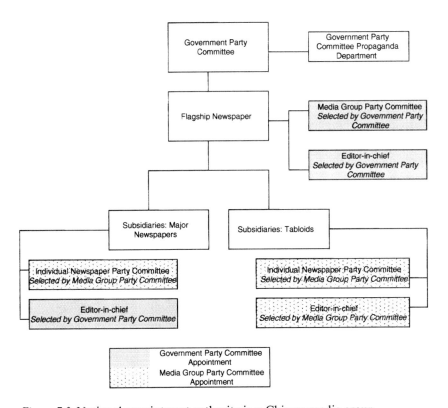

Figure 7.3 Notional appointment authority in a Chinese media group.

Shanghai Daily – an English language newspaper targeting foreigners living in Shanghai – is a fine example of a "commercial" enterprise that makes little economic sense. The newspaper is expensive to run and by most accounts will never earn a profit. It is rumored to only cover one third of its operating costs with advertising and subscription revenue. It exists because the Shanghai government wants to have an English-language vehicle for conveying propaganda messages to foreigners living in Shanghai. In another time, such a newspaper may have received government funding. However, the Shanghai Party Committee has attached it to Shanghai's Wenxin Media Group, which subsidizes *Shanghai Daily* with income from the sale of tabloids and other high-circulation media. Such indirect subsidy arrangements, it is said, are considered the price of doing business in the Chinese media sector.

Conclusions

This chapter outlined several major trends in the evolution of China's media sector: there has been dramatic growth in the numbers of PRC media organs and an increase in the types of topics considered acceptable for publication. State subsidies to media enterprises have also declined and market forces gained in prominence. As a result of these developments, the state's capacity to oversee media content has diminished, though the CCP retains important levers. Most fundamentally, these trends hinged on China's decision in 1978 to shift away from class struggle and toward modernization and economic development.

The story of China's media complex during the reform era is fairly simple. As China relaxed controls on content and made it easier to establish media outlets, a period of rapid growth occurred in China's media industry. This growth was not matched by an increase in resources to govern the media and oversee its management. Rather, the CCP tried new approaches and began to focus on codifying its expectations and standards in the form of formal, written laws, regulations, and directives. The institutions charged with administering these directives, however, were not sufficiently staffed, and the CCP became unable to consistently apply these rules and guidelines. Instead, the CCP focused on being inconsistent. It enforced its oversight powers seemingly at random in defense of what it saw to be core principles.

At the same time, the incentive structure media editors and reporters faced was affected by the CCP's decisions to allow the sale of advertisements, reduce government subsidies, and make media enterprises responsible for their own profits and losses. Market competition became a driver of editorial criteria and reporters and editors began to include and discard news items in order to appeal to the interests of ever more segmented niche audiences. The inclusion of obligatory content was increasingly viewed as a financial burden, while discretionary content rapidly became the key to commercial success. These developments allowed the borders of forbidden content to be pushed back, expanding the realm of discretionary content.

China's capitalist transition has not only enabled market forces to reshape media content, but also led to the development of new media institutions. Tabloids have risen to meet the needs of audiences thirsty for information. In some cases these media outlets cater to the lowest common denominator – such as xenophobic nationalism – and publish only the tantalizing and sensational. However, the same forces that put these news outlets into place ensured the emergence of cutting edge investigative reporting that has been singled out by some scholars as a harbinger of a brighter future for China's media industry.

In parallel, media conglomerates have emerged as an innovative solution to the conflicting demands of both party and pocketbook. Rather than fund unprofitable media outlets in order to ensure a mouthpiece, China's leaders have phased out many party papers that receive direct financial support and relied more on an indirect subsidy arrangement. This arrangement uses tabloid revenues to support the promulgation of political messages in other less profitable news sources, enabling the CCP to transmit its propaganda to wider audiences.

Of course, the CCP and state agencies have retained tools to guide, and when deemed necessary, control China's media professionals. Through its use of pre- and post-publication review, written and verbal guidance, and administrative rights over business establishments, the CCP has yielded a regime of self-censorship. At the time of this writing, China's political leaders maintain the ability to suppress reporting on any topic that they deem to be a threat to core party principles. Despite tremendous expansion in the amount of discretionary content found in PRC news media, a restrictive environment remains.

This chapter painted a picture of the Chinese media system that reflects the broader political tensions underlying China's emergent capitalism. These tensions pit CCP dominance emphasizing political control and stability against a capitalist logic emphasizing commercial viability and unfettered information. So far, these tensions have been carefully balanced in China's media complex, allowing the CCP to retain ultimate control, while fostering a thriving media sector.

When viewing the evolution of this system, one cannot help but wonder how much of what is in place now is the result of intentional choice, and how much is the result of chance. Did leaders in Beijing really set out to build a regime of self-censorship, or was that simply the best they could come up with when faced with the daunting task of providing oversight to overwhelming numbers of new media outlets? More importantly, is the system that is in place now sustainable into the future?

Convincing evidence can be found to support either a positive or negative assessment. Although only an assertion, this observer of the PRC media suspects that the balanced tensions between the political and commercial realms, especially the practice of controlling the media through self-censorship, are in the end not sustainable. The CCP can do many things to slow the process, such as manipulating licensing rules and creating additional barriers of entry into the media market. Ultimately, all this accomplishes is to slow the process of relinquishing control. As long as the boundaries between obligatory, discretionary, and forbidden content remain blurred, the area of discretionary content will continue to grow. As long as the prospects for material gain remain, media professionals will continue to push the envelope and seek to produce news that meets consumer demands. Not only will crackdowns on those who circumvent or challenge party media policies fail to stop this tide, they might even embolden those who resist and increase the rate of change.

As with the broader evolution of China's emergent political economy, the ultimate result of China's media evolution remains indeterminate. One should not expect to see a wholesale adoption of Western-style press freedoms, and one should not expect to see change come quickly. Indeed, the leadership in Beijing has been quite effective at slowing the pace of media independence to date. How long the carefully balanced tensions between commercial pressures and CCP controls can continue, however, remains to be seen.

Notes

1 Historical examples abound. During the Ming and Qing dynasties the adoption and use of State Confucianism to impart social control was clearly manifest. Republican China under the Kuomintang (KMT) government did not shy away from censorship as well. In 1934, the KMT established a censorship commission, which prohibited all works that violated Sun Yat-Sen's "Three People's Principles" and censored all work that contained "erroneous" or "reactionary" utterances. For a more detailed discussion, see Lynch (1999: 19–21).
2 The author of this chapter was unable to identify specific documents that outlined standing guidance on reporting on corruption in China. However, many have observed that reporting on corruption appears to be limited to individuals and institutions below ministerial level.
3 Unless otherwise noted, all discussion on mechanisms for control of PRC media content was informed by a series of interviews that took place between 2002 and 2005. Subjects interviewed included PRC journalists and editors, foreign correspondents working in China, scholars, and other knowledgeable observers of the PRC media complex.
4 Three key meetings that seem to occur every year are: (1) end-of-year national meetings of directors of propaganda departments; (2) provincial- and municipal-level propaganda meetings – occurring shortly after the national-level meeting; and (3) the All China Journalist Association annual meeting.
5 There has been a fair amount of variation in descriptions of the post-publication review process. For one recent description, see Bandurski and Hui (2006).
6 Perry Link has written and spoken extensively about this phenomenon of self-censorship. For one example, see Link (2002).
7 The website of the Congressional Executive Commission on China (2003) in the United States is an important resource for discussions of PRC media regulations

to constrain free expression. In particular, they have published a useful flowchart on the publication process in China.

8 In English, some refer to this newspaper as the "flagship" paper.
9 If a locality has more than one media group, only one will be lead by a party paper, since each locality can have only one party paper. However, if a locality has only one media group, it will be lead by a party paper.
10 Interview.
11 Interview.
12 Interview.

References

Bandurski, D. and Hui, L. (2006) "Freezing Point," *Wall Street Journal*, March 6, p. A4.

Beijing Review (2003) "Breaking News – State Media Reform," August 28, pp. 11–17.

Cambreleng, B. (2003) "China Flooded with Information, But it is Tightly Controlled," *Agence France* (Hong Kong), December 9.

Cody, E. (2004) "Party Censors Leave a Chinese City to Speculate on Corruption Scandal," *Washington Post*, November 1, p. A13.

Congressional Executive Commission on China (2003) "Choices and Consequences Faced by Authors in the PRC," February 15. Online. Available HTTP: cecc.gov/pages/virtualAcad/exp/bookflow.php (accessed November 17, 2006).

Link, P. (2002) "China: The Anaconda in the Chandelier," *New York Review of Books*, April 11. Online. Available HTTP: www.nybooks.com/articles/article-preview?article_id=15258 (accessed November 20, 2006).

Lynch, D. (1999) *After the Propoganda State: Media, Politics, and "Thought Work" in Reformed China*, Stanford, CA: Stanford University Press.

People's Daily (2005) "China Focus: Natural Disaster Death Toll Statistics No Longer State Secrets," September 13. Online. Available HTTP: english.people.com.cn/200509/13/eng20050913_208168.html (accessed November 17, 2006).

Polumbaum, J. (1990) "The Tribulations of China's Journalists after a Decade of Reform," in C.C. Lee (ed.) *Voices of China: The Interplay of Politics and Journalism*, New York: Guilford Press, pp. 33–68.

Stevenson-Yang, A. (2003) "The Absent-minded Reform of China's Media," in D. Finkelstein and M. Kivlehan (eds) *China's Leadership in the 21st Century*, Armonk, NY: ME Sharpe, pp. 223–248.

Watts, J. (2005) "Print and Be Damned – China's Paper Tigers Fight On," *Guardian*, July 1. Online. Available HTTP: www.guardian.co.uk/print/0,3858,5228578-108142,00.html (accessed November 17, 2006).

Zhao, Y. (1998) *Media, Market, and Democracy in China: Between the Party Line and the Bottom Line*, Chicago, IL: University of Illinois Press.

8 Why does capitalism fail to push China toward democracy?[1]

An Chen

The conventional wisdom in political science holds that a capitalist market economy is a necessary, though not sufficient, condition for democratic politics. Despite numerous cases of nondemocratic capitalist societies, history shows that capitalism is the sole economic system compatible with a democratic system of government. With the exception of formerly communist Eastern Europe and the Soviet Union, democratic transitions have taken place and been completed in a free-market capitalist context.

For all the principled discrepancy between capitalism and democracy, the democracy-fostering logic of capitalism is widely accepted. "Historically," Joseph Schumpeter found, "the modern democracy rose along with capitalism, and in causal connection with it. ..." Democracy is therefore "a product of the capitalist process" (Schumpeter 1950: 296–297). Capitalism emphasizes individual choice and peaceful competition (in the market-place) – values shared by democracy. By separating economic and political spheres, capitalism creates a balance of power between state and society. Capitalism, too, gives rise to class politics that can support social dynamics fostering democratization.

From a theoretical perspective, China's ongoing transition toward capitalism is of particular significance. Just a few years before democratization took place in Eastern Europe and the Soviet Union, Samuel Huntington predicted its "likelihood" there as "virtually nil" (Huntington 1984). Given the widely accepted capitalist prerequisites of democracy, this lack of premonition is hardly astonishing. Communist states characterized by command economies were seen as the least likely to move toward democracy.

As market reforms are pushing China toward full-fledged capitalism, China's state-society relations are changing in ways that make a transition toward democracy more plausible. First and foremost, capitalism is bringing class politics back into China's political equation. Furthermore, the expansion of individual freedoms and socioeconomic pluralism is undermining the social foundations of communist party hegemony. Albeit still exceedingly powerful, the Chinese Communist Party (CCP) can no longer afford to be entirely unresponsive to society. It depends increasingly on social support for governance and policy implementation, if not for survival. Societal changes emanating from the market process therefore distinguish China from a prototype communist state and render the experiences of many authoritarian regimes transitioning toward democracy germane to the study of China's political transition.

However, China's one-party system has emerged almost unscathed from the fundamental transformation of its command economy. Capitalism's advance has not brought any substantial democratic progress. While organized political opposition existed in varying degrees under other authoritarian regimes, it is completely absent in reform China. The thriving of the private sector has not given rise to a civil society in its true sense, nor has it significantly undermined the capacity of the party-state to dominate Chinese society. To the extent that the CCP has allowed Chinese citizens to enjoy more freedoms or yielded some of its economic powers to the market, it has not been forced to do so by social pressure, but largely according to its own reform agenda. If China's communist regime has truly evolved from totalitarianism to authoritarianism as some scholars argue, then the degree of its political repressiveness – particularly its organizational capacity for imposing its will upon society – far exceeds that of nearly all authoritarian regimes.

The politics of China since 1949 have been treated by many China specialists as *sui generis*, failing to fit into any totalitarian, communist, or developing country model. It would therefore be unsurprising if China's political transition would be equally unique. The main thrust of this chapter, though, will not directly explore the future of China's polity. Rather, I will build on structural models of democratization to offer an explanation for why the pro-democratic logic of capitalism has not emerged in China.[2] I will argue that China's capitalist transition has been a party-initiated and party-dominated process. As a result, no separation of the spheres of economic and political power has transpired, in turn undermining the creation of a civil society with powerful pro-democratic forces and class alliances.

Capitalist transition within a special context

The development of the private sector and its expanding weight in the economy is perhaps the most effective measure for the advance of capitalism in China. During the 1980s nearly all Chinese private enterprises were small in scale, yet from 1989 to 2003 their registered capital multiplied 417 times, an annual increase of 53.9 percent, while their number increased from 90,000 to 3.55 million. Therefore, the average capital of each private enterprise increased 13 times during the same period – from 90,000 *yuan* to 1.17 million *yuan* (Liu and Xu 2004: 22–23).

After the 1997 party congress accelerated the sell-off of state-owned enterprises (SOEs), many private enterprises grew larger by purchasing or annexing money-losing SOEs. In the mid-1990s the bulk of China's private sector was concentrated in light industry, construction and transportation, and services. A decade later, some heavy industries, infrastructure, and public facilities were in private hands, and private capital dominated twenty seven of China's forty industrial sectors (Yang *et al.* 2005). Meanwhile, the tax paid to the state by private enterprises increased from 455 million *yuan* in 1992 to 94.6 billion *yuan* in 2002 – multiplying 208 times (Zhang *et al.* 2004: 3).

Basically, the private and state sectors reversed their positions in terms of economic weight, thus altering China's employment structure. Between 1994 and 2002, private sector employment jumped from 8 percent (54 million) of the total workforce (including agriculture) to 22 percent (160 million), although the entire workforce increased only by 9.6 percent. Together with foreign-funded enterprises, the nonstate sector hired 2.3 times the number of workers in 2002 that SOEs and collective-owned enterprises (COEs) hired (Xiao 2005). The political implications of this change in employment patterns are enormous: the vast majority of urbanites in China do not work in party-controlled SOEs or COEs and therefore do not depend on the party-state for a living.

Despite the considerable advances of Chinese private firms, the country's political economy remains in the midst of a capitalist transition. Before this transition is complete, it would be premature to test the applicability of Western tenets linking capitalism and democracy on China. Clearly, the failure of capitalism to push China's polity toward democracy should in the first place be ascribed to the short history of China's capitalist transition. Capitalist modes of production are certainly not new to China, but they were thoroughly interrupted during the "socialist transformation" of the 1950s. The development of a market economy had to start from scratch under the reform regime. A long time period might therefore have to pass before China's new commercial classes gain the political weight paralleling that of their counterparts in mature market economies (Bobbio 1990: 80–81; Friedman 1962; Hirschman 1977; Weber 1978).

Nonetheless, we cannot accept *a priori* that China's capitalism-driven transition toward democracy is simply a waiting game. We need to delve deeper into the nature and logic of China's capitalist transition, especially what form of capitalism is developing in China and whether China will become a "normal" capitalist country in the future.

One of the key distinguishing features of China's capitalist transition is that it has not evolved as a spontaneous but rather a party-sponsored and party-controlled process. The CCP set out on the capitalist road not out of ideological conviction, but motivated by an understanding that capitalism is "superior" at least in one respect: it is economically more efficient than socialism. This political pragmatism has translated into a pro-capitalist strategy generating an enormous dilemma. On one hand, the survival of the regime hinges on its economic performance whose success entails the dominant role of the market. On the other, the CCP cannot entirely forsake, at least officially, its anticapitalist rhetoric, since it remains instrumental in maintaining its organizational cohesion and ideological legitimacy.

This dilemma has prompted central decision-makers to take great pains to wrap capitalism in a socialist package.[3] Although the post-Deng regime is only rhetorically tied to Marxism, there are no signs of it abandoning socialism as one of its legitimizing symbols. As such, it cannot be determined whether full-fledged capitalism will be the destination of China's ongoing economic transition.

The partial or perhaps "halfway" nature of market reforms accounts to a large extent for why China's new economy is far removed from an ideal-typical capitalism. Exactly as the official term "socialist market economy" denotes, market and command mechanisms have been fused and the expansion of the private sector constrained by discriminatory state policies. For example, 62 percent of private sector capital was self-raised in Beijing, while only 22 percent came from state banks (Zhang *et al.* 2004: 74).[4] In addition, the private sector is unfairly treated by the state in a number of other areas, such as land acquisition, access to market information, and the approval of business licenses.

While some of these constraints may just be transitional, others will probably persist because they are inseparably associated with state-guided capitalism. Indeed, China's powerful state and other legacies of China's not-too-distant Maoist past should caution one against drawing a parallel between China and other authoritarian-capitalist countries where organized political opposition and civil society posed constant challenges to authoritarianism.[5] To countervail the pro-democracy effects of capitalism, the CCP has allowed party cadres to retain considerable powers to control the market. This in turn has introduced commercialized patron-client ties between state agents and private entrepreneurs, continuing the dependence of private business on state agents (Wank 1999).

Capitalism and China's new social structure

Despite the state-led nature of China's capitalism, the requirements of market-driven economic growth have compelled the party-state to withdraw somewhat from society and to accept the increasing dominance of private ownership. These developments have eroded some of the regime's traditional control mechanisms and its economic source of political hegemony. Changing patterns of economic ownership and employment, however, have neither changed highly imbalanced state-society relations nor caused a substantial separation between political and economic powers.

Why does Chinese society remain so weak *vis-à-vis* the state even in regions where the bulk of economic power has at least statistically fallen into private hands? The party-state's grip on most power resources and its efforts to prevent China's capitalist transition from threatening the one-party system tell only part of the story. For all their causal linkage, the repressive capacity of the regime alone cannot explain the failure of capitalism to generate social pressures for democratization. There is one rule of capitalism to which China is no exception. Capitalism's development brings about a highly stratified society with large wealth differences among social groups and sharp class conflicts.

According to the structural model of democracy, democracy most likely emerges out of social stratification and class struggle. Democracy could be a product of the compromise reached among various groups that cannot destroy one another to gain complete power, and thus have to agree to democratic rules for peaceful competition (Lipset *et al.* 1956: 15–16). Barrington Moore, for instance, explicitly linked democracy to a particular pattern of class alliances that was built on economic class interests and the allocation of political power (Moore 1966). In short, democratic institutions have historically resulted from, served as a vehicle for, and in turn consolidated peaceful class struggle. In China, however, this scenario has not or probably will not occur in the foreseeable future. To account for China's slim chances of developing democracy, one needs to examine the social structure that is taking shape under China's new capitalism.

Social stratification and economic polarization

China's private industry and commerce had been mostly nationalized by 1956, although the "bourgeoisie" existed nominally until 1966 when the state stopped paying them a fixed interest on their private capital (Riskin 1991: 97). Urban small capitalists, handicraftsmen, and businesspeople were reemployed by SOEs. The collectivization of agriculture culminated in the establishment of the rural commune system in 1958 that confiscated most of each peasant household's farm implements, subjecting the productive activities of the entire peasantry to direct state control. The "socialist transformation" was further radicalized during the Cultural Revolution. On the eve of market reforms, the number of self-employed "individual laborers" constituted a tiny 0.01 percent of the Chinese population (Zhu *et al.* 1998: 6–7).

Chinese society was first re-stratified in the countryside where economic reforms started. Before 1978, peasants were all commune members engaged in agriculture. Rural reforms implementing the household responsibility system resulted in the division of the peasantry into two major categories. Peasants who were still tied to the land and farmed for a living were defined as "agricultural laborers" (*nongye laodongzhe*). Though still the largest part of the rural population, they constituted only 46–50 percent of this population in 1999. At the same time, nonfarm peasants reached 32–35 percent of the rural stratum – the second largest group in the countryside (Lu 2002: 160–198). These peasants left their land and sought employment in industry and services, working in nearby township and village enterprises (TVEs), private enterprises, or joining the "floating population" that is crowding into cities looking for jobs. Despite the fact that most of these are industrial workers by occupation, they are still treated as rural residents both in official statistics and in the implementation of welfare policies (Chan and Zhang 1999). Since their rural *hukou* (household registration) status remains unchanged, they are somewhat disparagingly referred to as "peasant workers" (*nongmin gong*). For a variety of reasons, such as the decline in farm produce prices, the livelihood of peasants whose income derives mainly from farming has deteriorated since the early 1990s, driving more of them to become *nongmin gong*.

Prior to market reforms, nearly all urban citizens were SOE or COE employees belonging to the "working class." Constituting the core of the working class were industrial workers – mostly SOE workers.[6] Thanks to multiple avenues for mobility in the reform era and more open labor markets for urbanites, the traditional "working class" fractured. Those who were well educated and possessed professional skills joined foreign or private companies as managers or white-collar employees. Others became private entrepreneurs or individual business owners, while some former workers have been appointed as contract-based SOE managers with substantially higher incomes than ordinary workers. As some workers climbed the social ladder, the incomes of a large proportion of the former working class, including most blue-collar workers, either stagnated or sank, even falling below subsistence levels. Since the late 1990s, massive SOE privatization has thrown large numbers of "redundant" or "unproductive" workers out on the streets, thereby swelling China's underclass to a politically significant size.

The foregoing class-based analysis of China's social stratification is reflected in official indices of inequality. Under the Maoist regime a high degree of economic egalitarianism was achieved. China's Gini index of inequality was 0.20 during the 1970s, lower than that in developing market states (0.54) and the average socialist state (0.22) (Parish 1984: 84–120). As China moved toward a market economy, a vast majority of Chinese benefited in terms of absolute income levels and quality of life. However, social stratification developed in tandem with market reforms and inequality grew with stunning speed, approaching the dangerous levels one finds in some Latin American and sub-Saharan African countries. A World Bank study indicates that from 1981 to 1998 China's Gini index jumped from 0.288 to 0.403, even exceeding increases recorded in Eastern Europe and the former Soviet Union, including their period of "deep structural transformation" (World Bank 1997: 7–13; World Bank 2000: 66; Xu 2000). In recent years, urban income discrepancy has continued to deteriorate and the Gini index was "estimated" at 0.47 in 2005 according to a government source (Wang 2005).

The inequitable distribution of wealth is sharply revealed in the widening gaps of income and assets between top and bottom. The 20 percent of households at the bottom of the income ladder took up 9 percent of total urban incomes in 1990. This dropped to only 3 percent in 1997. Meanwhile, the relevant percentages for the top 20 percent increased from 38.1 to 53.7

(Shi 2000). A sample survey among urban residents found in late 1999 that less than 5 percent of them contributed to almost half of the entire personal savings in banks (Xu 2000).

Although Hu Jintao assumed the top party post in 2002 with a commitment to poverty reduction, inequality continued to worsen. Recent statistics from the Ministry of Labor and Social Security reveal that the richest and poorest 10 percent of urban households own 45 percent and 1.4 percent of urban wealth, respectively (*China Daily* 2005). Equally telling, Wang Weiguang, vice president of the Central Party School, noted that his students – mostly local party-state officials – ranked the widening income gap (43.9 percent) before public security (24.3 percent) and corruption (8.4 percent) as China's gravest problem (Ji 2005).

The bourgeoisie: the appendage of political power

Although Barrington Moore used "democracy" to denote the liberal state with "no necessary connection with democracy" (Macpherson 1972: 47), his historical insights are pertinent (Dahrendorf 1967; Goldblatt 1997; Moore 1966). The fight of commercial classes for their right to economic freedom and access to government resulted in the establishment of some basic elements of democracy, such as parliamentary sovereignty and constitutional rule. Despite its somewhat doubtful if not negative role in contemporary processes of democratization, the bourgeoisie possesses some class-defined traits that are incompatible with dictatorship. For instance, its class interests require a parsimonious state that guarantees legal certainty, especially the sanctity of private property rights. Indeed, the bourgeoisie prefers "being left alone to practice democratic self-restraint" and is more likely to tolerate political differences (Schumpeter 1950: 297–298).

To be distinguished from the middle classes, China's new bourgeoisie can be simply defined as comprising the country's wealthiest people. Understanding precisely who this includes, though, remains difficult. There are no relevant statistics in China's official documents and censored publications. To defend its Marxist image and the "socialist" nature of its economy, the CCP has consistently denied that market reforms have produced a bourgeoisie. If the criterion for the bourgeoisie was the millionaire, China had three million of them who, if joined by their family members, constituted one percent of the population in 1998 (Chen 2002a).

Since it is composed of groups with varying political interests and backgrounds, China's new bourgeoisie should not be viewed as an undifferentiated aggregate. Nonetheless, two major groups can be distinguished. The first comprises family members of central or local leaders and former bureaucrats who have relied on their political lineage to derive commercial prerogatives. This group is positioned to manipulate political power to gain exclusive access to state-monopolized resources. The "crony" nature of China's new capitalism is most manifest in this special group who share a personal stake in preventing regime change. They represent perhaps the largest and most influential portion of the new bourgeoisie and espouse neither economic liberalism nor political democracy.

By contrast, most other members of China's new bourgeoisie accumulated wealth through self-help and are endowed with entrepreneurial qualities. But their liberal leanings have been diluted by their enmeshment in the political establishment. Usually these entrepreneurs started their businesses by taking advantage of chaotic markets and legal loopholes characteristic of the earlier reform phases. Once they established a foothold in the market-place, they sought patrons in the party-state both for political protection and for accessing public resources. To continue their advantages accruing from *guanxi* (personal connections) with party-state officials, they prefer no substantial change in the existing power arrangement.

Unlike the bourgeoisie with political lineage, China's self-made entrepreneurs share some of the pro-liberal features of Moore's classical bourgeoisie. Most of their efforts to forge clientelist ties with officialdom are part of a strategy for business survival. In uncertain market settings they are compelled to buy political power whilst competing against more privileged rivals. The high price of cultivating *guanxi* with party-state officials has led them to place a premium on the rule of law in the hope that it can constrain nepotism prevalent in political circles and circumscribe the party-state's interference in market activities. Their attitudes toward the CCP are therefore ambivalent at best.

The middle classes: a liberal but politically inactive force

In general terms, the middle classes share some of the pro-democratic qualities of the bourgeoisie, such as a preference for economic freedom, political pluralism, the rule of law, and opposition to traditional status hierarchies. Middle classes thus contrast as a force for democracy favorably with other classes. For example, the reliance of lower classes on the state for social security provisions may in some circumstances strengthen their allegiance to the authoritarian regime or make it easier for the regime to bribe them into quiescence. Similarly, under "crony capitalism" bourgeois interests gain access to state-monopolized resources and can resort to state power to maintain their monopolistic positions in the marketplace. Therefore, the middle classes usually represent the most liberal forces, since their economic interests are best served by market forces and the minimal role of the state.

In contrast to the political sensitivity associated with the concept "bour-geoisie," the Chinese government and academic circles tend to highlight the emergence of China's new middle classes in an effort to showcase significantly improved standards of living. With all affluent Chinese being thrown into the "middle-class" basket, different criteria have led to different assessments of its size. A recent investigation set the standard as follows: a monthly salary of at least 5,000 *yuan*, university education, and employed as managers/professionals in both the public and private sectors. According to this standard, the proportion of the middle classes in the entire population was 11.9 percent in 2005 (Li 2005). The figure seems more acceptable as it adopts the income standard used by the State Statistical Bureau, which defines 60,000 to 500,000 *yuan* as the annual income of urban middle strata. Another study estimates that the percentage of middle-class members in the entire workforce is 20 and may reach 40 in 20 years (Liu *et al.* 2005).

Unlike the bourgeoisie, China's middle classes benefited from pro-market reforms by relying on their acumen rather than bureaucratic patron-client ties. Their linkages with the communist state are thus weak, impersonal, and unaffectionate – one of the conditions for developing class autonomy. Under authoritarianism, any pro-liberal disposition among social groups contains by definition an antistate bias, since economic liberalism invariably correlates positively with a preference for political pluralism and checks on state power. China's middle classes should therefore be seen as a genuine liberal force.

Naturally, China's middle classes give the CCP credit for China's economic boom. However, they tend to lack confidence in the CCP's commitment to an ideal-typical capitalism, in part because of the party's bizarre socialist discourse. Even more importantly, they dislike the omnipresent clientelist symbiosis of the bourgeoisie with the party-state that constricts the space of development for lower layers in the social hierarchy. Members of the middle class thus protest the bureaucratic allocation of resources more strongly than China's self-made bourgeois. In fact, political corruption constitutes one of the root causes for the alienation of China's middle classes from the party-state.

Despite their pro-liberal inclinations, China's middle classes can hardly be expected to become a leading force in establishing and strengthening legal-institutional constraints upon party-state power. If we follow the stereotypical image in classical social science literature and construe class autonomy as collective self-government without superimposed political domination, China's middle classes do not fit the bill. Rather, according to several empirical studies they are most likely to resort to political inaction (Chen 2002a; Pearson 1997: 100–115). Political apathy is to some extent attributable to the lack of adequate economic weight on the part of China's middle classes, and hence confidence in their class power. More importantly, the formidable sanctions the CCP holds to forestall any societal challenges to its hegemony make China's middle classes politically risk-averse. This complicates considerably the development of China's civil society, since the middle classes are unable or unwilling to resist the CCP's attempts to maintain control. As a result, China's middle classes view the communist party-state with a complex blend of hate and fear.

Nonetheless, the intermediate position of the middle classes in the social structure makes their choice of allies decisive. This choice can tilt the balance of class power in favor of either democracy or authoritarianism. In most cases of regime change in Latin America and East Asia, the degree of radicalization of or the perceived threat from lower classes decisively influenced whether middle classes sought a pro-democracy coalition with the working classes or stood with the state and dominant classes in defending authoritarian rule.[7] China's social structure and the revolutionary thrust of the lower classes indicate that a pro-democratic alliance is unlikely.

Radicalized lower classes and intensified class struggle

SOEs used to be by far the largest urban employers with their performance affecting the livelihood of most urban families. As market reforms proceeded, many SOEs, for a lack of competitiveness, struggled on the verge of fiscal bankruptcy. Many SOE workers were laid off or bonuses and other benefits that augmented employees' basic wages cut. Some SOEs couldn't even pay basic wages and instead provided workers with unsold products as compensation. A research team found in 2000 that only 20.5 percent of SOE employees evaluated their livelihood as "improving," whereas 46.6 percent reported an absolute deterioration (Chen 2000).

The shift of employment patterns from state firms to the private sector bolstered China's general income levels. Market reforms and the booming economy also reduced poverty levels in China with people living in absolute poverty falling from 270 million in 1978 to 70 million in 1995 (World Bank 1997: 45). Since the late 1990s, however, re-impoverishment has developed in some segments of China's urban society.

Put differently, market reforms have not guaranteed a better material life individually. Especially those laid off from SOEs who find employment in the private sector often experience a drop in their material conditions. This is reflected in the growing number of capital-labor tensions in private firms, especially in coastal provinces. Employees are often underpaid and forced to work overtime, while employers tend to ignore demands for labor protection and improved welfare. In 2000 alone the number of judicial proceedings triggered by capital-labor tensions reached 200,000 (Reporter 2002).

China's new urban poor can be divided into three distinct segments: the disabled and elderly without family support; jobless workers; and migrant workers. Although numbers cannot be estimated precisely, relevant data suggest that the three groups combined make up a rapidly growing percentage of the urban population. Around 2000, the urban unemployment rate skyrocketed to 15–20 percent nationwide.[8] If rural laborers seeking urban jobs and "off-duty" workers who stay at home with part of their wage are included, the jobless rate is pushed to a staggering 27.76 percent (Long 2000).

Social stratification inevitably gives rise to class conflicts that, if moderate or manageable, can become a catalyst for democratization. Conversely, extreme socioeconomic polarization can make class conflict too intense for a democratic compromise. In that sense, the correlation between capitalism and democracy is not invariably positive. A country with extreme economic inequalities, as Robert Dahl argues, "stands a very high chance of having extreme inequalities in the exercise of power, and hence a hegemonic regime" (Dahl 1971: 81–82).[9]

The radicalization of China's lower classes is manifest first and foremost in the rising tensions between rich and poor. A recent report by the Chinese Academy of Social Sciences (CASS) provides some survey data verifying the escalation of class tensions. According to this report, only 10.6 percent of the surveyed found no "conflict of (social or class) interests," whereas 89.4 percent thought that "conflicts" existed among some or all social strata. The social groups whose "class-struggle" consciousness was the strongest were private entrepreneurs (100 percent) and laid-off workers (90.5 percent) (Lu 2002: 42–43; 80). Another report finds that Mao's class-struggle doctrine has gained growing support among impoverished workers and peasants (Forney and Gough 2002).

If the bourgeoisie and to a lesser extent middle classes represent China's conservative social forces in favor of authoritarian stability, the lower classes are apparently moving in the opposite direction, showing a strong revolutionary disposition. The experiences of some bureaucratic authoritarian regimes in Latin America show that the revolutionary orientation of subordinate classes is determined not so much by the intensity of class antagonism as by the extent to which the government is taken as the source of mass grievances (Collier 1999: 183–185; Stepan 1985: 317–343). In some of these regimes (e.g. Chile), the state's efforts to extricate itself from the economy considerably reduced the intensity of political opposition (Stepan 1985). In others (e.g. Brazil), wage demands by workers led to strong anti-government actions, mainly because government played a major role in wage determination (Collier 1999: 183–185).

In China, the bitterness of the lower classes about the income gap has translated into anti-regime sentiments for both cultural and pragmatic reasons. Although Confucianism regards hierarchical political and social relationships as the key to social harmony, it places a high value upon economic egalitarianism, which is associated with the justice of a social order. Unsurprisingly, from the Taiping Rebellion to the communist revolution, few revolutionary movements could succeed in China without recourse to the ideal of "equity of wealth" (*jun fu*) for social mobilization. This culture of egalitarianism has shaped China's political tradition. A tacit contract specifies that the ruler provides minimal subsistence insurance for the ruled in exchange for their acceptance of the "legitimacy" of the ruler. The failure of the ruler to do so would be interpreted as the loss of his "mandate of heaven" and hence justify a rebellion. As Western scholars found, socialist egalitarianism incorporating somewhat guaranteed subsistence – at least for the urban populace – did not just offer "legitimacy" to the Mao regime but inspired the Chinese to "extraordinary sacrifices" (Pye 1985: 323).

China's political tradition and contemporary circumstances therefore cause poor people at the bottom of society not to attribute their poverty to their weak market power, as the CCP would want them to. Rather, they hold the party-state responsible. For example, elderly pensioners clearly blame the management of SOEs, many of which operate on deficit spending, for their inability to pay the funds that support retired employees. A survey conducted in Hubei found that SOE retirees who received regular pensions saw their living standards decline by 20 percent, as their pensions could not keep pace with inflation (Chang 1998: 206).

Unemployed workers who lost their SOE jobs due to economic restructuring equally blame SOE management. Indeed, due to the peculiar nature of SOE employment, laid-off SOE employees tend to suffer a severe drop in their living standards. Before reforms, the government adopted a policy of low wages/high welfare benefits for SOE workers. SOEs covered all expenses for a worker's housing, health care, pension, etc. There was an implicit understanding that after a worker was laid off he/she would be paid an amount virtually equivalent to what he/she would have received in welfare benefits without terminating employment. However, this arrangement was not institutionalized. Laid-off workers therefore usually get a severance pay based on the length of their service, but this amount is usually too small to be an adequate compensation (Xia 2000).[10]

Laid-off SOE and "off-duty" workers make up the overwhelming majority of urban jobless and urban poor (Chang 1998: 202; Long 2000). Their grievances against the regime stem mainly from the circumstances leading to their unemployment. Although incompatibility with market mechanisms explains the collapse of many SOEs, the corruption of SOE directors and their collaborators in the party-state constitute major factors triggering SOE bankruptcies and sell-offs. Indeed, it is well known that many SOE directors purposely let their enterprises lose money so as to gain approval for bankruptcy or privatization proceedings, processes that afford those in charge ample opportunity to acquire bribes and other personal benefits (Chen 2002b).

Besides SOE retirees and laid-off workers, the third urban group that tends to be poverty-stricken are peasants based in urban areas – the "peasant workers" or *nongmin gong*. Due to their lack of education, skills, or connections, many of these can only find low paying "3-D" (dirty, difficult, and dangerous) jobs (Solinger 1995).[11] Adding to their plight is the party-state's policy of discriminating against them based on their place of birth. Since *nongmin gong* generally do not have the right of legal urban registration, they face grave difficulties in finding decent urban jobs and have no access to the benefits and subsidies connected with an urban "identity" or *hukou*.

Originally, the *hukou* or registration system used to serve as a check on rural-urban migration. Since the 1990s, the government has gradually opened cities to peasants but refused to offer them a legal urban identity – except in towns and small cities (Chan and Zhang 1999). Although this allows the state to excuse itself from additional financial burdens, this "let-alone" policy, as Solinger argues, has caused the "emergence of parallel, largely nonintersecting realms of dailiness within the city" and a "hollowing out of the state and a narrowing down of its authority in regard to the migrants" (Solinger 1999: 220–240). Living in a "vacuum of authority," the welfare of peasant migrants is neither taken care of by rural nor urban governments.

The class realignment of the communist regime

The widening income gap has generated stronger and stronger appeals for economic redistribution. According to a CASS report, 84.9 and 84.3 percent of Hefei City's industrial workers and unemployed, respectively, urged the government to levy higher income taxes upon the rich and increase welfare benefits for the poor. Yet, 75 percent of private entrepreneurs vehemently opposed this (Lu 2002: 115). So far, the party-state has failed to adequately address the lower classes' mounting grievances. Since China lacks institutionalized channels for effectively expressing social grievances, protests and riots have become more widespread. According to Zhou Yongkang, the public security minister, 3.76 million Chinese took part in 74,000 protests and riots across China in 2004 – an increase from 58,000 in 2003 and only 10,000 a decade ago. To echo the leadership's calls for stability and "social harmony," the party mouthpiece *People's Daily* warned against any attempts to use protests to correct social injustices (French 2005). Clearly, the evolution of class relations in China is driving social pressures for economic equality in a more radical direction.

To do justice to the reform regime, China's present leaders recognize the dangers posed by growing economic disparities and would like to neutralize the potential for revolutionizing impoverished lower-classes. However, reforms have diminished the fiscal capacity of the state considerably. Like its counterparts in other capitalist societies, the communist state will be hard pressed to find alternative solutions and is likely to adopt a more redistributive policy by transferring poverty alleviation costs to the rich. The state is therefore no longer able to stay away from the conflicts of class interests. It will be increasingly forced to take sides and show a manifest class orientation in the making of socioeconomic policy.

For the CCP, a self-proclaimed working-class party, "to rob the rich to pay the poor" (*jiefu jipin*) should be a logical option. Yet, the leadership seems to have ruled out this option or decided not to go too far in this direction. The CCP's pro-business policy should not be taken as evidence that China's business classes have "bribed" the political elites or achieved considerable influence over policy-making, as was the case in a number of bureaucratic authoritarian regimes in Latin America. Instead, with the unstoppable decay of the public sector, the private sector is becoming the sole hope for sustainable economic growth.

At present, private firms account for 70 percent of China's GDP (Engardio 2005), 60 percent of China's exports, a majority of retail sales, and the creation of over 70 percent of urban jobs (Shan 2005). In more and more regions, the private sector is the primary source of government revenue, the largest employer, and the primary donor to local public welfare activities (*Qian Shao* 1999). Over 95 percent of Zhejiang's economy was in private hands in 2002 and the tax payment of the private sector made up 60 percent of the entire tax revenue (Liu and Xu 2004: 25). By contrast, most remaining SOEs are struggling and cannot survive without heavy state subsidies, gobbling up scarce government budget resources.

Despite the anticapitalist nature of the CCP's guiding ideology, SOE privatization is proceeding on a large scale. This suggests that the reform regime intends to shift its base of legitimacy to economic performance. Since the bourgeoisie and middle classes are powering the most dynamic parts of the Chinese economy and hold the key to enhancing its competitive edge, the party-state encourages a trickle-down policy that places their interests above all other class interests. Political pragmatism is forcing the CCP to ally itself with China's emerging economic elites.

Although some fundamental, especially ideological, constraints remain under China's communist party-state, the leadership's class realignment has been evident in a sequence of steps taken since the late 1990s. During the 1997 party congress, the private sector was pronounced as "an important component part of China's socialist market economy" (Jiang 1997). In 1999, this alleged ideological breakthrough was incorporated into an amendment to China's constitution. In early 2001, China's private firms were given better access to raise capital on China's stock markets. And in a July 1, 2001 speech by Jiang Zemin, the party's door was officially thrown open to membership by capitalists or the bourgeoisie – a crucial step toward altering the CCP's class nature (Pomfret 2001).

In the past, the regime attempted to accommodate the new rich in recognition of their economic weight and in an effort to prevent them from developing into a force opposed to CCP rule. Now the regime has found in them a new and principal, if not exclusive, social basis of support.[12] The alignment of the party-state with the rich is especially visible at local levels, embodied in the typical pro-capital stance of local governments in labor-capital clashes. In a hardly veiled symbiosis, private businesses generate tax revenues and employment, which are crucial for the promotion of local officials. They also offer local officials direct material benefits in exchange for tax breaks, government contracts, and bank loans.

While its growth-without-equity strategy may be understandable from an economic perspective, the regime must face its political consequences. Indeed, since Hu Jintao succeeded Jiang Zemin as the CCP general secretary, the leadership seems to have turned somewhat to the left. With heavier emphasis on the welfare of disadvantaged and impoverished social groups, the government has recently increased its budgets earmarked for poverty relief and made greater efforts to establish social security networks.

Nonetheless, the new leadership seems constrained by the same structural factors as its predecessor. They have found that it is very difficult to reverse the widening income gap and prevent the further political alienation of China's poor majority. The inability or reluctance of the CCP to bring income redistribution to satisfactory levels without offending the rich has compelled the new leadership to use more heavy-handed tactics when confronting the resentment of lower classes. As poverty and income inequality are widely perceived as connected to the "injustice" of state policy, a revolutionary situation is looming. This situation terrifies both the CCP and its class allies, tending to strengthen the antidemocratic or "pro-stability" nature of their alignment. As a result, there is a distinct possibility that political repression and the revolutionary inclinations of lower classes will reinforce each other, trapping China in a vicious cycle.

Conclusion

A number of factors account for the failure of market reforms to push China toward democracy. Unlike most capitalist countries to which the structural model of democracy applies, China's capitalist development under the reform regime is not an uninterrupted historical process but was initiated, guided, and controlled by an ideologically anticapitalist party-state. Largely because of this inherent political dilemma, market reforms have not and perhaps will not lead to an ideal-typical capitalism. For all the pro-democracy socioeconomic changes it has achieved, China's capit-alist transition has not caused any significant separation of political and economic powers. Neither a Western-type civil society has emerged, nor have the social foundations of party hegemony been shaken.

In addition, social stratification and spiraling class conflicts have not generated powerful social dynamics for democratization in China. On one hand, the dominance of an all-powerful party-state in the marketplace has forced the business classes and other affluent social groups to depend on varying degrees on the government to prosper or survive, making it hard for them to develop autonomy. On the other, the intensification of socio-economic polarization has radicalized the lower classes and intensified class struggle to an extent that prevents the formation of a pro-democratic class alliance. In fact, threats perceived from the poor majority have pushed the affluent minority into the arms of authoritarian stability.

Growing pressures emanating from lower classes for economic redistribution are posing a grave threat to the communist party-state. Political corruption and policy failures are held responsible for massive unemployment, worsening income inequality, and urban poverty. The CCP has therefore become the target of seething popular discontent, but lacks the required institutional infrastructure or financial capacity to stop the income gap from widening further, curb corruption effectively, or reverse the public sector's decay. The strategy of relying on the private sector and market forces to maintain China's high-speed economic growth makes the CCP reluctant to alleviate poverty or narrow wealth differences at the cost of the affluent classes. The alignment of the state with the rich in the game of economic redistribution is driving the lower classes, especially the poorest, in a revolutionary direction.

The transition toward capitalism has thus placed the reform regime in a great dilemma. As Marxist ideology has sunk into irrelevance with the failure of China's socialist command economy, the CCP has attempted to rebase its ruling legitimacy on economic performance. Although capitalism has made China one of the world's fastest growing economies, the deteriorating socioeconomic polarization has undermined, rather than strengthened, the regime's legitimacy among the poor majority of Chinese. Since China's political direction is to a large extent controlled by the party leadership, a top-down process of democratization seems unlikely.

East Asian experiences of capitalist industrialization and democratization under state-dominant systems may offer some clues to China's political trajectory. Nonetheless, China's unique model of capitalist development generates two major differences. First, the transitional nature of the Chinese economy causes much uncertainty about the sustainability of China's high-speed growth. Second, the structural restraints upon the growth of democratic social forces in the Chinese context are far tighter and stronger than in its East Asian counterparts, making a transition toward democracy so much more remote.

Notes

1 This chapter draws on some arguments and information of my previous articles, particularly Chen (2002a; 2003).
2 Thus far, two patterns of transitions toward democracy have been identified and elaborated. One is the structural model that emphasizes the central importance of socioeconomic conditions. Another is the pattern of "pact-based" or "negotiated" democratization, in which the strategic choices and interactions of political elites are deemed decisive. This latter pattern does not make the structural one irrelevant or obsolete, though.
3 The refusal to alter the public discourse is not simply a theoretical matter but politically consequential. As Arnold Buchholz (1988) suggests in reference to the Soviet experience, if ideology undergoes little substantive change in reform, then "there is no fundamental change in the basis of the system."
4 The cadre power at local levels may not necessarily inhibit capitalism but distort it into what some scholars define as "politically oriented capitalism." James Scott (1972: 49–52) defines capitalism of this kind as involving "the granting by the state of privileged opportunities for profit."
5 David Potter (1997: 1–40) argues that a very powerful and almost entirely autonomous state in relation to social classes and groups provides "a most uncongenial setting for democratization."

6 SOE employees made up 71 and 69 percent of the entire workforce in 1979 and 1988, respectively, whereas collectively owned enterprises hired 29 and 30 percent (National Bureau of Statistics 1990).

7 A prevailing view is that militant lower-class pressures for radical reform undermine middle-class commitments to democracy, making a coalition of lower and middle classes less likely (Rueschemeyer *et al.* 1992). But a different scenario is also possible. As protests against authoritarian rule escalated and threatened social order in South Korea, the middle classes joined the protesting students and workers, regarding democratization as the only way to restore government authority (Jang 1993: 13–50). This situation also occurred in some Latin American countries. The middle classes joined the pro-democratic movement once they believed that the restoration of "democratic legitimacy" would avoid a revolutionary situation (O'Donnell and Schmitter 1986).

8 This percentage derives from calculations conducted by economists and is significantly higher than the government's official 3.4 percent unemployment rate (Forney and Gough 2002).

9 However, Przeworski *et al.* (2000: 117) suggest another likely scenario: "Under dictatorships, high income inequality may stimulate movements attracted by the egalitarian promise of democracy."

10 This information is also based on personal interviews with laid-off workers.

11 The factors motivating rural-urban migration are discussed in Croll and Ping (1997).

12 The CCP's turn to the political right has incurred attacks from China's Marxist fundamentalists who warned that the CCP was being degenerated into "the political spokesman of the capitalist class" ("Pi Jiang wanyanshu" 2001).

References

Bobbio, N. (1990) *Liberalism and Democracy*, London: Verso.

Buchholz, A. (1988) "Perestroika and Ideology: Fundamental Questions as to the Maintenance of and Change in the Soviet System," *Studies in Soviet Thought*, 36(3) (October): 149–168.

Chan, K.W. and Zhang, L. (1999) "The Hukou System and Rural-Urban Migration in China: Processes and Changes," *China Quarterly*, (160): 818–855.

Chang, X. (1998) *Jingji biangge zhongde "heixiang" [The "Black Box" in Economic Transformation]*, Zhuhai, Guangdong: Zhuhai chubanshe.

Chen, A. (2002a) "Capitalist Development, Entrepreneurial Class, and Democratization in China," *Political Science Quarterly*, 117(3): 401–422.

——(2002b) "Socioeconomic Polarization and Political Corruption in China: A Study of the Correlation," *The Journal of Communist Studies and Transition Politics*, 18(2): 53–74.

——(2003) "Rising Class Politics and its Impact on China's Path to Democracy," *Democratization*, 10(2): 141–162.

Chen, W. (2000) "Fubai manyan de tedian jiqi yanzhong weihai [The Features of Spreading Corruption and its Damages]," *Zhenli de Zuiqiu [In Search of Truth]*, (122) (August 11): 22–31.

China Daily (2005) "Urban Rich-poor Gap Rings Alarm Bells," June 22. Online. Available HTTP: www.chinadaily.com.cn/chinagate/doc/2005-06/22/content_453588.htm (accessed February 20, 2007).

Cody, E. (2005) "China Grows More Wary over Rash of Protests," *Washington Post*, August 10, p. A11.

Collier, R.B. (1999) *Paths toward Democracy: The Working Class and Elites in Western Europe and South America*, New York: Cambridge University Press.

Croll, E.J. and Ping, H. (1997) "Migration For and Against Agriculture in Eight Chinese Villages," *China Quarterly*, (149): 128–146.

Dahl, R. (1971) *Polyarchy: Participation and Opposition*, New Haven, CT: Yale University Press.

Dahrendorf, R. (1967) *Society and Democracy in Germany*, Garden City, NY: Doubleday.

Engardio, P. (2005) "China Is a Private-Sector Economy," *Business Week*, Online. Available HTTP: www.businessweek.com/magazine/toc/05_39/B3952magazine. htm (accessed August 22, 2005).

Forney, M. and Gough, N. (2002) "Working Man Blues," *Time*, 159(12): 26–27.

French, H.W. (2005) "Land of 74,000 Protests (but Little Is Ever Fixed)," *New York Times*, August 24, p. A4.

Friedman, M. (1962) *Capitalism and Freedom*, Chicago, IL: University of Chicago Press.

Goldblatt, D. (1997) "Democracy in the 'Long Nineteenth Century', 1760-1919," in D. Potter, D. Goldblatt, M. Kiloh, and P. Lewis (eds) *Democratization*, Cambridge: Polity Press.

Hirschman, A.O. (1977) *The Passions and the Interests: Political Arguments for Capitalism before its Triumph*, Princeton, NJ: Princeton University Press.

Huntington, S.P. (1984) "Will More Countries Become Democratic?" *Political Science Quarterly*, 99(2): 217–218.

Jang, J.C. (1993) "Political Cleavages in South Korea," in H. Koo (ed.) *State and Society in Contemporary Korea*, Ithaca, NY: Cornell University Press.

Ji, J. (2005) "Zhongguo zhuanjia jinggao shouru fenpei chaju yi jinru 'huangdengqu' [Chinese Experts Warn that the Income Gap has Entered the 'Yellow-light District']." Online. Available HTTP: www6.chinesenewsnet. com/MainNews/Forums/BackStage/ 2005 8_22_18_58_8_953.html (accessed August 22, 2005).

Jiang, Z. (1997) "Hold High the Great Banner of Deng Xiaoping Theory," *Beijing Review*, 40(40): 10–33.

Li, S. (2005) "Shuju xianshi woguo zhongchan jieceng zhan jiuye renkou 11% [Data Show that the Middle Strata Make up 11% of the Working Population of our Country]," *Zhongguo Qingnian Bao [China Youth]*, September 2.

Lipset, S.M., Trow, M., and Coleman, J. (1956) *Union Democracy: The Inside Politics of the International Typographical Union*, New York: Free Press.

Liu, Y. and Xu, Z. (eds) (2004) *Zhongguo minying qiye jingzhengli baogao no. 1: jingzheng zhiliang yu jingzhengli zhishu [A Report on the Non-state Sector's Competitiveness, no. 1: Competitive Quality and Competitiveness Index]*, Beijing: Social Sciences Academic Press.

Liu, J., Mo, L., and Lin, L. (2005) "Ershi niannei Zhongguo zhongchan jieceng guimo kedadao zongjiuye renyuan de 40%" ["China's Middle Strata May Reach 40% of the Entire Workforce in 20 Years"]. Online. Available HTTP: www 7.chinesenewsnet.com/MainNews/EntDigest/Life/zxs_2005-09-15_626009.shtml (accessed September 20, 2005).

Long, H. (2000) "Zhongguo zhengzhi fazhan keneng yinqi de shehui wenti [The Social Problems that China's Political Development Might Bring About]," *Xin Bao [Hong Kong Economic Journal]*, September 13.

Lu, X. (ed.) (2002) *Dangdai Zhongguo shehui jieceng yanjiu baogao [A Research Report on Social Strata in Contemporary China]*, Beijing: Shehui kexue wenxian chubanshe.

Macpherson, C.B. (1972) *The Real World of Democracy*, New York: Oxford University Press.

Moore, B. (1966) *Social Origins of Dictatorship and Democracy: Lord and Peasant in the Making of the Modern World*, Boston, MA: Beacon Press.

National Bureau of Statistics (1990) *Zhongguo gongye jingji tongji nianjian, 1989 [The Statistical Yearbook of China's Industrial Economy, 1989]*, Beijing: Zhongguo tongji chubanshe.

O'Donnell, G. and Schmitter, P.C. (1986) *Transitions from Authoritarian Rule: Tentative Conclusions about Uncertain Democracies*, Baltimore, MD: The Johns Hopkins University Press.

Parish, W. (1984) "Destratification in China," in J. L. Watson (ed.) *Class and Social Stratification in Post-Revolution China*, Cambridge: Cambridge University Press.

Pearson, M.M. (1997) *China's New Business Elite: The Political Consequences of Economic Reform*, Berkeley, CA: University of California Press.

"Pi Jiang wanyanshu [An Anti-Jiang 10,000-Word Memorial]" (2001) Online. Available HTTP: www1.Chinesenewsnet.com/cgi-binMon_Jul_30_15_06_47_2001.htm (accessed July 30, 2006).

Pomfret, J. (2001) "China Opens Door to Its Businessmen," *International Herald Tribune,* July 2.

Potter, D. (1997) "Explaining Democratization," in D. Potter, D. Goldblatt, M. Kiloh, and P. Lewis (eds) *Democratization*, Cambridge: Polity Press.

Przeworski, A., Alvarez, M.E., Cheibub, J.A., and Limongi, F. (2000) *Democracy and Development: Political Institutions and Well-Being in the World, 1950-1990,* New York: Cambridge University Press.

Pye, L.W. (1985) *Asian Power and Politics: The Cultural Dimensions of Authority,* Cambridge, MA: The Belknap Press of Harvard University Press.

Qian Shao [Frontline] (1999) "Feigong jingji nashui zhan Zhongguo banbi jiangshan [Tax Payment by the Non-public Sector Makes up Half of China's Total Tax Revenues]," (104): 135.

Reporter (2002) "Zhongguo dalu shehui chongtu anjian dafu zengjia [Legal Cases of Societal Conflicts Have Increased by a Big Margin in Mainland China]." Online. Available HTTP: www.secretchina.com/news/sc.asp?id=11933 (accessed February 15, 2006).

Riskin, C. (1991) *China's Political Economy: The Quest for Development since 1949,* New York: Oxford University Press.

Rueschemeyer, D., Stephens, E.H., and Stephens, J.D. (1992) *Capitalist Development and Democracy*, Chicago, IL: University of Chicago Press.

Schumpeter, J.A. (1950) *Capitalism, Socialism and Democracy*, New York: Harper Torchbooks.

Scott, J. (1972) *Comparative Political Corruption*, Englewood Cliffs, NJ: Prentice-Hall.

Shan, D. (2005) "Wei minying jingji zhuqi fazhan pingtai [Pave the Way for the Development of the Private Economy]," *Dangdai Jingji [Contemporary Economics]*, (3): 4.

Shi, T. (2000) "The Gap between Rich and Poor: A Severe Challenge," *The 21th Century*, 39(4): 54–55.

Solinger, D. (1995) "The Floating Population in the Cities: Chances for Assimilation?" in D. Davis, R. Kraus, B. Naughton, and E.J. Perry (eds) *Urban Spaces: Autonomy and Community in Contemporary China*, Cambridge: Woodrow Wilson Center Press and Cambridge University Press.

——(1999) "China's Floating Population," in M. Goldman and R. MacFarquhar (eds) *The Paradox of China's Post-Mao Reforms*, Cambridge, MA: Harvard University Press.

Stepan, A. (1985) "State Power and the Strength of Civil Society in the Southern Cone of Latin America," in P.B. Evans, D. Rueschemeyer, and T. Skocpol (eds) *Bringing the State Back In*, Cambridge: Cambridge University Press.

Wang, Z. (2005) "Measures Called for to Narrow Income Gap," *China Daily*, July 9. Online. Available HTTP: www.chinadaily.com.cn/english/doc/2005-07/09/content_458663.htm (accessed February 20, 2007).

Wank, D. (1999) *Commodifying Communism: Business, Trust, and Politics in a Chinese City*, New York: Cambridge University Press.

Weber, M. (1978) *Economy and Society*, New York: Bedminster Press.

World Bank (1997) *Sharing Rising Incomes: Disparities in China*, Washington, DC: World Bank.

——(2000) *World Development Indicators 2000*, Washington, DC: World Bank.

Xia, J. (2000) "SOEs' Implicit Unemployment Is Becoming Explicit," *Gaige*, 102(2): 56–60.

Xiao, G. (2005) "Zhongguo siying qiye de jueqi: chengjiu, wenti, ji zhengce [The Rise of China's Private Enterprises: Their Achievements, Problems, and Policy]." Online. Available HTTP: www.econ.hku.hk/~xiaogeng/research/Paper/Private%20Sector%20Development%20in%20China.pdf (accessed August 2, 2005).

Xu, X. (2000) "Income Gap Is Further Widened in Mainland China," *Xin Bao* [*Hong Kong Economic Journal*], October 26.

Yang, Z. *et al.* (2005) "*Minying jingji baogao: cong bucong dao weiguan jichu de lishixing kuayue* [*A Report on China's Private Economy: A Historical Leap from the Complement to the Basis*]." Online. Available HTTP: finance.sina.com.cn/roll/20050729/19201848024.shtml (accessed September 10, 2005).

Zhang, H., Ming, L., and Liang, C. (eds) (2004) *Zhongguo siying qiye fazhan baogao no. 5, 2003* [*A Report on the Development of China's Private Enterprises, No. 5, 2003*], Beijing: Social Sciences Academic Press.

Zhu, G. *et al.* (1998) *Dangdai Zhongguo shehui de jieceng fenxi* [*An Analysis of Various Strata in Contemporary Chinese Society*], Tianjin: Tianjin renmin chubanshe.

Part 4

China in the global capitalist system

9 China's rise as a trading power

Christopher Edmonds,
Sumner J. La Croix, and Yao Li[*]

Since China began economic reforms in 1978, its economic growth has been exceptional (see Table 9.1). The average income of a Chinese citizen has risen from US$717 in 1980 to US$4,726 in 2003.[1] The country's increased global trade reflects this exceptional development record. During the period 1980 to 2003, China's exports and imports increased at average annual rates of 10.2 percent and 9.4 percent, respectively. In fact, export growth has regularly outpaced output growth, with the share of exports in Gross Domestic Product (GDP) rising from 13.9 percent in 1985 to 30.1 percent in 2003.[2]

China's trade expanded rapidly during the period 1980 to 2000, only to achieve even faster trade growth since 2001 – growing at annual growth rates of 26 and 28 percent in 2002 and 2003. This rapid export growth has raised tensions with major trading partners, many of whom have initiated antidumping actions and imposed safeguard quotas on imports from China. It has also raised the specter of increased competition from Chinese firms and consumers for scarce oil supplies and other natural resources. Policymakers in China's largest trading partners therefore appear increasingly preoccupied by the implications of China's spectacular trade growth. China has moved aggressively to cement and advance its emerging regional leadership through a variety of measures, such as negotiation of Preferential Trading Agreements and construction of regional infrastructure. It is in this context that we analyze China's trade policies, the surge in its trade flows, and their impact within China.

We begin with a review of changes in China's trade policies since the start of reforms in 1978. The next section examines trends in the composition of China's trade and its trading partners. Finally, we compare China's export boom and the policies supporting it with the export booms of other Asian countries.

China's policies toward international trade

Since the start of the reform era, China's policies toward international trade have rapidly evolved, moving from strict state control over foreign

Table 9.1 China's output and trade, 1978–2004 (millions, in year 2000 $US)

	1978	1980	1985	1990	1995	1998	2000	2001	2002	2003	2004
GDP (millions, in yr. 2000 $US)	146,412	169,828	282,637	412,729	726,859	934,348	1,080,741	1,161,797	1,258,226	1,375,178	1,508,937
Average annual growth rate (%)	11.7	7.7	10.7	7.9	12.0	8.7	7.5	7.5	8.3	9.3	9.7
GDP in PPP $US	644,331	748,030	1,241,218	1,812,589	3,255,583	4,188,219	4,824,695	5,200,987	5,606,735	6,089,508	7,262,000
Average annual growth rate (%)	11.7	7.7	10.7	7.9	12.4	8.8	7.3	7.8	7.8	8.6	19.3
Exports (millions, in yr. 2000 $US)	6,208	10,433	27,581	72,914	153,963	181,379	249,117	263,481	323,648	425,863	541,393
Average annual growth rate (%)	1.7	29.6	21.5	21.5	16.1	5.6	17.2	5.8	22.8	31.6	27.1
Export/GDP (%)	4.2	6.1	9.8	17.7	21.2	19.4	23.1	22.7	25.7	31.0	35.9
Imports (millions, in yr. 2000 $US)	9,985	11,218	42,871	62,516	136,606	138,578	224,870	240,629	293,569	401,168	512,246
Average annual growth rate (%)	17.9	6.0	30.8	7.8	16.9	0.5	27.4	7.0	22.0	36.7	27.7
Import/GDP (%)	6.8	6.6	15.2	15.1	18.8	14.8	20.8	20.7	23.3	29.2	33.9
Net Exports/GDP (%)	-2.6	-0.5	-5.4	2.5	2.4	4.6	2.2	2.0	2.4	1.8	1.9
Net FDI Inflows (million, in yr. 2000 $US)	0	33	1,674	4,051	37,054	43,188	38,387	43,707	48,996	51,993	55,571
Average annual growth rate (%)			119.6	19.3	55.7	5.2	-5.7	13.9	12.1	6.1	6.9
FDI/GDP (%)	0.0	0.0	0.6	1.0	5.1	4.6	3.6	3.8	3.9	3.8	3.7

Sources: Data on exports and imports (1978-2003) come from International Monetary Fund (2005). China's GDP deflator, GDP, FDI, and PPP conversion factor data (1978-2004) come from World Bank (2005).

Note
Numbers expressed in monetary units show nominal values converted to $US at the official exchange rate and deflated to year 2000 values using the GDP deflator for China. Purchasing Power Parity (PPP) converts the value of China's GDP to $US using an exchange rate derived from the United Nations International Comparison Programme's (ICP) PPP estimates. For background and explanation of the ICP, see: HTTP://pwt.econ.upenn.edu/icp.html (accessed January 23, 2005).

trade to a relatively open trade policy. The changes occurred gradually over 25 years and were initiated by trade agreements and by decisions of the Chinese government to unilaterally liberalize, reducing both tariff and nontariff barriers to trade. China's rapid trade liberalization was accompanied by a similar transformation in its policies toward Foreign Direct Investment (FDI). However, unlike the gradual evolution of trade policy, FDI policy evolved in fits and starts with long periods of relative inaction. The two liberalizations are closely tied in practice, as much of the increases in exports and imports have been related to the growth of Foreign Invested Enterprises (FIEs) in China.

China's initial trade reforms in the early 1980s were measured and gradual, yet represented a major departure from the system of central state planning and control over trade. Setting aside direct controls, the Chinese state came to rely on a variety of policy instruments to regulate the nation's trade: from conventional tariff and quota policies to more tacit trade controls such as state licensing of trading rights and commodity inspections. Until the mid-1980s, China applied very high taxes on imported goods. Lardy (2002) estimated that the average tariff rate applied to imported goods fell from 56 percent in 1982 to 43 percent in 1985, and to about 15 percent in 2000. While the reduction in tariff rates in the 1980s was partially offset by a big increase in the use of quotas, the large tariff reductions of the 1990s were accompanied by big cuts in the use of quotas. The 1990s dismantling of trade barriers was largely unilateral, initiated by China to bolster its efforts to gain membership in the World Trade Organization (WTO). The pace of China's gradual liberalization of trade can be seen via the lens of the number of Chinese firms allowed to engage in international trade: it rose steadily, from 12 in 1979, to 800 in 1985, to 12,000 in 1995, and to 35,000 in 2001 (Branstetter and Lardy 2006).

China's rapid liberalization of FDI flows proceeded less smoothly and was strongly influenced by the size and composition of China's trade flows (Zhang and Song 2000). The activities of foreign firms in China were initially highly restricted. In most instances foreign firms were required to export most of their production or to have a Chinese partner with more than 50 percent ownership. Relaxation of these requirements in many industries led to massive FDI flows, first from East Asia, then from Europe and North America. The resulting accumulation of capital fundamentally altered China's trade flows. New FIEs built manufacturing plants designed to utilize China's cheap labor to assemble imported intermediate goods into final products, most of which were then exported. Thus, FIEs quickly assumed a large role in China's international trade and the share of exports produced by FIEs has continued to grow (Zhang and Song 2000).

An important policy component in China's trade liberalization was the government's decision to grant competitive advantages to firms engaged in export-processing activities. For example, these firms were allowed to import, without duties, the raw and intermediate inputs needed to manufacture final goods for export. Indeed, the share of duty free imports entering China under this favored treatment grew, and by 2000 an estimated 60 percent of imports were not subject to tariffs. However, the policy regime strongly favoring export processing firms weakened in the mid-1990s when exemptions from import duties were extended to some firms producing for the domestic market (Lardy 2002; Naughton 1996).

There are notable differences in China's approach to trade liberalization prior to its WTO accession in December 2001 and during the five subsequent years. In general, policy shifted from trade liberalization measures that applied to all trading partners, to trade liberalization that applied to particular trading partners or groups. Sustained strong growth in China's economy after 2000 has also induced the national government to devote considerable resources to finding and contracting for long-term supplies of raw materials and energy inputs.

Prior to its WTO accession, China negotiated access to overseas markets through a network of bilateral Most Favored Nation (MFN) agreements. These agreements stipulated that China provide its trading partners with the most favorable trade arrangements negotiated with other trading partners, and vice versa. Europe in 1978, followed by the United States in 1980, granted MFN status to China soon after it initiated economic reforms. This gained China immediate access to the world's two largest export markets.[3] The trade orientation of China's economy responded rapidly to this market access.

While the MFN treaty network was successful in jump-starting China's trade, it provided a flawed institutional foundation for the development of China's long-run trade and investment relationships. One particular problem clouding China's MFN status with the United States was the Jackson-Vanik amendment to the 1974 Trade Act. It requires that the MFN status of communist countries be linked to a review of their immigration policies. After the 1989 Tiananmen Square Incident, US legislators used the annual vote on MFN renewal to criticize China's human rights record. Since votes were closely contested, future access to the US market by China's manufacturing firms was far from assured. Among other things, this put a break on FDI in manufacturing plants that would have primarily produced goods for export to the US.

After the successful conclusion of the Uruguay Round of trade negotiations and establishment of the WTO in 1995, new procedures for resolving trade disputes between members raised the value of WTO membership for China. In response, China announced and implemented numerous policy reforms during the mid-to-late 1990s that allowed the world's major trading countries to accept its application to become a WTO member. These reforms committed the Chinese government to adopting many of the economic institutions that the WTO requires of members. They include bound tariff rates, national treatment of foreign products and firms, and minimum standards of intellectual property rights and public and private procedures for enforcing these rights. A 1999 trade agreement with the United States ended US objections to China's WTO membership and provided a signal to businesses around the world that China would enter the WTO.

China became a member of the WTO in December 2001. Its accession protocol included nearly 700 commitments made in 38 bilateral trade agreements with WTO members to reduce import barriers in specific product markets, and to end discrimination against FIEs in most sectors. Most of China's WTO protocols were front-loaded and were scheduled for implementation by December 2004. Other commitments, including completion of promised tariff cuts, quota removals, and the end of geographic restrictions on some types of foreign investment, are still in process and are not scheduled to be fully implemented until 2010.

Have the commitments made in the accession protocol been implemented on schedule? There is general agreement that the major WTO compliance issue is weak enforcement of intellectual property rights; many infringers of intellectual property in China operate undeterred. Implementation of required regulatory changes also slowed in 2005. While several major commitments for 2005 have been fulfilled (e.g. financial services liberalization and acquisition of trading rights by foreign companies), others (e.g. rules on distribution services and direct sales) were not implemented on schedule.

China's admission to the WTO occurred because it made several important concessions that allow member countries to restrict Chinese exports during specified transition periods. For example, article 16 of China's WTO Accession Protocol allows WTO members to impose safeguard quotas when "imports of a product from China are increasing rapidly, either absolutely or relatively, so as to be a specific cause of material injury or threat of material injury to the domestic industry" (USTR 2000). This special safeguard provision—applying only to Chinese exports—does not expire until December 2013. China's accession protocol also specifies that China will be treated as a "nonmarket economy" in antidumping cases through December 2016. Nielsen and Rutkowski (2005) concluded that these WTO provisions tend to bias the results of antidumping cases strongly against China. Both China's treatment as a "nonmarket economy" in antidumping cases and the special safeguards provision provide China's trading partners with wide latitude to pursue WTO-sanctioned protectionist measures against Chinese imports. China's decision to accept such unfavorable and asymmetric terms of WTO entry reflect the leadership's expectation that WTO membership would bring both short-term and long-term growth to China by placing its economic relationships with other countries within the WTO's fundamental framework governing global trade and investment.

Prior to its 2001 WTO accession, China did not belong to any Preferential Trading Agreements (PTAs). After accession, China quickly turned its attention to negotiating PTAs as a mechanism for fostering trade liberalization and securing access of newly ascendant Chinese firms to important foreign markets.[4] As of July 2005, China was negotiating or had proposed PTAs with Australia, Chile, India, Indonesia, New Zealand, Pakistan, Singapore, South Africa, Thailand, and four regional groupings – the Association of South East Asian Nations (ASEAN), the Gulf Cooperation Council, Mercosur, and the Shanghai Cooperation Organization (SCO). In November 2002, China and ASEAN announced an agreement to implement a PTA. This will cover the original six ASEAN member countries by 2010 and the less developed ASEAN members by 2015.[5] As part of the PTA implementation process, China and ASEAN embarked on the "Early Harvest" program, which committed both parties to reductions in tariffs on selected agricultural products.

China's push to conclude PTAs with Australia, Chile, New Zealand, the Gulf Cooperation Council, Mercosur, and the SCO is tied to its ongoing efforts to secure long-term supplies of critical natural resources (oil, minerals, and intermediate agricultural inputs). State-owned trading and resource enterprises have entered into long-term contracts with resource suppliers around the globe, thereby replicating similar contracts entered into by the developed countries. The contracts' prices are typically tied to world market prices and entail significant risks for the Chinese companies committing to them.

The future impact of China's PTA push is still unclear, but a number of economists have suggested some possibilities. Antkiewicz and Whalley (2004) find that China's PTA agreements have focused on preferential reductions in tariff rates and elimination of nontariff barriers. These have avoided addressing broader issues, stressed in US PTAs, such as investment and intellectual property rights. Lee *et al.* (2004) also point to Chinese frustration with the slow progress in the Doha Round of WTO negotiations as an important reason underlying China's PTA drive.[6]

China's PTA push may further reflect its strategic interest in promoting economic integration with its neighbors, fostering economic growth in its "backyard," and increasing its influence on neighboring countries. McLaren (1996) and La Croix and Grandy (1997) cautioned that although PTAs tend to provide larger benefits to the smaller PTA partners, they can also make the small country dependent on the large country's willingness to renew the agreement, especially if industries in the small country make specific investments to serve the larger country. Without good alternative markets for their products, these industries are likely to urge that their governments cater to Chinese conditions to renew the PTA. China's smaller neighbors have clearly recognized this and have taken measures to secure PTAs with other major trading partners.

Trends in China's international trade

Between 1978 and 2004, the value of exports as a share of total GDP in China increased greatly, playing a major role in shaping the country's overall growth rate (see Table 9.1). In 1978 China's exports comprised only 4.2 percent of GDP while in 2004 they comprised 35.9 percent. Chinese imports also grew rapidly during this period, broadly keeping pace with export increases until 2004. Since 2000, the annual growth rate of both exports and imports has exceeded 20 percent, with both series expanding at about the same pace until 2004, when export growth rates began to exceed import growth rates.

China's modest trade deficits of the 1980s and early 1990s turned to modest trade surpluses from the late 1990s through 2003. Large trade surpluses (measured as a share of GDP) have emerged since 2004. However, critics who label China's trade policies as neo-mercantilist – designed to garner export market share and produce trade surpluses – cannot find ready support in the trade balance data for their arguments. Even with the rise of substantial trade surpluses over the 2004–2006 period, China's surpluses should be distinguished from the large trade surpluses maintained by Japan at the height of its export boom. The greater presence in China of foreign invested firms serving export markets and the presence of assembly operations that use imported intermediate goods and raw materials account for much of China's recent surpluses.

As China's trade soared, its trading partners and the number and type of goods traded also underwent dramatic change. Through the late-1970s, China's foreign trade was primarily oriented toward other Eastern Bloc countries and displayed a pattern typical of these planned economies. Over the course of the 1980s and 1990s, the importance of the Eastern Bloc as a trading partner diminished, and trade with the large market economies, Asian economies, and countries with rich natural resource endowments soared. The growth rate of China's exports to both Europe and North America increased three-fold after the mid-1990s, while its imports from low-income and middle-income countries grew even more rapidly.[7]

The changes in the identity and importance of China's trading partners since 1978 closely mirrored its simultaneous transformation into a more capitalist market-oriented economy. The most striking changes included the rise of the US as a leading market for Chinese exports; the secular decline of Japan as a market for Chinese exports; the remarkable rise of Korean exports to China after trade opened in 1989; and rapid growth in trade between China and its East and Southeast Asian neighbors. These changes have cumulated to produce an overall pattern of trade that closely resembles those of other export-oriented capitalist economies in East and Southeast Asia.

The spectacular growth in China's trade and the rise of a new group of trading partners prompted us to investigate whether its import and export flows exceed those that a standard model of international trade would predict for an economy with China's characteristics. A large, geographically diverse country with a large population might be expected to have lower ratios of exports to GDP, as interregional trade within the country would substitute for international trade. Also, the country's large population would allow it to absorb the output of large specialized manufacturing plants subject to economies of scale. China's ratio of exports to GDP does not fit this pattern, as it soared to 33 percent in 2005. This ratio is more typical of those observed in smaller Asian countries and stands in sharp contrast to the 9.0 to 11.0 percent range observed in Japan between 1960 and 1977.[8]

Now consider bilateral rather than overall trade. We use an econometric model, known as the gravity model, to estimate how trade flows between pairs of countries over the 1982 to 2003 period were influenced by economic, social, and political factors suggested by international trade theory. These include the distance between the two countries, the relative size of the two economies, and their linguistic and cultural affinity.[9] We use the model's estimates to predict bilateral trade flows between China and its trading partners and then compare our predicted flows with China's actual trade flows. We find that the share of countries for which actual exports exceeded predicted exports rose from just under 35 percent in 1985 to 57.5 percent in 2002. The gaps between actual and predicted levels for China's exports and imports were particularly large for economies in Africa, South America, and the Middle East and smallest for countries in East and Southeast Asia.

The gravity model's results for Asian economies – that actual trade flows between China and its neighbors are lower than would be expected given the economic, social, and political characteristics of these countries and China – sharply contrast with results obtained from a simple comparison of the shares of trade between China and other Asian economies (which have grown rapidly since the onset of reforms in 1978). While a comparison of trade shares suggests little opportunity for further growth, our gravity model estimates suggest that there may be room for additional growth in trade between China and its Asian neighbors despite their high and increasing trade shares.

This analysis supports the conclusion that the Chinese economy overemphasizes foreign trade, an orientation that can be understood as logically following from the country's policies promoting international trade and FDI. By setting up separate regulatory regimes for export-oriented firms – often FIEs – these firms gained competitive advantages. More of the country's resources were thus channeled into export sectors. The relatively undervalued Chinese currency also stimulated investments in export-oriented businesses.

We conclude that China's trade and FDI policies have been major factors underpinning a highly dualistic development: China's export-oriented (coastal) provinces have boomed while interior provinces have grown at a slower pace. This dualistic development has helped spur China's overall economic growth and global market integration, but has also produced potential impediments to future economic growth. For example, government subsidies of investment in export-oriented enterprises may have had the unintended side effect of lessening market integration within China. Young (2000) and Wedeman (2003) have documented the impacts of interprovincial trade barriers within China.[10] They found that in the presence of interprovincial trade barriers, and limited transportation infrastructure linking Chinese provinces, successful domestic manufacturers quickly exhausted the demand for their products in their home provinces. Rather than pursue highly restricted markets in other Chinese provinces, they ventured into export markets.

The changing product composition of China's trade

China's rapid increases in trade and strong GDP growth have reshaped the country's economic endowments, fostered the development of new technologies, and, in turn, changed the very composition of China's trade flows. Our analysis suggests that over the reform period China's trade has become more diversified, more capital-intensive, and more technology-intensive. Detailed data on the products comprising China's imports and exports are only available for broad categories of highly aggregated goods (Foreign Trade Division 2005). To circumvent this problem, we analyzed detailed data collected by the US government on the value of US-China trade for 17,000 categories of goods during the years 1992–2004.[11] We found that the number of products imported by the US from China nearly doubled, increasing from 6,602 in 1992 to 11,995 in 2004. Similarly, the number of products exported from the US to China increased from 3,447 to 6,551 over the same period. To put this increase in perspective, the number of goods exported by the US to all economies increased from 8,036 in 1992 to 8,856 in 2004, and the number of import goods sent to the US increased from 14,762 in 1992 to 16,824 in 2004. These small increases in the overall number of products imported and exported by the US pale in the face of the huge increases registered in the number of goods traded by the US and China over this period.

Tables 9.2 and 9.3 characterize the composition of China's exports and imports over the years 1985 to 2002 by dividing them across six broad categories of labor-intensity, capital-intensity, and sophistication of technology used in production: 1) primary commodities; 2) labor-intensive and resource-based manufactures; 3) manufactures with low skill and technology; 4) manufactures with medium skill and technology; 5) manufactures with high skill and technology; and 6) unclassified products (UNCTAD 2002: 87–92). We draw several conclusions from Tables 9.2 and 9.3. First, the shares of primary commodity and labor-intensive/resource-based manufactured exports declined over the sample period. Second, the export share of manufactured goods with low skill and technology inputs rose from a low base over the 1985 to 1995 period and fell thereafter. Third, the value of China's manufactured exports based on production processes relying

Table 9.2 Changing composition of China's exports across types of goods, 1985–2002

Year	Categories of goods									
	Primary commodities		Labor-intensive and resource-based manufactures		Manufactures with low skill and technology intensity		Manufactures with medium skill and technology intensity		Manufactures with high skill and technology intensity	
	Value	*Share*	*Value*	*Share*	*Value*	*Share*	*Value*	*Share*	*Value*	*Share*
1985	5,959	24.6	12,295	50.8	552	2.3	303	1.3	1,407	5.8
1990	14,618	19.4	34,346	45.6	4,121	5.5	9,167	12.2	9,961	13.2
1995	20,264	13.1	67,811	43.7	14,440	9.3	17,536	11.3	28,640	18.5
1997	21,282	11.7	79,886	43.8	15,525	8.5	22,320	12.2	36,845	20.2
1998	20,342	10.6	78,813	41.2	16,615	8.7	25,322	13.2	42,872	22.4
2000	24,703	9.2	102,122	38.2	22,641	8.5	41,562	15.5	67,917	25.4
2001	26,875	9.2	106,099	36.4	22,943	7.9	46,636	16.0	79,697	27.4
2002	29,589	8.3	124,076	34.8	27,443	7.7	57,000	16.0	108,038	30.3
Average annual growth rate	9.9		14.6		25.8		36.1		29.1	

Source: Authors' calculations based on data from Statistics Canada (2005).

Notes
The definition of sectors follows UNCTAD (2002). The columns labeled "Value" show the real value of exports (in thousands of year 2000 $US). The columns labeled "Share" show the category's share of country's total exports.

Table 9.3 Changing composition of China's imports across types of goods, 1985–2002

Year	Categories of goods									
	Primary commodities		Labor-intensive and resource-based manufactures		Manufactures with low skill and technology intensity		Manufactures with medium skill and technology intensity		Manufactures with high skill and technology intensity	
	Value	Share	Value	Share	Value	Share	Value	Share	Value	Share
1985	5,190	12.9	3,635	9.0	7,165	17.8	10,662	26.4	10,784	26.7
1990	10,825	16.4	12,934	19.6	5,377	8.1	16,007	24.2	18,159	27.5
1995	26,759	15.5	32,690	19.0	12,159	7.1	43,888	25.5	50,424	29.2
1997	26,259	14.5	38,922	21.5	11,051	6.1	39,456	21.8	55,918	30.9
1998	23,482	13.3	35,011	19.9	10,428	5.9	36,488	20.7	62,801	35.6
2000	32,994	12.8	40,398	15.7	14,093	5.5	51,212	19.9	98,145	38.2
2001	34,646	12.9	39,128	14.6	13,831	5.2	56,186	21.0	108,166	40.4
2002	39,024	12.0	41,251	12.7	18,976	5.8	72,393	22.2	136,504	41.9
Average annual growth rate	12.6		15.4		5.9		11.9		16.1	

Source: Authors' calculations based on data from Statistics Canada (2005).

Notes
The definition of sectors follows UNCTAD (2002). The columns labeled "Value" show the real value of imports (in thousands of year 2000 $US). The columns labeled "Share" show the category's share of country's total imports.

on high skill and technology inputs was initially very small but has grown steadily through 2004. Finally, beginning in 1999, the share of exports supplied by FIEs increased sharply (National Bureau of Statistics 2004).

Our overall conclusion is that from 1985 to 2002, the composition of China's exports changed rapidly, from the production of goods using low-skill or medium-skill labor and relatively simple technologies to production of more skill-intensive, capital-intensive, and technically advanced products. Such an evolution was the usual pattern amongst East Asian export economies that "climbed the quality ladder" during their periods of most rapid export growth. Rapid increases in the import of intermediate inputs provide another signal that skill-intensive, high technology sectors are growing rapidly, as these sectors tend to make the most use of specialized international production chains.

The sweeping implications of China's trade growth for its domestic economy

China's economic reforms have been astoundingly successful in raising output, personal incomes and wealth, and reducing poverty. Trade and investment policies have been critical parts of China's overall development strategy. Since the beginning of China's export boom, per capita GDP has risen at an average annual rate of 8.1 percent and poverty incidence has fallen substantially.

Using the official national income poverty line, the number of poor people in rural China fell from 250 million in 1978 to just over 29 million in 2001. This corresponds to a change in the rural poverty incidence from 33.1 to 3.2 percent during this period (National Bureau of Statistics various years). Nearly half of this decline was achieved immediately following China's initial economic reforms, with poverty incidence falling to just 15.1 percent in 1984. The World Bank's poverty standard (US$1 PPP per day), generally used for international comparisons of poverty incidence, records smaller but still very large declines in poverty incidence, from 28.5 percent in 1987 to 16.6 percent in 2001 (World Bank 2005).

The large increase in average incomes in the reform period has been accompanied by a sharp increase in income inequality across households, provinces, and urban and rural areas.[12] One reason for the growth in inequality across provinces is that Chinese export industries are concentrated in a small number of high-income coastal provinces.[13] Guangdong alone accounted for over 35 percent of China's exports and 33 percent of China's imports in 2003. The next largest trading provinces were Jiangsu (14.25 percent), Shanghai (13 percent), Zhejiang (nearly 8 percent), and Shandong (nearly 6 percent). These four provinces and one city accounted for 75.6 percent of the total value of China's exports in 2003.

The geographic concentration of trading activities in coastal areas comes into sharper focus when comparisons of the value of trade across provinces are expressed in per capita terms. The value of exports per resident of

Shanghai, Guangdong, and Tianjin in 2000 was equivalent to US$2,854; US$1,979; and US$1,391 respectively. This compares to per capita values of exports of only US$21 and US$29 in Guizhou and Gansu, interior provinces which are the least trade-oriented. Since provincial rankings in terms of value of exports and value of imports are generally the same, it is unsurprising that a cross-provincial comparison of the value of imports per capita yields similar results.

Competition between FIEs for scarce skilled workers with foreign language skills has led to the emergence of new urban elites. In contrast, average incomes are lower and poverty incidences are higher in rural areas, particularly in interior provinces. According to the World Bank's (2001) estimates, in 1996 about 70 percent of China's rural poor lived in its western provinces. Inequality within rural and urban areas has also increased sharply since 1980 (Ravallion and Chen 2004: Tables 10, 11, 15).

Finally, China's trade and investment policies have fundamentally altered the ownership structure of Chinese firms over the last 25 years (see Table 9.4). Both negotiated and unilateral tariff reductions by the Chinese government have facilitated the emergence of globally competitive export industries. Trade policies have also sped the relative decline of state-owned enterprises and aided domestic private firms by opening overseas markets spurring FIE growth. Table 9.4 highlights both the shift away from public ownership and the shift toward the use of production processes that are closely integrated with a foreign owner's design, production, and marketing networks. Overall, this has favored higher export growth, as it allows FIEs to use low-wage Chinese labor to produce and export goods that meet technical and style demands of foreign consumers.

Chinese policymakers' willingness to accept FDI that brought only part of the value addition from the overall production process has clearly increased the speed of China's ownership transformation and integration into global production networks. However, it also appears to have increased the specialization of Chinese firms, lessened the overall growth impact of FDI, and inflated China's export figures. Recently, the Chinese government issued a series of regulations that effectively raised Chinese tariffs on imported automobile parts from a range of 10–14 percent to 28 percent, and in 2006, the imposition of domestic input requirements for FIEs involved in assembly-for-export activities was seriously considered.[14]

Export growth: China versus other export-oriented Asian economies

Next, we compare the extent of China's trade growth during its export boom with the trade growth of other Asian economies that experienced prolonged export booms after the Second World War. Figure 9.1 displays export growth for China and selected Asian economies, with the initial year normalized as the year in which rapid export growth began in each

Table 9.4 Composition of China's trade across mode of production and enterprise ownership

	Value ($US billions)		Shares	
	2001	2004	2001	2004
EXPORTS	266	593	100.0	100.0
BY MODE OF PRODUCTION				
Conventional trade	112	244	42.1	41.1
Processing trade	147	328	55.4	55.3
Processing trade with supplied material	–	69	–	11.6
Processing trade with imported material	–	259	–	43.7
Other mode	7	22	2.5	3.7
BY ENTERPRISE OWNERSHIP				
State-owned enterprises	113	154	42.5	25.9
Foreign-invested enterprises	133	339	50.1	57.1
Other enterprises	20	101	7.4	17.1
Collective enterprises	–	32	–	5.4
Private enterprises	–	69	–	11.7
IMPORTS	244	561	100.0	100.0
BY MODE OF PRODUCTION				
Conventional trade	113	248	46.6	44.2
Processing trade	94	222	38.6	39.5
Processing trade with supplied material	–	54	–	9.6
Processing trade with imported material	–	168	–	29.9
Other mode	36	91	14.8	16.3
BY ENTERPRISE OWNERSHIP				
State-owned enterprises	1,036	1,765	42.5	31.4
Foreign-invested enterprises	1,259	3,246	51.7	57.8
Other enterprises	142	604	5.8	10.8
Collective enterprises	–	177	–	3.2
Private enterprises	–	420	–	7.5

Source: Ministry of Commerce (2007).

economy. The figure shows that China's export boom was larger than those in other Asian economies except South Korea. It is also notable that the long-term growth in the exports of several other Asian economies was just 10–15 percent below China's rate.

In early 2007, China's export boom motors on, seemingly locked in high gear after 20 years of spectacular growth. Using the earlier export booms as a guide, how long might we expect China's boom to run? On average, these booms lasted at least 30 years before tapering off. The implications of another ten years of Chinese export growth are astounding. Even if export growth slows to an annual rate of 20 percent, China's exports will double every 3.5 years. Thus, by 2016, Chinese exports would be about eight times larger than in 2006. The effects on China's trading partners

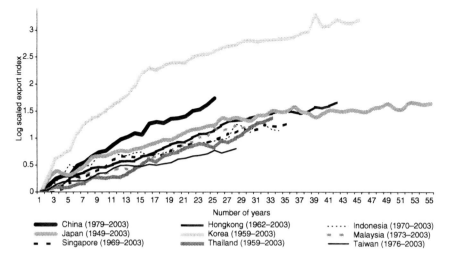

Figure 9.1 Export growth experiences of selected export-oriented economies of Asia.

Sources: Authors' calculation based on trade data from International Monetary Fund (2005) and US GDP deflator from International Monetary Fund (2006).

Note
The base year is defined as the first year in which the three-year moving average of the annual export growth rate was greater than or equal to 5 per cent for at least three years in succession. When countries first begin to export goods, export growth rates tend to be very high due to the small denominator in the growth calculation; accordingly, the figure does not consider growth rates based on export values of less than US$100 million (in year 2000 $US).

of such massive increases would be enormous, generating unprecedented, persistent structural change in both developing and developed economies.

The rapid growth in the value of China's imports, which generally followed its export trend until 2003, contrasts sharply with Japan's experience. Japan's exports and imports grew at similar rates from 1955 to 1964 when its export-to-import ratio ranged from .87 to 1.18. However, from 1964 to 1972, its exports expanded much faster than imports. On the eve of the first OPEC oil crisis in 1972, Japan had already experienced 23 years of booming exports, while achieving a high export-to-import ratio of 1.47. One likely source of the differences in import growth rates between China and Japan may be the higher propensity of FIEs in China to import intermediate inputs, add labor services to these imports, and then export them as final products. During Japan's export boom, FIEs played only a small role.

China's record of running small overall trade deficits and surpluses has, however, obscured some large imbalances with particular trading partners. China's large surpluses with the US since 1997 and its large deficits with Korea and several ASEAN countries since 2001 are particularly noteworthy.[15] In 2004, the ratio of China's exports to the US over imports from the US was five to one.

There are several explanations for the individual imbalances and the overall balance of China's trade. First, an imbalance between savings and investment rates in the economies of some key trading partners, particularly the US, has contributed to individual imbalances. Second, subsidies and business loans to China's state-owned enterprises have reduced these firms' costs and allowed them to charge lower prices that undermine the ability of foreign producers to compete in these markets. Third, the close relationship between foreign investment and China's external trade orientation, as well as barriers to trade both within China and in foreign countries, have led to China's preeminence as a global source of manufactures. Finally, the relatively undervalued yuan, in part a result of China's decision to accumulate additional foreign reserves to insulate the currency from speculative attacks, has provided a cost advantage to Chinese exports.

A comparison of China's trade policies with those of other East Asian economies may be useful, as China has adopted and modified a number of policies used successfully by its Asian counterparts. Economists have been at odds over the relative importance of such trade policies in generating earlier Asian export booms.[16] Dani Rodrik summarized the debate succinctly:

> Observers with a favorable take on industrial policy saw in East Asia a confirmation of their theories on the importance of state intervention. Advocates of free markets saw instead the triumph of small government and unfettered private initiative. Trade economists viewed it as a miracle based on outward orientation, labor economists stressed the early emphasis on education, and macroeconomists pointed to the region's fiscal conservatism. Growth theorists debated the respective contributions of human capital, physical capital, and technology adoption.
>
> (Rodrik 1999)

Recognizing the lack of consensus regarding the foundations of East Asian growth, we nonetheless offer a number of observations regarding to which extent Chinese trade policies were exceptional. First, during their earlier export booms, Asian economies (with the exception of Hong Kong) adopted policies that featured a substantial role for the state in directing development. In this respect, China was no exception. Policymakers employed a variety of policies to spur growth and investment in particular industries. Among the most widely applied state interventions were export subsidies – often in the form of subsidized credit – that targeted particular industries. State coordination and target setting for investments, public support for education, and subsidies to research and development activities also played prominent roles.

Second, China's trade liberalization demonstrated a level of policy discipline that rivaled that of its predecessors in Asia. Indeed, China's unilateral reductions in trade barriers greatly exceeded those carried out during earlier Asian export booms. The increase in competition from imported products is important, as import competition typically raises the productivity of domestic firms (Weinstein and Lawrence 2001). This is particularly important in China, as improving the efficiency of its state-owned enterprises has been an ongoing goal of its reform program.

Finally, most of East Asia's successful economies employed exchange rate controls and maintained undervalued exchange rates during their earlier export booms. In addition, East Asian states generally maintained fiscal balance and encouraged high rates of domestic savings. This facilitated high rates of investment in physical, technological, and human capital, all of which aided their development and ability to build industries for which they had a comparative advantage. China's use of monetary and fiscal policies has, in its broad brush patterns, mirrored earlier policies adopted by East Asian governments.

We conclude that trade outcomes and policies of China and East Asia's earlier developers are similar along many dimensions. The differences are also worth considering: China's trade sector is 3.5 times the size of Japan's, and China's program of unilateral and negotiated trade liberalization was larger and proceeded quicker than those initiated by the earlier Asian boom economies. Ultimately, though, there might be a distinct parallel between Japan's past and China's future. If China's trade sustains its expansion at the same rate as in the last 20 years, and, more importantly, if China's sizeable export surpluses for 2005 and 2006 continue, then there is the likelihood that China could face big protectionist backlashes in the not so distant future.

Prospects and implications of China's rise as a trading power

The implications of China's growth for the global economy are much greater than those of earlier export booms. Quite tellingly, China's population in 2005 (1.3 billion) was 15 times larger than that of Japan circa 1953 (87 million). If China's export boom (measured from 1984) lasts as long as Japan's export boom (33 years), then global implications are astounding. Indeed, if Chinese GDP grows to the levels achieved by Korea or Malaysia during their export booms, it would reach US$5.59 trillion (in year 2003 US$) or 36.2 percent of US projected GDP in 2017 – nearly triple the 12.4 percent share of US GDP that China represented in 2003 (Wilson and Purushothaman 2003). If a tripling in the relative size of its economy also implies a tripling in China's export shares, then the required global structural adjustment will be enormous, transforming not just China's economy but also those of its trading partners.

The rapid and sustained growth in China's exports across a broad range of markets has prompted trade disputes and raised prospects for serious trade conflicts with important trading partners. The modern history of export booms suggests that we should not hesitate to predict a protectionist backlash if Chinese exports continue to grow at post-2001 rates. Already, incipient protectionism is evident against a particular category of Chinese exports: the surge in China's exports of textiles and apparel following the end of the Multi-Fiber Arrangement in 2005 has prodded both the US and EU governments to take quick and unforgiving actions. Both imposed "safeguard" quotas severely limiting the growth of Chinese textile and apparel exports (Buckley 2005).

Nonetheless, there are grounds for optimism concerning China's trade prospects. Opposition to Chinese exports could lessen if increases in Chinese household incomes lead to increases in demand for US and EU goods that target higher-income consumers. These firms and their workers would then join the coalition of US firms favoring open trade with China. Perhaps more importantly, FIEs play a weighty role in China's economy, especially the export-processing arrangements driving much of Chinese foreign trade. The large role of FIEs in China's economy creates constituencies in foreign countries that support liberalized trade with China. These constituencies are not limited to the corporate headquarters of FIEs active in China, but also include their labor forces, domestic suppliers, and financial backers.

Another factor that may reduce overseas protectionism is that some trading partners, for example the United States, have already "lost" most of their low-skill-intensive manufacturing industries. Thus, increased Chinese exports are more likely to reduce exports from other developing countries. Jobs and output in developed countries with very small low-skill manufacturing sectors should be less affected, although this could change as China moves up the value-added ladder to produce more sophisticated goods.

Finally, China has become a stronger advocate of more liberal global trade policies, especially after its entry into the WTO. China's global weight as a trading power is such that its stance could sway future WTO negotiations, including new or revived negotiations under the Doha Round. China could also trigger more concerted regional endeavors toward free trade. In this manner, Chinese efforts might sustain both a liberal global trading environment and its own export boom.

Notes

* We thank Matt Pennaz for excellent research assistance and discussion of China's trade.
1 The income figures are purchasing power parity (PPP) estimates, adjusted to reflect international price differences.
2 These estimates do not incorporate recent revisions in China's GDP that have substantially raised its level.
3 China's initial exports of agricultural goods encountered high EU and US tariffs and restrictive quotas even with its MFN status. As Chinese exports shifted toward labor-intensive manufacturing goods, they encountered lower tariffs and fewer restrictive quotas.

4 For a more complete analysis of the effect of PTAs on China's trade, see Clarete *et al.* (2004).
5 See Tongzon (2005) for an optimistic assessment of potential gains from the ASEAN-China PTA.
6 See Rutherford and Martinez (2000) for an overview of the distributional impact of a PTA.
7 Between 1995 and 2003, the value of Chinese exports to EU countries and the US rose from 54.2 to 180.1 billion in constant year 2000 US dollars.
8 Authors' calculation based on International Monetary Fund (2006).
9 See Edmonds *et al.* (2005) for a more detailed discussion of the gravity model and its application.
10 Naughton (2000) and Bai *et al.* (2004) are less convinced that internal trade restrictions had a large effect on inter-provincial trade.
11 Our analysis uses the 10-digit definition of products in the Harmonized System – HS.
12 The role of trade opening in altering rural-urban economic disparities in China is assessed in Anderson *et al.* (2003), and Huang and Rozelle (2003).
13 The role of China's trade policies on firm location is discussed in Batisse and Poncet (2004) and Jin (2004).
14 In its March 30, 2006 complaint to the WTO, the United States argues that China's regulations governing tariffs on auto parts are WTO inconsistent. See United States Complaint (2006).
15 Analysis of China's overall trade accounts is complicated by difficulties in accounting for Chinese imports and exports that use Hong Kong's entrepôt services and by the unique treatment of Taiwan by China's trade accounts (Fung and Lau 2003).
16 Kokko (2006) and Noland and Pack (2005) revisit this question with the aim of assessing the implications of East Asia's development experience for other regions.

References

Anderson, K., Huang, J., and Ianchovichina, E. (2003) "Long–Run Impacts of China's WTO Accession on Farm-Nonfarm Income Inequality and Rural Poverty," *World Bank Policy Research Paper,* No. 3052, Washington, DC: World Bank.

Antkiewicz, A. and Whalley, J. (2004) "China's New Regional Trade Agreements," *NBER Working Paper,* No. 10992.

Bai, C. E., Du, Y., Tao, Z., and Tong, S. (2004) "Local Protectionism and Regional Specialization: Evidence from China's Industries," *Journal of International Economics,* 63(2): 397–418.

Batisse, C. and Poncet, S. (2004) "Protectionism and Industry Location in Chinese Provinces," *Journal of Chinese Economic and Business Studies,* 2(2): 133–154.

Branstetter, L. and Lardy, N. (2006) "China's Embrace of Globalization," *NBER Working Paper Series,* No. 12373.

Buckley, C. (2005) "Textile Exports Haunt US-China Trade Talks," *International Herald Tribune,* July 11. Online. Available HTTP: www.iht.com/articles/2005/07/10/business/trade.php (accessed February 3, 2007).

Clarete, R., Edmonds, C., and Wallack, J. (2004) "Preferential Trade Agreements and China's Trade," in C. Wiemer and H. Cao (eds), *Asian Economic Cooperation in the New Millennium: China's Economic Presence,* Singapore: World Scientific Publishing, pp. 385–423.

Edmonds, C., La Croix, S., and Li, Y. (2005) "China's International Trade: Past Patterns and Emerging Issues," *East-West Center Working Papers, Economics Series,* No. 88, East-West Center: Honolulu, HI. Online. Available HTTP: www.eastwestcenter.org/stored/pdfs/ECONwp088.pdf (accessed February 3, 2007).

Foreign Trade Division, US Census Bureau (2005) *USA Trade Online,* Washington, DC: US Census Bureau. Online. Available HTTP: www.usatradeonline.gov (accessed February 3, 2007).

Fung, K.C. and Lau, L. (2003) "Adjusted Estimates of the United States-China Bilateral Trade Balances: 1995-2002," *Journal of Asian Economics,* 14(3): 489–496.

Huang, J. and Rozelle, S. (2003) "Trade Reform, Household Effects, and Poverty in Rural China," *American Journal of Agricultural Economics,* 85(5): 1292–1298.

International Monetary Fund (2005) *Direction of Trade Statistics,* Washington, DC: International Monetary Fund.

——(2006) *International Financial Statistics,* Washington, DC: International Monetary Fund.

Jin, J. (2004) "On the Relationship between Openness and Growth in China: Evidence from Provincial Time Series Data," *World Economy,* 27(10): 1571–1582.

Kokko, A. (2006) "Export-Led Growth in East Asia: Lessons for Europe's Transition Economies," in S. Söderman (ed.) *Emerging Multiplicity – Integration and Responsiveness in Asian Business Development,* Basingstoke: Palgrave Macmillan.

La Croix, S. and Grandy, C. (1997) "The Political Instability of Reciprocal Trade and the Overthrow of the Hawaiian Kingdom," *Journal of Economic History,* 57(1): 161–189.

Lardy, N. (2002) *Integrating China into the Global Economy,* Washington, DC: Brookings Institution.

Lee, H., Roland-Holst, D., and van der Mensbrugghe, D. (2004) "China's Emergence in East Asia under Alternative Trading Arrangements," *Journal of Asian Economics,* 15(4): 697–712.

McLaren, J. (1996) "Size, Sunk Costs, and Judge Bowker's Objection to Free Trade," *American Economic Review,* 87(3): 400–420.

Ministry of Commerce (2007) *Trade Data.* Online. Available HTTP: zhs.mofcom.gov.cn/tongji2001.shtml (accessed February 3, 2007).

National Bureau of Statistics (2004) *China Statistical Yearbook,* Beijing: Statistical Publishing House.

——(various years) *China Rural Poverty Monitoring Report,* Beijing: China Statistics Press.

Naughton, B. (1996) "China's Emergence and Prospects as a Trading Nation," *Brookings Papers on Economic Activity,* No. 2: 273–345.

——(2000) "How Much Can Regional Integration Do to Unify China's Markets?" *Working Paper,* No. 58, Stanford, CA: Center for Research on Economic Development and Policy Reform.

Nielsen, J.U.M. and Rutkowski, A.J. (2005) "The EU Anti-dumping Policy towards Russia and China: Product Quality and the Choice of an Analogue Country," *World Economy,* 28(1): 103–136.

Noland, M. and Pack, H. (2005) "The East Asian Industrial Policy Experience: Implications for the Middle East," *Institute for International Economics Working Paper,* No. 05-14, Washington, DC: Institute for International Economics.

Ravallion, M. and Chen, S. (2004) "China's (Uneven) Progress Against Poverty," *World Bank Policy Research Working Paper*, No. 3084, Washington, DC: World Bank.

Rodrik, D. (1999) "East Asian Mysteries: Past and Present," *NBER Research Summary*, Spring. Online. Available HTTP: www.nber.org/reporter/spring99/rodrik.html (accessed February 3, 2007).

Rutherford, T.F. and Martinez, J. (2000) "Welfare Effects of Regional Trade Integration of Central American and Caribbean Nations with NAFTA and MERCOSUR," *World Economy*, 23(6): 799–826.

Statistics Canada (2005) *Trade Analyzer Database*, Ottawa: Statistics Canada.

Tongzon, J.L. (2005) "ASEAN-China Free Trade Area: A Bane or Boon for ASEAN Countries?" *World Economy*, 28(2): 191–210.

UNCTAD (United Nations Commission on Trade and Development) (2002) *Trade and Development Report*, New York and Geneva: United Nations.

United States Complaint (2006) *China – Measures Affecting Imports of Automobile Parts*, DS340, March 30. Online. Available HTTP: www.wto.org/english/tratop_e/dispu_e/cases_e/ds340_e.htm#top (accessed February 3, 2007).

USTR (United States Trade Representative) (2000) *United States-China Bilateral Market Access Agreement*, Washington, DC: USTR.

Wedeman, A. (2003). *From Mao to Market: Rent Seeking, Local Protectionism, and Marketization in China*, New York: Cambridge University Press.

Weinstein, D. and Lawrence, R. (2001) "Trade and Growth: Import-Led or Export-Led: Evidence from Japan and Korea," in J.E. Stiglitz and S. Yusuf (eds) *Rethinking the East Asia Miracle*, New York: Oxford University Press.

Wilson, D. and Purushothaman, R. (2003) "Dreaming With BRICs: The Path to 2050," *Goldman Sachs Global Economics Papers*, No. 99. Online. Available HTTP: www.gs.com/insight/research/reports/report6.html (accessed February 3, 2007).

World Bank (2001) *World Development Report*, Washington, DC: World Bank.

——(2005) *World Development Indicators*, Washington, DC: World Bank.

Young, A. (2000) "The Razor's Edge: Distortions and Incremental Reform in the People's Republic of China," *Quarterly Journal of Economics*, 115(4): 1091–1135.

Zhang, K. and Song, S. (2000) "Promoting Exports: The Role of Inward FDI in China," *China Economic Review*, 11(4): 385–396.

10 Energy security in China's capitalist transition

Import dependence, oil diplomacy, and security imperatives

Kang Wu and Ian Storey

The People's Republic of China (PRC) had been a net energy exporter since the 1960s. In 1993, however, China became a net oil importer. Largely as a result of China's capitalist transition, China's thirst for energy resources has continued to grow massively in recent years. This is deepening the country's energy import dependence, which in turn is changing many aspects of China's energy markets and accelerating China's integration with the rest of the world. However, with higher dependence on energy imports, particularly imports of oil, energy security has emerged as a top issue for the Chinese leadership. Indeed, the exigencies of energy security have come to influence the conduct of China's foreign relations.

There are in general four dimensions of energy security. The first is the economic dimension. Energy security means smoothly securing adequate supplies of energy efficiently and at the lowest cost. This requires governments to have an energy policy that is transparent and reduces barriers to the efficient operation of markets. The second is the geopolitical dimension. Promoting energy security means that oil or energy diplomacy plays a key role in a country's foreign policies. The third is the national security and military dimension. Energy security can be an important component in formulating a country's national security and defense policies. The final is the environmental dimension. To manage energy consumption while simultaneously protecting the environment and avoiding ecological degradation, any country, particularly a large and fast growing developing country like China, faces huge challenges.

The purpose of this chapter is twofold. First, we will analyze the nature and seriousness of China's energy vulnerabilities, especially rising dependence on energy imports. Second, we will examine the economic, geopolitical, and, to a lesser extent, military dimensions of the dilemmas shaping China's energy security. Unfortunately, a detailed analysis of the environmental issues associated with energy security is beyond the scope of this chapter, though these issues will be touched on.

Increasing energy needs and resulting vulnerabilities

China is a large energy producer and more importantly, a giant energy consumer. From the global perspective, China ranks second, after the United States, in total energy consumption. On a per capita basis, however, China's primary energy consumption was nearly 30 percent below the world average in 2005.

Coal plays a dominant role. China is the world's largest coal producer and consumer. In 2005, coal accounted for 70 percent of China's primary commercial energy consumption.[1] China is also the second largest oil consumer after the United States, though oil accounts for just under 21 percent of China's total primary energy consumption.

Currently, the share of natural gas in China's primary energy consumption remains low at under 3 percent. Its importance, however, is growing. Similarly, China's nuclear power program only gained traction at the end of the 1990s, but the country now plans to increase nuclear power generation capacity by a factor of 4 to 5 over the next 15 years. The aim is to reduce China's dependence on coal, which generates greenhouse-gas emissions. Finally, the Chinese government is exploring ways to improve energy efficiency and to increase the use of renewable energy sources such as solar, wind, biomass, and hydroelectric power.

China's energy vulnerabilities

At present, China's energy system remains vulnerable in six major areas. First and foremost, the Chinese economy has been growing at spectacular rates for nearly three decades and is expected to enjoy high growth rates for at least the next 15 years. China will therefore have enormous energy requirements over the long-term. This rising energy use is causing a major vulnerability: a structural mismatch between energy resource availability and energy consumption.

While increasing energy requirements are themselves challenging, an equally great challenge is determining the right energy mix. China needs clean, high-quality energy to support continued economic growth, but, despite the relative abundance of coal and other energy resources, China currently lacks high-quality premium fuels. For instance, the shares of natural gas and nuclear power are still very low in China's energy production.

In addition, there are structural problems within individual energy sectors. In coal, for instance, upstream mining is well developed but investment is lacking in coal washing, shaping, transportation, distribution, and coal-water slurry. Similarly, in the power sector, power generation, transmission, and distribution are not well coordinated, leading to bottlenecks in many markets (Yan and Zhao 2003).

Closely associated with the deep structural mismatch between energy needs and energy production is China's second energy vulnerability. It centers on the fact that China's per capita energy consumption is below the world average and far below the levels of developed countries. For instance, China's per capita primary energy consumption was only 15 percent of that in the United States during 2005. Low per capita energy consumption implies that as the Chinese economy develops, an increase in per capita energy consumption is inevitable.

As a result, the promotion of energy efficiency has taken on enormous importance in China. Already, China has applied various energy conservation technologies and achieved impressive results. The task, however, is becoming increasingly difficult (Xuan 2004). As a priority, China intends to establish a market-oriented policy framework and invest substantially in new energy technologies to further promote energy conservation. If China fails to effectively implement these conservation strategies, energy demand may rise to levels that are impossible to meet in the future.

The third area of vulnerability is China's growing oil demand and the lack of domestic supply. In terms of energy security, oil supply security is the most important issue for China. While natural gas imports may add to the security problem, they may also be viewed as a way to mitigate the growing dependence on oil through energy diversification.

The fourth energy vulnerability is the conflict between energy use and environmental protection. China is currently the world's largest sulfur dioxide polluter and the second largest carbon dioxide emitter. In November 2006, the International Energy Agency predicted that the PRC would surpass the United States in 2009 as the biggest emitter of carbon dioxide (Quek 2006). Moreover, at the beginning of this decade about two-fifths of China's land territory was affected by acid rain, with the Lower Yangtze region the most heavily disturbed (Zhang 2002).

Much of these problems can be traced back to China's reliance on coal to meet the bulk of its energy needs. The massive use of coal is causing serious problems with the environment and public health. At present, nearly 80 percent of coal is burned raw, either as a fuel or for power generation. Although the Chinese government has made great efforts to promote the use of clean and premium fuels, it is inevitable that coal will remain the primary source of energy. In fact, it will take decades before China is able to reduce coal to under 50 percent of total energy consumption and apply basic clean coal technologies.

The fifth vulnerability is that for all energy sectors a well-functioning management and regulatory framework either does not exist or is incomplete. The Chinese government has tried for decades to address this problem. Reform of the coal, oil, and gas industries, for example, started as early as the mid-1980s. However, the coal sector remains beset with low efficiency, heavy pollution, railway congestion, and production safety issues, while in oil and gas, competitive markets are far from fully established. Power sector reform, on the other hand, is relatively new, but also faces a major uphill battle in ending decades of monopoly. As of today, there is still a long way to go toward establishing regulatory frameworks that allocate energy according to market-based systems.

The last vulnerability is the inefficient supply of energy to China's vast rural areas. China currently has over 20 million people in rural areas who have no access to electricity. The massive use, often in primitive ways, of non-commercial biomass (mainly stalks and firewood) is ecologically destructive and economically inefficient. As a result, rural energy development has long been one of the foci of China's energy policy. The government has tried for decades to promote the commercialization of biomass use and extend the electric power grid to remote areas. But the government continues to face enormous challenges. Even now 61 percent of China's total population, or over 780 million people, live outside of urban cities and towns.

Among these vulnerabilities, the structural mismatch between energy production and consumption, as well as rising oil imports and their impact on energy security, are considered the most challenging. While China's total energy needs during the coming decades are problematic, the country's lack of clean, premium, and high-quality fuels is an even bigger predicament. Indeed, adequate supplies of clean and high quality energy could support the Chinese government's goals of fostering rapid economic growth while improving China's environmental and ecological conditions. However, to obtain sufficient clean, premium, and high-quality energy products, China not only has to substantially increase its investment in oil, gas, hydroelectricity, nuclear power, and clean coal technologies but also import more oil and gas. This will, in turn, increase the importance of energy security.

Put differently, energy security will soon become the biggest energy vulnerability facing the PRC. If China feels that its energy security is jeopardized, many of the other policy goals such as the use of clean and high-quality fuels, environmental protection, and improving the efficiency of the energy sector through reform will be negatively affected.

Deepening energy import dependence

As represented in Figure 10.1, China became a net oil importer in 1993 following nearly 15 years of rapid economic growth. Currently, China is a net energy importer on an overall basis, mainly due to rising oil imports and shrinking coal

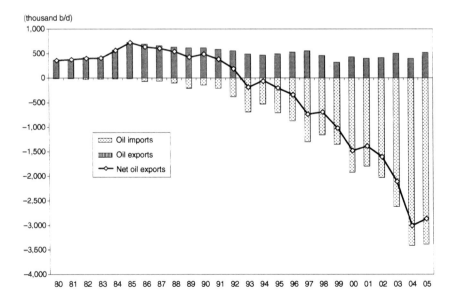

Figure 10.1 China's oil (crude and products) exports and imports, 1980–2005.

exports. Moreover, China's coal exports are likely to decline further during the coming decades, while natural gas and oil imports will continue to grow.

As the world's largest coal producer, China has long exported coal to Asia. However, the rapid rise of domestic coal demand since 2003 has threatened China's position as a large coal exporter. Coal imports have been on the rise, and, within the next five to ten years, China is likely to become a net coal importer.

To diversify its sources of energy, China has rapidly developed its natural gas industry since the late 1990s. The pace of development has been particularly fast in recent years, as China's overall energy supply tightened. Spurred by high demand for energy, especially electric power, domestic natural gas pipelines have been built at a rapid pace. At the same time, one liquefied natural gas (LNG) terminal for imports is up and running, another is under construction, and several more have been approved.

China's current natural gas consumption is supplied almost entirely from domestic production, but future natural gas supplies are expected to come from three sources: higher domestic gas production; current and future LNG imports from Australia, Indonesia, Malaysia, and the Middle East; and emerging imports of pipelined gas from neighboring countries to start at the earliest between 2010 and 2015 (Wu and Fesharaki 2005a).

Finally, China's petroleum sector and oil markets are expected to change continuously over the next ten years and beyond. Crude production growth from within China is expected to be flat, yet demand for petroleum products is likely to grow strongly. As Figure 10.2 elucidates, this situation

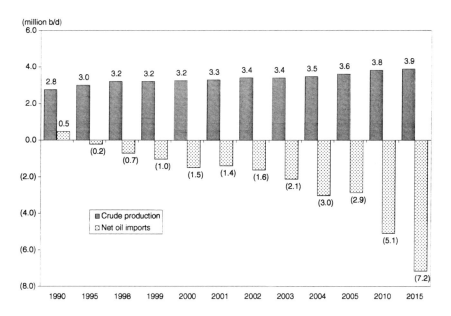

Figure 10.2 China's crude production and net oil import requirements, 1990–2015.

will require continuously rising imports of oil over the long term. Most troubling is that over 70 percent of China's net imports are likely to come from the geopolitically unstable Middle East.

Strategic policy proposals

China's growing importance of energy security is therefore first and foremost a consequence of rising oil imports. In the future, the decline of coal exports and stagnant domestic oil production will add to this problem (Wu and Fesharaki 2005b). Evidently, oil supply security in particular and energy supply security in general has become one of the top concerns for the Chinese government since the beginning of the new millennium.

This is reflected in recent government policy proposals. For the first time, two energy security items were incorporated in China's 10th Five-Year Plan (2001–2005) (Wu 2001). At the strategic level, the government set the goal to optimize the mix of energy while ensuring the country's overall energy security. Specifically for oil and gas, the plan contained the establishment of a strategic petroleum stockpile. This stockpile aims to ensure petroleum supply security and enhance the government's capacity to stabilize the market.

Concern with energy security took a step further when in November 2004 China's State Council approved the country's first "Mid- and Long-Term Energy Conservation Plan" (Hai 2005). In addition, the 11th Five-Year Program (2006–2010), where the term "plan" was replaced by "program," has made improving energy efficiency and conservation a top priority. The policy goals of the 10th Five-Year plan were expanded upon in this program, which mentions ensuring energy supply and managing energy demand, especially energy conservation, as enduring policy goals. Nonetheless, China still has a long way to go to before it can reach the ambitious targets contained in these policy documents.

Overall, the past years have seen the formulation of a plethora of additional policy proposals by the Chinese government (Chen 2003; Qin 2004; Xu and Yang 2004). One central thrust is to adjust energy consumption and production structures so as to reduce China's dependence on oil. Encouraging coal gasification, liquefaction, and the development of nuclear power are the most common proposals in this respect.

Another set of proposals is found in the realm of international relations, which will be discussed in detail in the next sections. A final set of proposals reflects clearly how China's energy production and distribution system remains dominated by state firms. Although subsidiaries of China's state oil giants have been listed on stock markets abroad and their corporate governance reformed, the process of reforming the state energy production and distribution systems remains ongoing. For example, there are calls to establish an oil futures market and to enhance the government's energy information gathering and research capabilities. There are also plans to form a centralized government agency for energy management and to draft a coherent national energy policy.

State oil companies are also seen as tools for the government to secure energy resources. These companies, for instance, should seek to strengthen overseas investments, particularly in the Middle East, Asia Pacific, Russia, Central Asia, Africa, and Latin America. There are also calls for China's state oil corporations to strategically cooperate with state shipping firms and to enhance government support for these shipping companies. The aim is to make ocean transportation of energy resources an important element of China's energy security.

Despite this wealth of policy proposals, progress on many fronts remains difficult, especially deeper reforms of China's internal energy production and distribution markets. China thus continues to search for ways to form a comprehensive and effective energy security strategy on the economic front.

Energy security, foreign policy, and national security

Energy security is as much a political issue as an economic one, and therefore has important consequences for a country's foreign and defense policies. In China's case, the political ramifications of energy security are profound. Since at least the early 1990s, the Chinese Communist Party's (CCP) continued legitimacy has depended in large part on its ability to improve the economic welfare of the Chinese people, something it has been able to do with considerable success. Yet, energy security is a prerequisite for sustained economic growth and is therefore viewed by the ruling elite as critical to its long-term survival.

The future of China's energy security has clearly become a source of some concern for China's political leaders. According to one Chinese analyst, the success or failure of China's modernization drive rests on the Chinese government's ability to achieve energy security (Friedberg 2006: 24). Indeed, the highest levels of the Chinese leadership have drawn attention to the country's energy security situation, resulting in the formation of the State Energy Leading Group, chaired by Prime Minister Wen Jiabao (Liu 2006: 4). And as a study by the policy research division of the CCP concluded: "The question of importing oil is not a pure economic issue, but more an issue involving international politics" (Tang 2006: 28).

As analyzed in previous sections, one of the outcomes of China's capitalist transition has been the country's growing dependence on energy imports. This dependence can be mitigated in part through domestic initiatives such as enhancing energy self-sufficiency and harnessing renewable energy sources. However, such programs will take decades to bear fruit, and in any case it is virtually impossible for a country like China to become totally self-sufficient in energy resources. As a result, China's dependence on imported energy is set to become a permanent reality with important consequences for the conduct of Chinese foreign and defense policies.

In this sense, the PRC is simply following in the footsteps of other capitalist developers, and is becoming a more normal country. During the 20th century, access to energy resources became a prime concern for major capitalist powers such as Britain, the United States, and Japan, exerting a strong influence on those countries' foreign and defense policies. In the early 20th century the Middle East assumed a new importance in Britain's foreign policy as the Royal Navy switched from coal to oil. Post-World War Two, the need to secure access to overseas oil fields became one of the central drivers of US foreign policy, particularly in the Middle East.

More recently, the Bush administration's decision to invade Iraq in 2003 may publicly have been justified by the need to destroy Saddam Hussein's alleged weapons of mass destruction program and also a desire to spread democracy in the Middle East. However, oil was certainly a major factor in these calculations. Access to oil has also been a critical component for resource-poor Japan's foreign and defense policies. Tokyo has thus pursued different means to obtain that end: from military expansionism in 1941 to diplomacy post-1945.

The following sections are divided into three parts. The first examines the influence of energy security on China's foreign policy, in particular on Beijing's increased interaction with resource-rich regions of the world. The second part focuses on how energy security is reshaping the parameters of the PRC's national security and defense policies, specifically the perceived need to reduce the country's strategic vulnerabilities. The final part then considers whether China's search for energy security will become a force for cooperation, competition, or possibly even confrontation with other powers such as America, Japan, India, and Russia.

Energy security and Chinese foreign policy

China's foreign policy may be said to consist of three interlinked core elements: great power diplomacy (*daguo waijiao*), good neighbor or peripheral diplomacy (*zhoubian waijiao*), and energy or resource diplomacy (*nengyuan waijiao*) (Tang 2006: 12). The first element centers primarily on the PRC's relations with the United States, followed by other major powers such as Japan, India, Russia, and the European Union. The aim of China's great power diplomacy has been to foster a stable international environment by avoiding confrontation.

The second element is based on China's desire to foster close and cooperative relations with its neighbors, particularly those it shares borders with in Northeast, Southeast, and Central Asia. The resolution of border disputes and the development of transport linkages to bolster increased trade relations have been the main thrusts of this second element.

The third element, energy diplomacy, is the newest of the three elements, and is aimed at securing energy and other natural resources to fuel China's modernization program. Since the dawn of the 21st century, energy diplomacy has acquired an even greater prominence. The travel itineraries of PRC leaders increasingly include energy producing countries, and the bilateral agreements secured invariably involve commitments by China to purchase energy resources or invest in these countries' energy production.

The most important geographical area for China's energy needs is the Middle East, which supplies nearly half of the country's crude oil imports. The two most important countries for China in this region are Saudi Arabia and Iran. Over the past several years Sino-Saudi relations have grown closer, as Riyadh seeks to reduce its dependence on the United States, and Beijing's thirst for oil has increased. Today, Saudi Arabia provides China with about 17.5 percent of its crude oil imports, a figure that is set to rise over the coming decades (*BBC News* 2006).

Iran is also a major producer of oil and gas, and the PRC is keen to increase imports of both. In March 2004 Beijing signed an agreement with Tehran to import 110 million tons of LNG for the next 25 years worth US$25 billion (*Wall Street Journal* 2004). This price tag can easily double if an actual contract is signed today. The PRC has also made a major investment in Iran's Yadavaran oil field (*Washington Post* 2004).

While China may have no choice but to increase energy imports from the Middle East, it also seeks ways to manage if not reduce its overall dependence on this region for two reasons: first, this region is politically unstable, which could lead to supply disruptions; and second, Beijing is concerned about the strategic vulnerabilities associated with the transit of energy resources from the Middle East through geographical choke points such as the Strait of Hormuz and the Strait of Malacca. The issue of strategic vulnerabilities will be explored in more detail later. What follows is a brief examination of China's attempts to reduce its dependence on the Middle East by securing energy resources in other parts of the world.

Since the collapse of the Soviet Union in 1991, Beijing has looked to neighboring Kazakhstan in Central Asia and Russia as important sources of energy supplies. Both countries share a land border with China and oil imports can be received *via* oil pipelines or by rail. In the late 1990s, China entered into negotiations with Kazakhstan to construct an oil pipeline. However, it was not until 2004 that construction of the pipeline actually began. Completed in late 2005, the US$700 million, 960-kilometer pipeline from Atasu in central Kazakhstan to Xinjiang Province in China is capable of delivering 10 million tons of oil every year, rising to 15 million tons by 2010, and up to 50 million tons over the long term (*Asia Times* 2005a; *People's Daily* 2004a).

China has also worked hard to cultivate close relations with other Central Asian Republics and has been the driving force behind the Shanghai Cooperation Organization (SCO). This organization links Central Asian Republics to China and Russia. For China, one of its main agenda items has been to secure Chinese access to regional energy resources.

One of China's top priorities in its relations with Russia has been tapping into that country's vast energy resources. Russia is the world's largest producer of crude oil, and is already an important supplier to China. Over the past decade Beijing has been trying to gain access to Russia's massive oil reserves located in eastern Siberia, an effort that has brought it into direct competition with Japan. Tokyo imports 80 percent of its oil from the Middle East, and, like China, is trying to lessen its dependence on that part of the world. Japan and China have competed with each other to build rival pipelines to transport the Siberian oil. Japan prodded Moscow to accept a route from Angarsk in eastern Siberia to the Pacific port of Nakhodka; the oil would then be transported to Japan by sea. As a sweetener to the deal, Tokyo offered to finance construction of the proposed pipeline, estimated at US$13–15 billion.

In opposition, China lobbied Russia to build a pipeline from Angarsk to the northeastern Chinese city of Daqing (*Economist* 2003). In order to extract maximum concessions, Moscow skillfully played the two sides off each other. In late 2004 Japan seemed confident that it had won the race. However, in April 2005 Moscow announced that the first stage of the oil pipeline would begin in Taishet, not Angarsk, and terminate mid-way at Skovorodino where oil would be shipped to China by rail (*Moscow Times* 2005). Although Moscow has indicated that the pipeline would eventually terminate at Nakhodka on Russia's Pacific coast, Tokyo was piqued by comments from Russian officials that China had priority over Japan, and threatened to withdraw its offer to finance the project (*Japan Times* 2005). It seems likely, therefore, that Japan has lost out and that China will purchase the bulk of Russia's Siberian oil.

China is also looking much further afield in its search for energy resources, including Africa and South America. Beijing has had interests in Africa since the establishment of the PRC in 1949. From the 1950s until the late 1970s these were primarily ideological: at the time, Beijing portrayed itself as the leader of the Third World and sponsored a number of revolutionary movements on the continent. During the 1980s and 1990s, China's interest in Africa waned as the country focused on economic development and relations with its Asian neighbors. Over the past few years, however, Africa has again become an area of intense interest for China, and oil has helped rekindle that interest. China has signed oil exploration or production agreements with the Sudan, Niger, Ethiopia, Egypt, Gabon, and Algeria, and is pursuing negotiations with Chad, Angola, and Congo over similar deals.

African countries now supply approximately 25 percent of China's oil imports (Hill 2004). However, it is important to note that China is expanding its presence in Africa for reasons other than energy resources. Africa represents a potentially large market for Chinese manufactured goods and constitutes a community of 53 countries able to extend diplomatic support to China at the United Nations and other multilateral forums, thus denying

Taiwan international space (Thompson 2004). China's sponsorship of the China-Africa Summit in Beijing in November 2006, attended by heads of state from 48 African countries, highlighted Africa's growing importance in Chinese foreign policy.

Finally, China's energy diplomacy extends to South America. Over the past few years Beijing has stepped up relations with Venezuela, Brazil, Ecuador, Argentina, Peru, and Cuba. In particular, China has courted Venezuela, one of the world's leading oil producers. Although Venezuela provides the United States with 1.5 million barrels of oil per day, Hugo Chavez has pursued an anti-American agenda since becoming president in 1998 (*BBC News* 2005). As US-Venezuela ties have chilled, Sino-Venezuelan relations have warmed. The backbone of this new relationship is oil: Chavez wants to reduce dependence on oil exports to the United States, while China wants to increase energy imports from Venezuela. However, like Africa, oil is only one factor in China's South America policy. Beijing sees South America as an important market for Chinese goods, as well as another significant diplomatic community of 14 countries.

Energy security and China's national security

China's growing dependence on energy imports has aroused strategic anxieties within the government and among the country's security analysts. The focus of this anxiety is the perceived vulnerability of seaborne energy imports. At present, China's navy is incapable of protecting the country's sea lines of communication (SLOC), the maritime arteries which enable ships to bring resources into the country and carry them out into the global market. Since the end of World War Two, the United States Navy has ensured freedom of navigation and kept the SLOCs open for international trade.

America's global naval preponderance is a double-edged sword for China. On the one hand, it enables China to thrive as a maritime trading power. On the other hand, Chinese security analysts fear that in the event of heightened tensions with America, say over Taiwan, the US Navy would be able to blockade Chinese ports and interdict vessels heading for China on the high seas with impunity. The disruption of seaborne energy supplies to the PRC would have two effects: first, it would severely hinder China's ability to prosecute a war; and second, the country's economic growth would be negatively impacted, if not derailed.

Emblematic of China's concern is the Strait of Malacca (SOM). Located in Southeast Asia, the SOM is a narrow and congested waterway separating Indonesia and Malaysia, with Singapore located at its southern entrance. As the shortest route between the Indian and Pacific Oceans, the SOM is one of the world's most important waterways: 65,000 vessels transit through it each year, carrying over one-third of global commerce and half of global energy supplies. As the Chinese economy continues to boom, the SOM's strategic significance for China increases each year.

As noted earlier, half of China's crude oil imports originate in the Middle East, with this figure expected to rise to 65 percent by 2015. Energy resources from the Middle East, plus those from Africa, are shipped to Chinese ports *via* the SOM, or the Lombok-Makassar Strait further to the east in Indonesia. The Chinese government increasingly views the country's reliance on these maritime choke points, especially the SOM, as a strategic vulnerability.

In late 2003 President Hu Jintao expressed concern at China's energy security situation, noting that "certain major powers" (a codeword for the United States) were trying to control the strait (*Wen Wei Po* 2004). China's state-run media soon dubbed the issue China's "Malacca dilemma." As one commentary put it, "It is no exaggeration to say that whoever controls the Strait of Malacca will also have a stranglehold on the energy route of China" (*Zhongguo Qingnian Bao* 2004). In fact, Chinese analysts have accused the United States, Japan, and India of using transnational threats (especially piracy) in the area as a pretext to bolster their regional naval forces. According to Lu Guoxue, Washington's intention is to curtail China's rising power by restricting its access to energy supplies through the SOM (*Zhongguo Qingnian Bao* 2004).

China's first line of defense to protect its SLOCs and ensure uninterrupted supplies of energy is the People's Liberation Army Navy (PLAN). Over the past decade, the operational capabilities of the PLAN have improved significantly due to a combination of acquisitions of high-technology naval platforms from abroad (mainly Russia) and an active indigenous construction program. These have equipped the PLAN with new and sophisticated destroyers, frigates, amphibious landing ships, and submarines (Goldstein and Murray 2004).

The primary driver for China's naval modernization has been potential contingencies in the Taiwan Strait, particularly the need to conduct amphibious landings and deter the US Navy from intervening in the dispute (Cole 2006). The surface vessels and submarines now in the PLAN's inventory also enable China to exert limited control over its SLOCs, particularly those close to the Chinese coast. However, while China has made some progress toward establishing a blue-water navy, that is, an ocean-going navy, it is still several decades away from realizing that goal.

As a blue-water navy might not be achieved for a generation, Chinese security planners have begun considering other ways to reduce the country's "Malacca dilemma." One suggested strategy is to establish a Chinese naval presence, either temporarily in times of crisis or permanently as the PLAN expands, at ports in countries friendly to the PRC. This would obviate the need for Chinese navy vessels to operate far from home. This "string of pearls" strategy includes ports in Cambodia, Burma, Bangladesh, and Pakistan (*Washington Times* 2005). Such a strategy would be dependent on China maintaining close relations with those countries, and might run the risk of fueling regional suspicions of China's intentions.

Other proposals call for China to bypass the SOM altogether. All of these proposals involve significant financial outlays, technical difficulties, and security concerns. One of the most fanciful proposals has been for China to finance construction of a canal across the Kra Isthmus in southern Thailand. The idea of an "Asian Panama Canal" has been around since the late 17th century, and was most recently revisited in 2001 by Thailand's Deputy Prime Minister Chavalit Yongchaiyudh. Initially, the project aroused some interest in China, but Beijing baulked at the US$25 billion price tag. In 2003 Thai Prime Minister Thaksin Shinawatra effectively killed the project in favor of a cheaper oil pipeline across the south of the country. Again China expressed an interest, but its enthusiasm waned due to cost concerns and escalating political violence in Thailand's southern provinces (*Nation* 2005). Moreover, neither the Kra Canal nor the energy pipeline would lessen China's sense of vulnerability. Tankers would still have set sail to and from Thailand, only shifting the geographical focus of the problem slightly (Storey 2006).

Two other proposals involve the construction of energy pipelines to the PRC, much like the Kazakh-China pipeline outlined earlier. The first is a US$2 billion 750-mile pipeline from Sittwe in Burma to Kunming in China's Yunnan Province. This project is appealing to China because oil tankers carrying energy supplies from the Middle East and Africa would be able to sail directly to Sittwe, bypassing the SOM (Cheong 2004). The two countries reportedly began talks on the financing and construction of this pipeline in 2004 (Beng 2004).

The second proposal is to build a pipeline from the Pakistani port of Gwadar to Xinjiang Province. Pakistan is a close ally of the PRC and Gwadar, partly financed by China, is very close to the Persian Gulf. Ships carrying energy supplies to China would be able to bypass all maritime choke points except the Strait of Hormuz. However, the China-Pakistan Energy Corridor, as the project has been dubbed, would be an expensive proposition given the long distances involved and the rugged terrain. The pipeline would also have to run through Baluchistan Province, which is prone to separatist violence.

Increasingly those who frame China's national security and defense policies have to consider strategies to reduce the country's energy import dependence. These strategies include achieving blue-water status for the PLAN and constructing pipelines that bypass the SOM and other maritime choke points. However, all strategic options are expensive, time-consuming, and politically problematic. In the meantime, China will have to contend with the dilemmas and insecurities posed by its dependence on the maritime security and control over international waters exerted by the US Navy.

Energy security and great power relations

As China's energy dependence deepens and Beijing looks to secure access to energy resources across the globe, security analysts and scholars of international relations have begun to consider the possible effects on

China's relations with other major powers, particularly the United States, Japan, and India. One such scholar, Aaron Friedberg (2006), has posited three possible scenarios. First, that energy security concerns will act as a catalyst for great power cooperation, especially in US-China relations. Second, that resource scarcity could lead China to adopt a more aggressive foreign policy, in which military force is used to secure energy resources. The final scenario lies somewhere in between: that "concern over access to resources will continue to act as a constraint on China's external behavior and an inducement for avoiding conflict with the United States" (Friedberg 2006: 32–34).

Based on current trends, it seems likely that for the foreseeable future China's efforts to achieve energy security will engender both cooperation and competition with other major powers. While the second scenario cannot be dismissed, it would be counterproductive to the PRC at this stage of its development.

There is no doubt that China's search for energy security has created some friction with other global powers. Tensions have arisen between China and Japan, for instance, over access to energy resources in the East China Sea. Since 2003, Chinese rigs have been drilling for natural gas near the median line between the PRC and Japan in the East China Sea. Japan has called on China to desist because it believes Chinese rigs are exploiting gas on the Japanese side of the median line (*Asia Times* 2005b). Talks between the two countries have thus far failed to resolve the dispute, and both sides have stationed warships in the area. The potential for a naval clash has aroused concern in both countries, as well as in the United States. China's *People's Daily* (2004b) has described the competition for Russia's Siberian oil and the East China Sea dispute as "only a prelude of the game between China and Japan in the arena of international energy."

However, it should be noted that competition for energy resources is one of a number of factors that have created strains in Sino-Japanese relations. Visits to the Yasukuni Shrine by Japanese politicians, the treatment of World War Two in Japanese school textbooks, the tightening of the US-Japan alliance and the implications for conflict over Taiwan, and the PRC's military modernization have also put strains on the relationship. Indeed, competition for energy resources is unlikely to spark a Sino-Japanese conflict, with both sides keen to protect annual bilateral trade of US$200 billion.

China's expanding overseas energy interests have also brought it into contention with the United States. Voices in Washington have been critical of China's relations with countries such as the Sudan, Iran, Burma, and Venezuela, either because of those countries' poor human rights records or because they have adopted policies or positions perceived as inimical to US interests. In all of these countries China has important and growing energy interests. In the Sudan, for example, China's state-run oil companies have been investing heavily in oil production and refining facilities since the late 1990s, and today China buys 50 percent of the country's output (Hill 2004). US oil companies have been prevented from investing in the Sudan since 1997 because of Khartoum's poor human rights record. Human rights groups have accused China of providing diplomatic support for Sudan at the United Nations in order to protect oil interests.

China's ties to Iran have also raised America's ire. As noted earlier, Iran has become an important energy supplier to China. The United States has discouraged other countries (including Japan) from investing in Iran's energy industry, and instead called on the international community to impose punitive sanctions on Tehran because of its alleged development of nuclear weapons. China has opposed a sanctions regime against Iran, preferring diplomacy. However, China has avoided rupturing relations with America over Iran by agreeing to discuss the issue at the United Nations. China's actions underscore the fact that in the hierarchy of foreign policy priorities, "great power diplomacy" trumps "energy diplomacy."

Energy security concerns have also led to other problems between China and the US. China's growing presence in South America has created some anxiety in the US that Beijing is attempting to challenge America's preeminent position in its own backyard (Thompson 2005). In terms of competition for energy resources, a troubling precursor of things to come might be the failed bid to purchase the US oil company Unocal Corp by state-owned China National Offshore Oil Corporation (CNOOC) in August 2005. After several months in the media spotlight, CNOOC dropped its bid in the face of sustained opposition from US lawmakers who objected to the sale on national security grounds.

China's bid for energy security has also engendered cooperation between the PRC and other countries. While Indian companies have lost out to their Chinese rivals in securing access to energy resources in countries such as Nigeria and Kazakhstan, energy companies from the two countries have actually joined forces in the Sudan and Syria. There is a growing realization in both Beijing and New Delhi that cooperation is more desirable than competition. As India's former Oil Minister Mani Shankar Aiyar stated in January 2006: "We must set the stage for India and China to cooperate where possible and compete where necessary, without any of this having any political, diplomatic, or military implications" (*Financial Express* 2006). In the same month, India and China signed a series of agreements designed to increase cooperation between their respective state-owned energy corporations (*International Herald Tribune* 2006).

Perhaps the most encouraging example to date is the March 2005 Joint Marine Seismic Undertaking (JMSU), signed between China, the Philippines, and Vietnam to explore for oil and gas in the disputed waters of the South China Sea.[2] One of the primary drivers of the JMSU was rising global oil prices, and the agreement suggests that energy security concerns have created the political will to shelve the sovereignty dispute and engage in joint exploitation. However, whether the JMSU is set to become a model for energy security cooperation in the Asia-Pacific region remains to be seen.

In sum, while energy security concerns have influenced China's foreign, defense, and national security policies, they have not transformed them. The PRC's number one priority will continue to be stability in the international system, a prerequisite for China's continued economic growth.

Conclusion

China's capitalist transition has resulted in the PRC's transformation from an energy exporting nation to a major energy consumer and importer. As a consequence, energy security issues have risen to the top of the Chinese government's agenda. The survival of the CCP depends in large part on its ability to sustain economic growth, which in turn rests on continued access to energy resources, both at home and abroad.

Domestically, the Chinese government has continued to promote reform of the country's energy markets and state energy firms. To manage China's growing dependence on imported oil, the government is actively pursuing alternative sources of energy generation, including nuclear power, hydroelectricity, and renewable energy resources. China is also looking to increase energy efficiency and conservation, two areas in which it lags behind the rest of the world. China's continued dependence on coal, though, will continue to pose major challenges for the country's environment, as well as the global community at large.

The impacts of energy security on China's international relations are multiple. China's energy import dependence has the potential to engender either greater cooperation or competition with other powers. For now, energy security has become one of the three core elements of Chinese foreign policy. Chinese leaders currently emphasize access to foreign energy resources, along with expanded trade and investment ties. As a result, China's interests are becoming increasingly global, albeit across a narrow range of concerns.

Energy security has also become an important factor in the PRC's national security and defense policies. Although Taiwan drives China's military modernization program, anxiety over the vulnerability of seaborne energy imports is focusing attention on the need to increase China's naval power, since a blue-water navy would enable China to secure its maritime trade routes. However, this will be a long-term process, and in the meantime China is studying means to reduce its vulnerabilities by trying to bypass maritime choke points.

It is important to bear in mind that energy security has not fundamentally altered China's foreign and defense policies. The central aim of Chinese foreign policy continues to be the maintenance of a stable international system. China may be competing for energy resources with other countries, but this competition is unlikely to lead to direct confrontation. Similarly, energy security concerns have not led the PRC to drastically increase its defense expenditure.

In the end, economic factors triggered by China's capitalist transition will continue to deepen China's energy import dependence, increasing the prominence of energy security in Chinese policy-making. Successfully assuring energy security, in turn, will depend in large part on whether China can manage its geopolitical environment and avoid confrontation over energy resources. It will also hinge on whether China's energy production and distribution system can be reformed to avoid ecological degradation and disasters.

While not all signs are clear, Chinese leaders' emphasis on energy security seems to be prodding some cooperative and even multilateral initiatives. One thing is for sure, China's rapidly deepening energy import dependence will integrate China further with the rest of the world. The process of assuring energy security will thus constitute a key force shaping the international ramifications of China's capitalist transition.

Notes

1 Primary commercial energy is defined as including coal, oil, natural gas, hydroelectricity, and nuclear power only.
2 For more details on the JMSU see Schofield and Storey (2005).

References

Asia Times (2005a) "Caspian Oil Exports Heading East," February 9. Online. Available HTTP: www.atimes.com/atimes/Central_Asia/GB09Ag02.html (accessed January 8, 2007).
——(2005b) "Japan and China Face Off Over Energy," July 2. Online. Available HTTP: www.atimes/com/atimes/Japan/GG02Dh01.html (accessed January 9, 2007).
BBC News (2005) "US Denies Plotting to Kill Chavez," February 22. Online. Available HTTP: news.bbc.co.uk/2/hi/americas/4289209.stm (accessed January 8, 2007).
——(2006) "Chinese President in Saudi Visit," April 22. Online. Available HTTP: news.bbc.co.uk/2/hi/middle_east/4935374.stm (accessed January 8, 2007).
Beng, P.K. (2004) "China Mulls Oil Pipelines in Myanmar, Thailand," *Asia Times*, September 22. Online. Available HTTP: www.atimes.com/atimes/Japan/GG02Dh01.html (accessed January 8, 2007).
Chen, X. (2003) "Nengyuan anquan yao zhongshi neibu yinsu, qiangdiao zhengce tizhi baozhang [Emphasis on Internal Factors and Policy Imperatives Needed for Energy Security]," *Zhongguo Nengyuan* [*Energy of China*], May 25: 4–14.
Cheong, C. (2004) "China Pipeline Plan to Secure Oil Supplies," *The Straits Times*, July 31.
Cole, B. (2006) "The PLA Navy's Developing Strategy," *China Brief*, 6(21), October 25: 4–6.
Economist (2003) "Your Pipe or Mine?" 368(8343), September 27: 40.

Financial Express (2006) "India, China Brotherhood On Oil?" January 10. Online. Available HTTP: www.financialexpress.com/latest_full_story.php?content_ id=113980 (accessed January 9, 2007).

Friedberg, A. (2006) "Going Out: China's Pursuit of Natural Resources and Implications for the PRC's Grand Strategy," *NBR Analysis*, 17(3).

Goldstein, L. and Murray, W. (2004) "China Emerges as a Maritime Power," *Jane's Intelligence Review*, October. Online. Available HTTP: www8.janes.com/Search/ documentView.do?docId=/content1/janesdata/mags/jir/history/jir2004/010708. htm@current&pageSelected=allJanes&keyword=%22China%20emerges%20 %22&backPath=http://search.janes.com/Search&Prod_Name=JIR& (login required; accessed January 8, 2007).

Hai, S. (2005) "Xiangjie jieneng zhongchangqi zhuanxiang guihua [Expert Elaboration on the Special Mid- and Long-Term Energy Conservation Program]," *Guoji shiyou jingji* [*International Petroleum Economics*], February: 17–21.

Hill, J. (2004) "China Covets African Oil and Trade," *Jane's Intelligence Review*, November. Online. Available HTTP: www8.janes.com/Search/documentView. do?docId=/content1/janesdata/mags/jir/history/jir2004/jir01078.htm@current &pageSelected=allJanes&keyword=%22China%20covets%20African%20 oil%20and%20trade%22&backPath=http://search.janes.com/Search&Prod_ Name=JIR& (log in required; accessed January 8, 2007).

International Herald Tribune (2006) "China and India: Bidding Partners, At Least on Paper," January 20. Online. Available HTTP: www.iht.com/articles/2006/01/20/ business.oil.php (accessed January 25, 2006).

Japan Times (2005) "China to Get Oil Before Japan: Russian Envoy," May 20, p. 32.

Liu, X. (2006) "China's Energy Security and its Grand Strategy," *Policy Analysis Brief*, The Stanley Foundation.

Moscow Times (2005) "Japanese Told China to Get Pipeline First," April 21, p. A7.

Nation (2005) "Energy Land Bridge: Beijing's Interest 'On the Wane'," February 14. Online. Available HTTP: www.nationmultimedia.com/search/page.arcview. php?clid=6&id=112092&usrsess (accessed January 9, 2007).

People's Daily (2004a) "Section of Sino-Kazak Oil Pipeline Breaks Ground in Kazakhstan," September 29. Online. Available HTTP: english.people.com. cn/200409/29/eng20040929_158673.html (accessed January 25, 2006).

——(2004b) "China-Japan Oil Race Inevitable," October 28. Online. Available HTTP: english.people.com.cn/200410/28/eng20041028_161984.html (accessed January 9, 2007).

Qin, X. (2004) "Zhongguo nengyuan anquan zhanluezhong de nengyuan yunshu wenti [China's Energy Security Strategies: The Issue of Transportation]," *Zhongguo Nengyuan* [*Energy of China*], 26: 4–7.

Quek, T. (2006) "China Will Be Worst Carbon Emitter," *The Straits Times*, November 11.

Schofield, C. and Storey, I. (2005) "Energy Security and Southeast Asia: The Impact on Maritime Boundary and Territorial Disputes," *Harvard Asia Quarterly*, Fall: 36–46.

Storey, I. (2006) "China's Malacca Dilemma," *China Brief*, 6(8): 4–6.

Tang, J. (2006) "With the Grain or Against the Grain? Energy Security and Chinese Foreign Policy in the Hu Jintao Era," *The Brookings Institute Analysis and Commentary*, October.

Thompson, D. (2004) "Economic Growth and Soft Power: China's Africa Strategy," *China Brief*, 4(24): 3–6.

——(2005) "China's Global Strategy for Energy, Security, and Diplomacy," *China Brief*, 5(7): 1–3.

Wall Street Journal (2004) "China and Iran Near Agreement on Huge Oil Pact," November 1, p. A3.

Washington Post (2004) "Iran's New Alliance with China Could Cost US Leverage," November 17, p. A21.

Washington Times (2005) "China Builds Up Strategic Sea Lanes," January 18. Online. Available HTTP: www.washtimes.com/national/20050117-115550-1929r. htm (accessed January 9, 2007).

Wen Wei Po (2004) "Hu Jintao Concerned Over Malacca Strait Factor in PRC Oil," Foreign Broadcasting Information Service Translation, January 14.

Wu, K. (2001) *China's National Energy Policies for Oil and Gas Under the Tenth Five-Year Plan*, prepared for the United States Department of Energy, Office of Natural Gas and Oil Import and Export Activities.

Wu, K. and Fesharaki, F. (2005a) "Higher Natural Gas Demand Has China Looking Worldwide," *Oil and Gas Journal*, 103(27): 50–57.

——(2005b) "As Oil Demand Surges, China Adds and Expands Refineries," *Oil and Gas Journal*, 103(28): 20–24.

Xu, Y. and Yang Y. (2004) "Zhongguo shiyou anquan zhanlue gouxiang [Strategic Framework for China's Petroleum Security]," *Zhongguo Nengyuan [Energy of China]*, 26: 4–11.

Xuan, N. (2004) "Woguo nengxiao wenti fenxi [An Analysis of China's Energy Efficiency Problems]," *Zhongguo Nengyuan [Energy of China]*, 26: 4–8.

Yan, C. and Zhao, Z. (2003) *Zhongguo nengyuan fazhan baogao 2003 [China's Energy Development Report 2003]*, Beijing: China Metrology Press.

Zhang, Z. (2002) "National Energy Security Strategies," in L. Chen (ed.) *Report on Issues of China's National Strategies*, Beijing: China Social Sciences Press, pp. 395–415.

Zhongguo Qingnian Bao (China Youth Daily) (2004) "China's Malacca Straits Dilemma," Foreign Broadcasting Information Service Translation, January 15.

11 The impact of China's capitalist transition on foreign policy

Yinhong Shi

China's enormous contemporary transformation

Since Deng Xiaoping launched China's economic reform policy in 1978, enormous changes have occurred in this huge country. This has been especially the case since Deng's famous inspection tour of Southern China (*nan xun*) in 1992, which led to a sustained soaring of the Chinese economy and a reformist social orientation. Most recently, the enormous transformations taking place in China have garnered quite intensive attention almost all over the world, above all among China's Asian neighbors and the advanced industrial countries of the West. Increased attention has resulted in many predictions and discussions about China's ascent to the status of a future world power. Implications have been outlined for the regional and global political economy, the prospects for American preponderance in the world's power structure, and the future of peace and prosperity, especially relations among the actual and potential great powers of the future.[1] These predictions have almost overshadowed previous predictions and discussions regarding the same topic.[2]

Among the enormous changes occurring in China, the one that results in the richest imaginations is undoubtedly the dramatic increase of China's economic strength. For every year in more than a decade China's GDP growth has been sustained at a rapid rate, first doubling and then redoubling the size of China's economy. Concurrently, China experienced a dramatic expansion of foreign trade, a leap-forward in its productive capacity, and increased influence on global commercial relationships, especially the supply of raw materials and energy. Closely connected with this economic ascent have been other developments that have received widespread global attention: the huge expansion of the Chinese private sector in the national economic structure; the replacement of a planned economy by market forces in most sectors; the new reality of expanding "economic liberty" never seen before in the history of the People's Republic of China (PRC); and related changes in popular social values and fundamental social relations. While the political operations of the party-state on all levels have experienced more limited change, reforms have nonetheless led to remarkable transformations. China's economic juggernaut has also exhibited many dark undersides, such as mounting developmental gaps, economic divisions, social injustices, and environmental degradation.[3]

The concept of "China's capitalist transition" and its relevance to China's foreign policy

All the major changes detailed above pose a major question: how to "devise" in an appropriate way a parsimonious "paradigm" for expounding China's contemporary changes and future orientation? Speaking more concretely, how to define the most fundamental nature of the monumental changes occurring in China in both a sufficiently comprehensive and reflective way? And how then to render this concept relevant to elaborating an understanding of fundamental social, political, and economic trends shaping China's future?

The "China's capitalist transition" project initiated by Dr Christopher A. McNally at the East-West Center attempts to make an innovative and valuable contribution to providing answers to these, indeed, very difficult questions. As outlined in the introduction to this volume, the critical political economy concept of a capitalist transition involves an effort to capture the basic dynamics of China's international ascent and recognize them as driven by the forces associated with the rise of Great Britain, the United States, Germany, and Japan to international prominence. Accordingly, China is in the midst of a capitalist transition because state institutions provide more and more support to market institutions and private ownership, creating a dynamic in which the government interacts with markets and private firms to support wealth accumulation by private individuals and institutions. The result is the empowerment of domestic and international private capital to an extent not seen before in the PRC, in turn conditioning the *modus operandi* of the Chinese party-state.

Manifestations of China's capitalist transition include the expansion of market forces; the growth of private capital; the emergence of a more open and pluralistic polity; the creation of new social forces and diverse cultural and ideational expressions; and the massive international integration of China's economy.

While the capitalist transition concept captures quite comprehensively the internal dynamics of China's transformation, we must inquire further as to where its relevance lies when discussing China's evolving foreign policy. First and foremost, it has to be recognized that domestic social conditions and dynamics are among the most important factors influencing a country's foreign policy. Few theorists on international relations or scholars on foreign policy would deny this sound proposition.

China's transition undoubtedly has produced or is producing various new social forces and conditions which can influence China's foreign policy directly or (much more often) indirectly. For instance, the fact that

China's economy has gradually outgrown state ownership and moved to a mixed economic model in which the most dynamic part is powered by private capital (both domestic and international) should be expected to have certain effects on China's foreign policy. Similarly, China's emergence as a major global economic player is shaping the foreign policy tools at the disposal of Chinese policy makers.

Therefore, a perspective focusing on China's capitalist transition should be of relevance to China's evolving foreign policy orientation. This is especially so since the concept stresses international causes and contents, making it relevant for understanding China's contemporary foreign policy. In fact, rising international trade and financial flows across China's borders allow global economic events to directly influence China's domestic political economy. More attention in the making of China's foreign policy is therefore paid to the nature and logic of international economic events.

Certain problems, though, remain with applying this concept. First, despite the fact that the primary social dynamics in China since 1978 can be conceived as being part and parcel of a capitalist transition, Chinese leaders from Deng Xiaoping to Hu Jintao would definitely refuse to accept this concept. This is for reasons greater than pragmatic political considerations.

Second, the concept of a capitalist transition focuses on the strengthening of "new social forces" in an environment of a market economy. This implies an emphasis upon the creation and expansion of a middle class, ideally accompanied by the development of a civil society. However, because of the relative separation between foreign policy and domestic society in China, the connections and interpenetrations of foreign and domestic policy are less prominent in China than in Western capitalist countries.[4] Up to now social changes and their societal agents have rarely influenced the making of China's foreign policy directly, except maybe in a limited range of foreign economic policies.[5] The international power structure and interactions with external forces still carry more weight.

Put differently, the degree of power centralization and "authoritarianism" in China's foreign policy-making and foreign policy implementation is generally still very high. This renders domestic changes relatively less influential. Just like domestic high politics, foreign policy decisions in China are not dominated by social forces, but rather remain under the purview of the closely knit leadership of the Chinese Communist Party (CCP).

A final point of caution with regard to applying the concept of a capitalist transition to discussions on China's foreign policy must be noted. The concept of a capitalist transition implies that the forces of social "liberalization" and "pluralism," as well as the development of civil society will unfold in China. Taking this implication at face value underestimates or even neglects those elements that might undermine prospects of "liberalization" and the growth of sociopolitical pluralism in China. I will come back to this point in the last sections of this chapter. For now, I would like to caution against an overly optimistic evaluation of China's prospects for political liberalization. An excessive focus on the concept of a capitalist transition, whose primary content is *economics*, can lead the observer to pay insufficient attention to the fundamental *political* nature of the Chinese state. Similarly, a focus on China's capitalist transition and its effects upon foreign policy-making might lead one to be unable to fully sense and understand the great complexities and inherent contradictions embedded in China's future orientation.

The "primacy of the economy" and China's increasing absorption into the world capitalist system

Evidently, the concept of a capitalist transition is quite pertinent for understanding in a theoretically systematic way the economic and social conditions in contemporary China, including the general repercussions of these conditions in China's polity. However, due to the limitations noted above in applying this concept, I will suggest an alternative or complementary perspective for discussing the particular subfield of China's foreign policy. This corresponding perspective builds on the concepts of "primacy of the economy" (or primacy of economic development based on the expansion and deepening of market forces) and China's increasing absorption into the world capitalist system.

These concepts are closely related to the concept of China's capitalist transition but still somewhat different. Using them will allow me to make accurate and less disputable observations while undertaking a not-so-theoretical analysis of China's evolving foreign policy orientation.

Following this modified approach within the framework of China's capitalist transition project, the essential questions are: in comparison with the prior era, what new characteristics are emerging in China's foreign policy? In fact, when taking the primacy of the economy and China's increasing absorption into the world capitalist system as background, what are the major trends shaping China's contemporary external orientation? These questions can be tackled on three analytical levels: first, the fundamental objectives of China's foreign policy; second, the making of China's foreign policy; and third, the instruments of China's foreign policy.[6]

After analyzing the evolution of China's foreign policy along these three analytical levels, I will in the final parts of this chapter emphasize the limits to change in China's foreign policy. Specifically, I will sound a note of caution concerning well-intentioned simplifications and exaggerations about the present and future of China's foreign orientation and, more generally, East Asia's international relations.

Fundamental objectives of China's contemporary foreign policy

The first major development that should be emphasized when discussing China's contemporary foreign policy is the remarkable degree of "economization" that has taken place over the past decade. Policies directly aimed at assuring China's economic security and development have emerged as one of the primary drivers of China's foreign policy orientation. Traditional national security objectives have therefore been permeated by a motivation of a fundamentally economic nature: to forge an enduring "peaceful international environment" that supports China's economic development. In tandem, traditional diplomatic objectives have attained a vital economic motivation, that is, to promote the import of foreign capital and technology, and the export of Chinese goods.[7]

The permeation of China's foreign policy by fundamentally economic objectives is closely connected with China's increasing involvement in the world capitalist system, a kind of connection between economic objective and economic effect. China's international identity has changed from being a "nation outside of the system" to "a nation within the system." The country has therefore moved from being against the international status quo to largely endorsing and even in many aspects committing to maintain the international status quo. Although there have been complexities, restraints, and ambiguities, the primary inclination is relatively clear.[8] In this sense, the transition unfolding in China is triggering a new era of diplomacy. Since China needs to retain a peaceful environment for socioeconomic development, Chinese foreign policy has taken an accommodating stance toward the regional power structure, especially the United States. China benefits from the present global economic system and therefore the status quo is increasingly in its interest.

During President Jiang Zemin's state visit to the United States in 1997 he and President Clinton reached an agreement (however rhetorical it was) to build up the China-US "constructive strategic partnership." This was despite the almost perennial vicissitudes of Sino-American relations. This agreement was then incorporated into nearly all public statements by the Chinese government, attaining the status of something like China's declared foreign policy program.[9] Underlying this agreement was the idea of *daguo waijiao* (great power diplomacy), a term or concept often used by Chinese and foreign scholars to describe the major objectives of Chinese foreign policy after that state visit.

Intriguingly, *daguo waijiao* is almost never used in official Chinese public documents, unlike the term *daguo guanxi* (relations with the great powers) or *yu fada guojia de guanxi* (relations with the advanced industrial countries). This is because the traditional doctrine of the PRC's foreign policy emphasized relations with developing countries. Consequently, there were misgivings in party circles of emphasizing *daguo waijiao* in official documents. However, by the late 1990s the Chinese government recognized more and more clearly that it had become imperative for China to conduct a strategy based on *daguo waijiao* with *daguo guanxi* as a first priority (Ye 2000; Zhang 2003).

There has naturally been a close connection between emphasizing great power diplomacy and China's increasing absorption into the world capitalist system. For instance, the establishment of institutionalized bilateral and multilateral economic arrangements with the biggest capitalist nation, the United States, has emerged as an increasingly weighty concern in China's diplomacy. Similarly, China's diplomacy toward major European powers (including the European Union) and, indeed, with the whole international capitalist system is motivated by economic priorities. Participation in international economic institutions has thus become a major foreign policy objective. And as great power diplomacy emerged as a new priority under China's deepening involvement in the capitalist international order, a politico-strategic "spill-over" effect transpired: economic priorities have promoted to a considerable degree China's eagerness to participate in established international security and political regimes.

China's increased dependence on external economic developments in the world capitalist system has produced strong restraints on the conduct and objectives of China's foreign policy. The result has been increased moderation and prudence due to considerations of vital economic security. This focus manifests itself repeatedly in China's conduct of foreign policy with the United States. It also constrains and influences China's policy objectives and actions *vis-à-vis* Southeast Asia, the Republic of Korea, and sometimes even Japan (Boyd 2004; Brooke 2004; Kynge and McGregor 2003; Li 2005; McGregor 2005).

The emergence of these constraints on Chinese foreign policy has led some Western observers to reach a simplified and excessively optimistic assessment of China's future external orientation.[10] Yet, economic priorities have had limited effects upon China's behavior in, for instance, the issue areas of Taiwan, Hong Kong, human rights, as well as arms control and non-proliferation. Traditional security objectives and an emphasis on national sovereignty continue to pose a considerable influence on China's external posture and therefore are worthy of serious consideration and analysis.

The making of China's contemporary foreign policy

To analyze and provide a general interpretation for how foreign policy-making has evolved in China, it is useful to start with the new and primary influence played by conceptions of the primacy of the economy and China's increasing absorption into the world capitalist system. I will start with the top level of foreign policy-making, especially several new characteristics found among China's contemporary leadership.

Despite profound changes in many other aspects of Chinese policy-making, top leaders still play an overwhelmingly decisive role in foreign policy-making, handling most major issues. The first remarkable development among top leaders is their new ideology. China's "traditional" ideology, which heavily influenced China's foreign policy orientation, consists of three basic components: (1) the traditional communist ideology, especially the Marxist-Leninist-Maoist perspective that shaped fundamental beliefs regarding the nature and logic of international relations; (2) Chinese patriotism or Chinese modern radical nationalism; and (3) the perspective of *realpolitik* or political realism in handling international politics and foreign policy. This last element is of course far from being unique to the Chinese or communists.

Over the past decade, a quite remarkable new component has been added to this set of ideological beliefs. This component could be called a "new internationalism," containing elements of "liberal internationalism" in its outlook and expressing the general context of China's increasing globalization and involvement in the world capitalist system. Although beliefs characterized by this new internationalism are still limited, they are developing rather rapidly. Naturally, the development of these new beliefs is not without some vicissitudes.

The new internationalism is characterized by a focus on multilateral cooperation, involvement in international organizations and regimes, and transnational nonpolitical communications. This focus is for both the inherent value attached to these engagements and their contributions in promoting China's national interests. In particular, much of the once hotly propagated and elaborated *xin anquan guan* (New Security Outlook) declared by President Jiang Zemin, which the Chinese government continues to advocate after his retirement, can be identified with this new internationalism (*People's Daily* 2002, 2004b). This is in addition to the much publicized and discussed *duobian waijiao* and *duobian zhuyi* (multilateral diplomacy and multilateralism).[11]

In addition, the general intensity of Chinese nationalism held by China's top leaders has been gradually reduced since Deng Xiaoping. This is with the clear exception of the Taiwan issue and the integrity of China's major frontier territories. Driven to a large degree by the primacy of the economy and China's increasing involvement in the world capitalist system, the resulting mitigated nationalism can be defined as "pragmatic nationalism."[12]

Similar conditions and influences have further created and strengthened some new contents in the *realpolitik* or realist ideology of China's contemporary leadership. "Economization" and "international socialization" have shaped to some degree their conceptions of national interest. China's national interests are now seen as partially merging or assimilating with the common interests of international society.

Memory moves people, more or even much more so than ideology. Put differently, the memories or historical experiences of China's top leaders, especially the lasting historical "lessons" learned during their formative years, are extremely important in shaping their fundamental policy outlooks and strategies. This point cannot be emphasized too much. Chinese contemporary leaders including Deng Xiaoping went through three extremely dramatic historical events, each of which shaped their perspectives as top leaders. These are: the Cultural Revolution; the initial period of reform following that turmoil; and the Tiananmen Event of June 1989. The prior two heavily influenced Deng Xiaoping; the latter Jiang Zemin and Hu Jintao.

The lessons learnt from the Cultural Revolution's huge disaster in combination with the very inspiring results generated by China's initial reform and opening up directly shaped Deng Xiaoping's essential belief in the primacy of the economy, thus launching China's process of absorption into the world capitalist system. For Jiang Zemin and Hu Jintao, the vital "regime-saving" effect of economic performance during the critical years after 1989 was equally influential. It strengthened their belief in the beneficial sides of market-oriented reforms and involvement in the global system of trade and finance, therefore prodding them to continue China's capitalist transition in the economic realm. This was despite "antiliberalization" measures taken after the Tiananmen Event in the political realm.[13]

In addition to these important domestic experiences, the historical memories of China's top leaders in international affairs are also important factors shaping their making of foreign policy. These international events include China's evolving relations with the United States, the country's participation in economic globalization, and increased involvement in international regimes. Evidently, these experiences are compatible with the central themes mentioned above and have produced primarily positive feedback loops, prodding China's increasingly moderate and responsible engagement with international society.

Besides directly influencing the thinking of central leaders, more than two decades of the primacy of the economy and increasing absorption into the world capitalist system have brought about fundamental transformations in China's system of government, including the mechanisms for foreign policy-making and implementation. Following enormous economic and social changes generated by China's transition, the task of managing domestic and international affairs has become ever more complex. As a result, governmental branches and institutions have multiplied, which in turn has had a decentralizing influence upon policy-making, including foreign policy-making. China never has had such a large bureaucratic system as the one that now exists. As it continues to expand, inefficiency, confusion, competition among various institutional self-interests, and all other phenomena of "big government" are natural results.

Among the prominent conflicts of interests caused by the multiplication of governmental branches, several are especially noteworthy. These include among others: civilian leaders who are chiefly concerned with national economic management and issues of domestic stability versus the Chinese military establishment; diplomatic branches who are strongly inclined to favor an expansion of China's engagement in international life versus the military branches; diplomatic branches versus branches managing economic affairs, triggered by the latter's increasing size and influence in foreign policy-making; and competition among the insufficiently differentiated branches of the various national intelligence systems which lack centralized control.

Closely connected with the above problems is the issue of establishing an effective mechanism for coordinating and centrally controlling foreign policy-making. Indeed, the capacity for centralized control over the overall policy-making/implementation process on noncrisis issues has been gradually declining since Deng Xiaoping. As an example, the establishment of a "National Security Council" to effectively coordinate national security policy has been a protracted process without any result.

One of the new variables influencing foreign policy-making in China is the rapid expansion of semiofficial and unofficial mass media, providing new avenues for the reflection of public opinion. The emergence of these new forces influencing foreign policy-making are closely related to China's capitalist transition, being generated by several of its component dynamics, such as the expansion of markets, the emergence of new social forces, and the growth of diverse cultural and ideational expressions. In other words, the dramatic development of market forces and the private economy, which in turn is generating social diversification, has led to a multiplication of semiofficial and unofficial mass media with rapidly growing influence.

Several major issues are pertinent regarding the expansion of mass media outlets and their reflection of public opinion. To begin with, it must be stressed that the influence of semiofficial and unofficial mass media conveying public opinions is increasing at quite a rapid pace. But then, what reflects official opinion? In China today, only very few media directly managed by the central government and provincial party branches can be regarded as reflecting purely official opinion. All others are semiofficial or nonofficial in nature.

With regard to foreign policy, semiofficial and unofficial media generally exhibit two types of influence. First, their editorial lines and policy proposals conform to the Chinese government's intentions and policy directions. Second, in some cases they advocate ideas that indirectly oppose central government policies due to both commercial and nationalistic motivations.

Why would semiofficial and unofficial media dare to indirectly oppose the government's foreign policies? The answer is that there are two distinct motivations. On one hand, media outlets want to earn money by selling as many newspapers and magazines as possible, thus increasing their profitability. Commercial considerations thus seriously affect their editorial policy. On the other hand, popular nationalism among both journalists and the general public has become a driving force for advocating policies different from those of the central government. In many cases, these two motivations are joined.

Can we speak of true public opinion under China's current political system? Although China's system is quite different from democratic systems, some form of mass politics already exists. As a result, the influence of public opinion on Chinese foreign policy-making is growing rather remarkably if compared to the past. Put differently, despite the fact that China is not a democracy, Chinese government leaders cannot neglect public opinion. For example, their understanding of public opinion concerning political issues is almost surely no less than that of their American counterparts. The degree to which and the manner in which individual Chinese leaders respond to public opinion, though, differs. Deng Xiaoping probably didn't care much about public opinion. The leadership headed by Jiang Zemin and Zhu Rongji that followed Deng and was in charge before the 16th Party Congress of the CCP cared already much more about public opinion. China's current leaders certainly care and worry about public opinion very much with varying results. Different political leaders also possess different instincts when treating and responding to public opinion. The Chinese leadership has therefore gradually become more responsive to expressions of public opinion, but depending on the political talent and character of individual leaders, there remain differences in how they strategically respond to and attempt to guide public opinion.

Here is a recent case to illustrate the dynamics discussed in the above paragraphs. After the Japanese Government took unilateral actions on Sino-Japanese political and strategic disputes, and in view of the frustrations over Japan's negative responses toward several limited initiatives by the Chinese government attempting to improve the bilateral relationship, China's leaders took an unprecedented permissive attitude toward China's media. Frequent and emotion-charged reports disparaging Japan, largely focused on Japan's nationalist tendencies and hard line behavior toward China, were permitted for weeks and months. This in fact partially transferred foreign policy-making *vis-à-vis* Japan to the increasingly agitated anti-Japanese Chinese public. The room of freedom for policy-making on the part of the Chinese government became restricted and belated efforts to partially control media reports on Japan proved insufficiently effective in calming public sentiments. Concurrently, historical grievances emerged as the primary issue shaping Sino-Japanese relations, which by their nature dictate an escalating hard line posture toward Japan. Action-reaction cycles started to operate at almost full force gaining self-strengthening momentum. The four issue areas shaping Sino-Japanese relations – growing economic interdependence; the day-to-day business of diplomatic relations; historical disputes; and the increasing strategic rivalry between China and Japan – melded into a somewhat confused whole, making a level-headed approach to this complicated and dynamic bilateral relationship almost impossible.

New instruments of China's foreign policy

As China became increasingly absorbed into the world capitalist system and developed its economy, new foreign policy tools, such as new avenues of economic and diplomatic cooperation emerged. However, not only cooperative economic and diplomatic resources were added. New tools of economic pressure and even punishment transpired for China's foreign policy makers, some of which began to be employed symbolically and temporarily over the Taiwan issue in mid-2004.[14] The foundation of these new instruments is China's heavier economic weight, greater degree of economic interdependence, and expanded channels for asserting economic influence.

In recent years, the prominence of economic diplomacy in China's foreign policy has increased at a dramatic pace.[15] Previously, the most remarkable cases were confined to relations with the United States. These included the huge and repeated government-sponsored commercial purchases of industrial equipment and civilian airplanes from US companies, mainly to attain major political and strategic objectives. Related to these developments has been the forming of a loose "China Lobby" by US corporations, especially by those with massive investment and trade relations with China. On occasion, China has been able to exploit this loose "China Lobby." With respect to Europe a similar form of economic diplomacy emerged. Another important case is the uniquely structured economic relationship with Russia, the predominant contents of which are the purchase and sale of advanced weaponry from Russia to China. This relationship has been of extraordinary strategic significance to China (Cody 2005a; Shi 2002b; and Sutter 2001).

Related to the special relationship with Russia is the emergence of China's military capability as another plank among China's strengthened instruments of foreign policy. Although the causal relationship is indirect, the strengthening of China's military capability is part and parcel of China's monumental economic transition. Improved military capabilities are making growing contributions to China's rise as a genuine great power, although its current employment is very limited. The one notable exception is how China's military capability acts as a credible deterrent against Taiwanese *de jure* independence.

In recent years, China's military build-up has been regarded as a priority on China's national agenda. In fact, almost all strategists in China see the strengthening of military capabilities as absolutely necessary, especially when considering the low capabilities China possessed over the previous two decades and China's expanding external security concerns. One upshot of this situation is the rising influence, both directly and indirectly, of the People's Liberation Army (PLA) over the distribution of national resources and foreign policy-making. This trend is likely to continue, although up until now the PLA as a representative of national interest and as an interest group with its particular ideational inclination, institutional culture, and financial demands has been effectively restrained and controlled by the civilian political leadership.

When assessing the future of China's military capability, every reasonable observer will agree with the following factual description: "The highest estimates of the annual Chinese defense budget are less than a quarter of the Pentagon's budget of more than $400 billion. Even so, the fast-growing Chinese economy and the country's rapid industrialization are giving Beijing previously unimaginable financial and technical resources to improve its armed forces" (Dickie *et al.* 2005). Nonetheless, the concern of US government officials at the highest level has increased dramatically (Sammon and Gertz 2005; Schmitt 2005). This indicates that at the distant horizon of the Sino-American strategic relationship storm clouds are gathering.

Finally, I would like to point out a fact that relates back to China's economic diplomacy. China's increasing absorption into the world capitalist system has generated an expanding need to focus economic diplomacy on the search for secure energy supplies. Triggered by the process of rapid economic growth, a strong sense of something like "energy obsession" has emerged in China in recent years (Bajpaee 2005; Howell 2005; Lam 2004). Accompanying this is a growing awareness of the probability of increased tensions in China's relations with some of its neighbors.

Reflecting this situation is, first, the competition over a Russian oil pipeline between China and Japan, including negative influences on Sino-Japanese and Sino-Russian relations; second, deteriorating and probably dangerous disputes between China and Japan over oil and gas deposits under the East China Sea and, related to this, disputes over the Diaoyudao (Senkaku in Japanese) Islands; and third and most significant in the long term, increasing US nervousness about China's worldwide search for energy, which carries with it broad negative strategic imaginations. The political firestorm that erupted over the attempted takeover of the US energy firm Unocal by the Chinese conglomerate China National Offshore Oil Corporation (CNOOC) in 2005 certainly indicates this. In fact, China's increasing "energy obsession" has generated appeals in some Chinese mass media to create a blue-water navy to protect vital sea lanes.

Concluding remarks: analytical limitations and prospects for China's external orientation

As mentioned at the end of section two, taking the concept of a capitalist transition with implications of social "liberalization," "pluralism," and the development of "civil society" as a means to analyze Chinese foreign policy is apt to underestimate some dynamics and potentialities. In particular, such an approach could miscalculate the degree to which China will become a liberal, moderate, or "internationalized" society and therefore lead to faulty conclusions concerning China's future foreign policy orientation, a miscalculation already prominent among some in the Western world.

To begin with, the fundamental assumption of most liberal theories that a free market economy has an overwhelming capacity to construct a liberal political state with a liberal internationalist foreign policy is far from wholly convincing. This is not much unlike the assumptions held by the realist school of international relations, which denies or seriously underestimates this kind of capacity. History has demonstrated repeatedly that, due to the nature of human social life, fundamental political forces possess a degree of independence and often produce dominant effects. This is especially the case in the arena of interstate relations and national foreign policy which tend to be influenced by both structural elements, such as the nature of geopolitics and the balance of power, and collective psychological factors, such as nationalist feelings and stereotyped mass perceptions. China will be no exception in this respect. The country's distinct political, cultural, and historical attributes make the outcome of its transition indeterminate.

It is easy to find close connections between the limitations of China's domestic political transition and the limitations of her foreign policy transition. However, this absolutely does not mean that the transitions and changes already taking place in these fields are not substantial. Stated differently, certain conditions and developments have to be taken into account when one tries to think about the prospects of China's foreign policy orientation. These are in addition to the belief in the primacy of the economy and China's increasing absorption into the world capitalist system that I have elaborated on in previous parts of this chapter.

First, China has experienced a rather rapid growth of popular nationalism, which has increasingly affected the making and implementation of foreign policy. We must view in this context the much greater need perceived by Chinese leaders to generate a succession of foreign policy achievements in order to gain the Chinese public's endorsement and support. Ideally, these achievements should be seen by the Chinese public as promoting the nation's greatness without incurring outlandish costs.

Second, as many Chinese scholars are prone to remark, the long-term "structural contradiction" or "structurally determined" strategic rivalry between the United States and China could lead to a future potential confrontation or even conflict. As already referred to in the last section, the storm clouds gathering on the horizon of the Sino-American strategic relationship could very well put a halt to China's gradual and increasing internationalization.

Third, the political and strategic antagonism between China and Japan, which has intensified dramatically in recent years, could end up having the same effect as the growing strategic rivalry with the United States. Indeed, the rivalry with Japan besides being "structurally determined" by big power dynamics also contains strong and seemingly irreconcilable psychological forces.

Fourth, there exist several major uncertainties in East Asia's international environment, all of which could adversely affect present trends in China's foreign policy orientation. These include the future of the Korean Peninsula; the future of Japan's role in Asia, especially as an assertive political and even military power; and the proliferation of weapons of mass destruction and their delivery systems.

Finally, the single most important "structural" change in the Asia Pacific region which will affect China in the predictable future is China's own international rise. Everyone knows that the surprisingly rapid pace of this rise is a consequence of the fundamental transition unfolding in China's political economy, whether one defines it as capitalist or not. At the same time, almost no one is really certain of its future repercussions and consequences, especially in consideration of the uncertainties surrounding China's continued military build-up.

Quite plainly, China's external environment could be severely complicated by the country's own continued development. Due to the basic nature of international politics, which since Thucydides has been characterized as basically anarchical in nature, China's dramatic increase of economic strength, diplomatic influence, and military prowess is likely to bring corresponding worries by its neighbors. Especially the United States and Japan are likely to feel strategically "threatened." Even if one supposes that all actors in the international system have their best possible intentions at heart, an assumption far different from the normal state of affairs, China's unrelenting rise will complicate the international political environment and thus create uncertainties over the prospects for sustaining China's development.

China's international ascent is also producing certain domestic ramifications. A new prevailing consciousness is emerging among the Chinese populace, which will constitute one of the most significant developments affecting the future of China's foreign policy orientation (Shi 2005b). First and foremost, Chinese public opinion has discovered almost suddenly that very rapid and sustained economic growth has allowed China to garner huge economic strength. This strength can now be used as a major strategic instrument of national power and be applied, in addition to diplomacy, as the most practical instrument of Chinese foreign policy.

Second, Chinese public opinion has again almost suddenly realized that there is a need for an active outward-oriented foreign policy. Specifically, such a policy is needed to secure the supply of required external resources and access to foreign markets. It is also needed to maintain related political influence abroad, in turn promoting China's domestic economic development and contributing to the management of certain domestic economic and social tensions. Associated with this realization is the rather sudden sense among Chinese leaders and the public that the country needs to develop policies to assure its energy security. Indeed, judging from recent press reports some Chinese mass media is afflicted with a kind of "energy obsession." These concerns about energy security are leading to a stronger sense that China needs to increase its sea power.

Third, following the lead of many Chinese scholars, the Chinese public has also come to the conclusion that there is a long-term potential for strategic rivalry between the United States and China. This is in large part due to developments concerning the Taiwan issue in 2004, which caused for the first time an unambiguous domestic realization that there might be a military conflict or limited war in the future with the United States.

Fourth, Chinese public opinion in late 2004 and early 2005 swiftly stumbled on a huge and dangerous "Japan Problem." As a result, a new and complex image of Japan is being established among the Chinese public. Japan is both perceived as a rising and declining power. In political and even military terms Japan is seen as becoming more assertive and threatening, while economically and demographically it is seen as a declining nation, especially when compared to China. Traditional hatred is fused with these images, leading to a perception that China in the future must and can overwhelm Japan (Shi 2005a).

Finally, another relatively new change is emerging which will have both profound domestic and international consequences. Quite a significant part of Chinese elite opinion seems to have developed a greater sense of urgency for external problems than for continuing domestic reform. On the part of many, the idea of "influencing the world by reforming ourselves," which during the Deng era virtually represented a consensus among China's foreign policy elite, seems to be retiring quietly from the mind. This serious recent development, as all the other changes described in this section, may sound somewhat inauspicious for the sustained unfolding of China's capitalist transition.

Notes

1 For different perspectives shaping these discussions, see, among others, Hoge (2004); Johnson (2005); Marcois and Miller (2005); Perlez (2004b); Shaplen and Laney (2005); and the special issue of *Foreign Policy - China Rising: How the Asian Colossus Is Changing Our World*, especially the contribution by Brzezinski and Mearsheimer (2005).
2 For a few influential books originally discussing China's rise see Swaine and Tellis (2000); Bernstein and Munro (1997); and Brown (1995).
3 I have described and analyzed most of these societal and political transformations in Shi (2004). See also the contributions in Marsh and Dreyer (2003); Gilboy and Heginbotham (2004); and for social injustice Pei (2002).
4 This kind of separation is almost taken for granted as a major assumption in the realist school of international relations. It is also implied, though to a much lesser degree, in various liberal or rationalist theories. See Wight (1991).
5 As with in so many things concerning China's foreign policy-making, empirical evidence for this point is difficult to pinpoint. Moreover, if detected by a Chinese scholar in China, it would be difficult to publish. I will here chiefly employ an impressionist approach using the analytical self-confidence of an experienced professional observer of China's foreign policy residing in China to generate a hopefully reliable and sometimes penetrating account.
6 These three levels constitute the typical or standard framework of foreign policy analysis. See Holsti (1977: parts 3 and 4).
7 The most authoritative and important contributions in Chinese supporting these points are, of course, the numerous statements on China's foreign policy by Deng Xiaoping. See Deng (1983, 1993, and 2000).

8 For the complexities, restraints, and ambiguities mentioned here see Wu (2004); Zhao (2004a); and Shi (2002a).
9 These statements include mainly "reports" and speeches by China's top leaders on major occasions, such as the CCP Congress, National People's Congress, and high-level national celebrations.
10 See *New York Times* (2003). A more balanced point of view is expressed by Cheow (2003).
11 For discussions by Chinese scholars of these issues see Wang (2001) and Su (2005). For a discussion outside of China on this topic, see Kuik (2005).
12 The characteristics and differences of this mitigated nationalism compared to other principal forms of Chinese nationalism are analyzed by Zhao (2003, 2004b).
13 Another factor influencing leadership perceptions was that due to China's increasing international economic importance it could to some extent withstand the Western economic and diplomatic sanctions imposed after June 4, 1989. This perspective is having a lasting effect upon the Chinese leadership's policy beliefs over the Taiwan issue and, by extension, the United States.
14 See *People's Daily* (2004a). For possible effects generated by this economic pressure, see *People's Daily* (2005).
15 See Wang (2004); Perlez (2004a); and Cody (2005b). For possibly the earliest strategic advocacy of China's economic diplomacy see Shi (2003).

References

Bajpaee, C. (2005) "China Fuels Energy Cold War," *Asia Times*, March 2. Online. Available HTTP: www.atimes.com/atimes/China/GC02Ad07.html (accessed September 29, 2006).

Bernstein, R. and Munro, R. (1997) *The Coming Conflict with China*, New York: A.A. Knopf.

Boyd, A. (2004) "Oil Worries Lubricate South China Sea Pact," *Asia Times*, September 4. Online. Available HTTP: www.atimes.com/atimes/China/FI04Ad04.html (accessed September 29, 2006).

Brooke, J. (2004) "China Fears Once and Future Kingdom," *New York Times*, August 25, p. A3.

Brown, L. (1995) *Who Will Feed China?* New York: W.W. Norton.

Brzezinski, Z. and Mearsheimer, J.J. (2005) "Clash of the Titans," *Foreign Policy*, 146: 46–50.

Cheow, E. (2003) "Hu Recasts China's Foreign Policy," *Japan Times*, June 25. Online. Available HTTP: www.japantimes.co.jp/cgi-bin/eo20030625a1.html (accessed October 4, 2006).

Cody, E. (2005a) "China's Quiet Rise Casts Wide Shadow," *Washington Post*, February 26, p. A1.

——(2005b) "China Builds A Smaller, Stronger Military," *Washington Post*, April 12, p. A1.

Deng, X. (1983) *Deng Xiaoping wenxuan [Selected Works of Deng Xiaoping]*, Vol. 2, Beijing: People's Publishing House.

——(1993) *Deng Xiaoping wenxuan [Selected Works of Deng Xiaoping]*, Vol. 3, Beijing: People's Publishing House.

——(2000) *Deng Xiaoping duiwai zhengce sixiang xuexi gangyao [A Program for Studying Deng Xiaoping's Thoughts on Foreign Policy]*, Beijing: World Affairs Press.

Dickie, M., Mallet, V., and Sevastopulo, D. (2005) "Washington Is Turning Its Attention From the Middle East," *Financial Times*, April 7. Online. Available HTTP: search.ft.com/searchArticle?queryText=Washington+Is+Turning+Its& y=7&javascriptEnabled=true&id=050407000889&x=6 (accessed September 22, 2006).

Gilboy, G.J. and Heginbotham, E. (2004) "The Latin Americanization of China?" *Current History*, September: 256–261.

Hoge, J.F. (2004) "A Global Power Shift in the Making," *Foreign Affairs*, 83(4): 2–7.

Holsti, K.J. (1977) *International Politics: A Framework for Analysis*, 3rd edition, Englewood Cliff, NJ: Prentice Hall.

Howell, D. (2005) "China's Global Impact Grows," *Japan Times*, January 29. Online. Available HTTP: www.japantimes.co.jp/cgi-bin/eo20050129dh.html (accessed October 4, 2006).

Johnson, C. (2005) "The Real China Threat," *Asia Times*, March 19. Online. Available HTTP: www.atimes.com/atimes/China/GC19Ad05.html (accessed September 29, 2006).

Kuik, C.C. (2005) "Multilateralism in China's ASEAN Policy: Its Evolution, Characteristics, and Aspiration," *Contemporary Southeast Asia*, 27(1): 102–122.

Kynge, J. and McGregor, R. (2003) "China Replaces Its 'Five Principles' with Foreign Policy Pragmatism," *Financial Times*, February 24. Online. Available HTTP: search.ft.com/searchArticle?queryText=China+Replaces+Its+%27Five +Principles%27&javascriptEnabled=true&id=030224000758 (accessed October 4, 2006).

Lam, W. (2004) "Beijing's Energy Obsession," *Wall Street Journal Asia*, April 2. Online. Available HTTP: taiwansecurity.org/News/2004/AWSJ-020404.htm (accessed September 29, 2006).

Li, S. (2005) "Zhongri guanxi de lixing siwei [Rational Thinking on the China-Japan Relations]," *Wen Hui Pao* (Hong Kong), April 11. Online. Available HTTP: www.e-economic.com/info/1907-1.htm (accessed October 6, 2006).

McGregor, R. (2005) "Beijing in Dilemma over Protesters," *Financial Times*, April 12. Online. Available HTTP: www.ft.com/cms/s/0c42d3d4-aaf1-11d9-98d7-00000e2511c8.html (accessed September 29, 2006).

Marcois, B.W. and Miller, L.R. (2005) "China, U.S. Interest Conflict (over the Middle East oil resources)," *Washington Times*, March 25. Online. Available HTTP: www.washtimes.com/op-ed/20050324-075950-4488r.htm (accessed September 29, 2006).

Marsh C. and Dreyer, J.T. (eds) (2003) *U.S.-China Relations in the Twenty-first Century: Policies, Prospects, and Possibilities*, Lanham, MD: Lexington Books.

New York Times (2003) "China's More Nuanced Diplomacy," October 14, p. A24.

Pei, M. (2002) "China's Governance Crisis," *Foreign Affairs*, 81(5): 96–109.

People's Daily (2002) "Zhongguo guanyu xin anquan guan de lichang wenjian [China's Position Document on the New Security Outlook]," August 2. Online. Available HTTP: news.xinhuanet.com/zhengfu/2002-08/06/content_512599.htm (accessed October 29, 2006).

——(2004a) "Guo Tai Ban: Bu huanying yi Xu Wenlong wei daibiao de 'lüse' taishang [Taiwan Affairs Office of the State Council: 'Green' Taiwanese Businessmen Represented by Xu Wenlong Not Welcomed]," May 31. Online. Available HTTP: news.sina.com.cn/c/2004-05-31/06022670680s.shtml (accessed October 29, 2006).

People's daily (2004b) "Guowuyuan Xinwen Bangongshi baipisu: 2004 nian Zhongguo de guofang [White Paper of the Information Office, PRC State Council – China's National Defense 2004]," December 27. Online. Available HTTP: news.xinhuanet. com/zhengfu/2004-12/27/content_2385569.htm (accessed October 10, 2006).

——(2005) "'Lüse' taishang Xu Wenlong fabiao gongkaixin zhichi 'Fan Fenlie Guojia Fa' [The 'Green' Taiwanese Businessman Xu Wenlong Issue – A Public Letter to Support 'Anti-Session Law']," March 28. Online. Available HTTP: news.sina.com.cn/c/2005-03-28/03595479155s.shtml (accessed October 10, 2006).

Perlez, J. (2004a) "Across Asia, Beijing's Star Is in Ascendance," *New York Times*, August 28, p. A1.

——(2004b) "As U.S. Influence Wanes, A New Asian Community," *New York Times*, November 4. Online. Available HTTP: taiwansecurity.org/NYT/2004/ NYT-041104.htm (accessed September 29, 2006).

Sammon, B. and Gertz, B. (2005) "Bush Warns of China Arms Sales," *Washington Times*, February 22. Online. Available HTTP: washtimes.com/national/20050222-115008-9802r.htm (accessed September 29, 2006).

Schmitt, E. (2005) "Rumsfeld Warns of Concern About Expansion of China's Navy," *New York Times*, February 18, p. A4.

Shaplen, J.T. and Laney, J. (2004) "China Trades Its Way to Power," *New York Times*, July 12, p. A19.

Shi, Y. (2002a) "A Rising China: Domestic Ambiguities and Controversies," speech given on February 12, 2002 at the Carnegie Endowment on International Peace, Washington, DC; published in a pamphlet by the Sasakawa Peace Foundation, USA.

——(2002b) "Arms Control and Non-proliferation in East Asia: Grave Situation and Possible Dangers," *Contemporary International Relations*, 12(8). Online. Available HTTP: www.cap.lmu.de/transatlantic/download/Shi.doc (accessed October 10, 2006).

——(2003) "Guanyu Zhongguo duiwai jingji zhengce de sikao [Reflections on China's Foreign Economic Strategy]," *International Economic Review*, (6): 50–51.

——(2004) "The Issue of Civil Society in China and Its Complexity," in Y. Sato (ed.) *Growth and Governance in Asia*, Honolulu, HI: Asia-Pacific Center for Security Studies, pp. 225–232.

——(2005a), "Zhongri guanxi weiji de xincheng ji kongzhi [The Making and Control of the Crisis in Sino-Japanese Relations]," *Wen Hui Pao* (Hong Kong), June 1. Online. Available HTTP: www.lfda.gov.cn/bbsxp/PrintPost.asp?ThreadID=501 (accessed October 10, 2006).

——(2005b) "Guanyu jinhou Zhongguo duiwai zhengce yulun fangxiang de sikao [Reflections on the Possible Future Orientations of the Chinese Foreign Policy Opinion]," *World Economics and Politics*, (2). Online. Available HTTP: www. iwep.org.cn/guojizhengzhi/shiyinhong.htm (accessed October 10, 2006).

Su, C. (2005) "Faxian Zhongguo xin waijiao: Duobian guoji zhidu yu Zhongguo waijiao xin siwei [To Find China's New Diplomacy: Multilateral International Regimes and the New Thinking on Chinese Diplomacy]," *World Economy and Politics* (Beijing), (4). Online. Available HTTP: www.xslx.com/htm/gjzl/ gjgx/2005-05-31-18819.htm (accessed October 10, 2006).

Sutter, R., (2001) "China's Recent Approach to Asia: Seeking Long-term Gains," *PacNet* (23). Online Available HTTP: www.csis.org/component/option,com_ csis_pubs/task,view/id,1125/type,3/ (accessed September 29, 2006).

Swaine, M.D. and Tellis, A.J. (2000) *Interpreting China's Grand Strategy: Past, Present, and Future*, Santa Monica, CA: RAND.

Wang, Y. (2001) "Xin shiji de Zhongguo yu duobian waijiao [The New Era China and Multilateral Diplomacy]," *The Pacific Journal*, (4). Online. Available HTTP: www.iwep.org.cn/pdf/duobianwaijiaoyuzhongguowaijiao.pdf (accessed October 10, 2006).

Wang, Y. (2004) "Jingji waijiao zhanxian Zhongguo meili [Economic Diplomacy Demonstrates China's Charisma]," *Global Times* (Beijing), December 3. Online. Available HTTP: www.internationalrelations.cn/Article/ShowArticle. asp?ArticleID=1062 (accessed October 10, 2006).

Wight, M. (1991) *International Theory: The Three Traditions*, Leicester, England: Leicester University Press.

Wu, X. (2004) "Four Contradictions Constraining China's Foreign Policy Behavior," in S. Zhao (ed.) *Chinese Foreign Policy: Pragmatism and Strategic Behavior*, Armonk, NY and London: M.E. Sharpe, pp. 58–65.

Ye, Z. (2000) "Zhongguo shixin daguo waijiao shizai bixin [*Daguo Waijiao* Strategy: An Inevitability for China]," *World Economy and Politics* (Beijing), (1). Online. Available HTTP: www.internationalrelations.cn/Article/cn/200411/15. html (accessed October 10, 2006).

Zhang, D. (2003) *Jiangou Zhongguo: Buqueding shijie zong de daguo dingwei yu daguowaijiao* [*Constructing China: Great Power Identity and Diplomacy in An Uncertain World*], Taipei: Yangzi Press.

Zhao, S. (2003) "Chinese Nationalism and Its Foreign Policy Ramifications," in C. Marsh and J.T. Dreyer (eds) *U.S.-China Relations in the Twenty-first Century*, Lanham, MD and Oxford: Lexington Books, pp. 63–84.

——(2004a), "Beijing's Perception of the International System and Foreign Policy Adjustment after the Tiananmen Incident," in S. Zhao (ed.) *Chinese Foreign Policy: Pragmatism and Strategic Behavior*, Armonk, NY and London: M.E. Sharpe, pp. 140–150.

——(2004b), "Chinese Nationalism and Pragmatic Foreign Policy Behavior," in S. Zhao (ed.) *Chinese Foreign Policy: Pragmatism and Strategic Behavior*, London and Armonk, NY: ME Sharpe, pp. 66–90.

12 Conclusion

Capitalism in the dragon's lair

Christopher A. McNally

Speed and scale

If we step back and consider China's rapid international ascent within the confines of the world's past 300 years of history, some intriguing parallels emerge. China's rise appears in many ways to be propelled by the same historical forces associated with the climb to international prominence of other great powers. Although each of these industrial powers charted its own course, buffeted by different historical and social currents, they all undertook a form of capitalist development.

China today is undoubtedly in the midst of such capitalist development. As noted in Chapter 2, this process is most fundamentally driven by the inherent human tendency to seek gain and accumulate capital. While this tendency exposes capitalism's less savory facets, from avarice to crass materialism, it also motivates diligence, thrift, and, perhaps most profoundly, human creativity. Of course, capitalism is in general distinguished by the rise of market institutions to organize the supply of our basic (and not-so-basic) livelihoods.

Ultimately, though, a political vantage point is perhaps the least understood and yet the most salient for developing countries. The unique historical process of capitalism is characterized by the rise of capital-owning social strata to economic, social, and political prominence. At first these social groups avoid, then cooperate, engage, and compete with state elites. If a capitalist transition proceeds, the increasing power of capital can balance the state's coercive means, establishing constitutional limits that assure the security of property rights and the predictability of economic rules.

While China is in the midst of a capitalist transition, the specific processes unfolding are often unmatched in speed and scale. In comparison to earlier instances of capitalist accumulation, China seems to be doing everything simultaneously in a much more condensed time frame. For instance, China's capitalism unites aspects of crude Victorian capitalism with 21st century technology and corporate organization. When comparing changes in US history with China's transition, then China has combined over the past decade:

> the raw capitalism of the Robber Baron era of the late 1800s; the speculative financial mania of the 1920s; the rural-to-urban migration

of the 1930s; the emergence of the first-car, first-home, first-fashionable clothes, first-college-education, first-family-vacation, middle-class consumer of the 1950s; and even aspects of social upheaval similar to the 1960s.

(McGregor 2005: 3)

One of the most conspicuous manifestations of Chinese development is an intense effort to establish a continental infrastructure. Roads, ports, railways, telecommunication systems, as well as power generation and transfer networks are being developed with breathtaking speed and scope. China has already built the world's second largest expressway network, with more than 4,000 km of expressway added each year since 1998. Total length of this network reached 34,000 km by the end of 2004, and plans for the future are even more ambitious. The Chinese State Council approved in December 2004 a blueprint for a national expressway system of 85,000 km in length, spanning the country to include all cities with 200,000 or more residents (Fang 2004).

China's establishment of a comprehensive national infrastructure parallels earlier instances of capitalist development, including America's westward expansion in the late 19th century and the building of the interstate freeway network in the 1950s. In similar fashion, China is experiencing a rapidly accelerating process of urbanization. About 220 million farmers have moved from the countryside to cities between 1990 and 2003 (National Bureau of Statistics 2004: Table 4-1) and the growth rate of urbanization is at nearly 2 percentage points annually (*People's Daily* 2005). This represents the biggest and fastest move from the land to the city in human history. In tandem with urbanization, the education system is expanding at a rapid pace. Between 1999 and 2004 admissions to and graduations from high school both more than doubled, while university enrollment grew from around 1.6 million to 4.5 million students, a 180 percent increase (*China Economic Quarterly* 2005: 22–23).

On the flipside, there is a very dark quality to China's capitalist transition. As in all cases of initial capitalist accumulation, the processes occurring in China are often cruel in nature and accompanied by social ills. China has seen the abuse of the weak and the prevalence of extremely harsh working conditions. China's development has also been uneven with urbanization and greater mobility amplifying social and regional inequalities.

One of the most fundamental contradictions facing China's capitalist transition is environmental destruction on a shocking scale (see Economy 2004). The largest industrialization witnessed in the history of civilization is causing rampant pollution and resource depletion. Pollution alone cost the Chinese economy about 3 percentage points of GDP growth in 2004. As an official with China's State Environmental Protection Agency put it, "China can't go the way of polluting first, and then treating it; the ecological system that shoulders economic development will be crushed" (Spencer 2006).

Urbanization, industrialization, national integration, environmental degradation, and social institutionalization and stratification can be found in all instances of initial capitalist development. China is no exception, exhibiting distinct parallels to its earlier predecessors. The first observation is therefore that China is fundamentally tracing the path of a capitalist transition. However, the second observation must be that the historical, geographical, and external conditions facing China's emergent capitalism are unique.

Up front is that China's capitalist transition is happening at breakneck speed on a massive scale. Phenomena unfolding are condensed in temporal terms and stunningly expansive in geographic terms. To one extent or another, all chapters in this volume engage with these two fundamental characteristics of China's transition.

Chapters 3 through 5 note how China's corporate sector is developing rapidly and on a scale that is already having an impact on the global competitive landscape. These chapters trace the development of an information technology (IT) sector with indigenous heavyweights, the emergence of a sizeable venture capital industry that is transferring knowledge, ideas and practices from abroad, and the advance of internationally competitive Chinese corporations that are in the process of mastering global expansion. Each in their own way thus expresses how both speed and scale are yielding a highly diverse political economy with considerable capacities at an early developmental stage.

Chapters 6 through 8 further elucidate the deep imprints speed and scale are leaving on China's transformation. Chapter 6 argues that China's large size creates considerable divergence in regional endowments, including disparities in access to global markets and capital. In turn, these differences are shaping a variety of locally embedded political economies. It makes therefore more sense to speak of varieties of capitalism within China. Chapter 7 provides a different facet of the influence of China's huge size. Although the party-state attempts to exercise hermetic control over the generation and dissemination of information, it is just impossible to master the resources to undertake such an effort. China is too large with by far too many media outlets. Finally, Chapter 8 expresses how the speed of China's economic transition has far outstripped the capacity of China's political system to deal with mounting socio-economic imbalances. China thus faces an increasingly polarized populace that could undermine the Chinese Communist Party's (CCP) future legitimacy.

The final three thematic chapters express the major roles that speed and scale play in China's enmeshment with the international system. Chapter 9 notes how the continuation of China's export boom along the lines of earlier export booms in East Asia will create a formidable trading power. The consequence: continuous structural economic change that will task global society's capacity to adjust. Chapter 10 observes the major contradiction between the energy resources available within China and the country's potential future needs. Quite simply, China's energy requirements are highly likely to stress the globe's geopolitical balances. Finally, Chapter 11 most precisely states China's dilemma of size. China is already so large at such an early stage in its development that continued expansion of its international weight is strategically "threatening" to neighbors and major world powers. China's geopolitical environment could thus be severely complicated by the very continuation of its developmental trajectory.

The speed and scale of China's capitalist transition constitutes a fundamental characteristic, shaping the institutions, politics, and international ramifications of China's emergent political economy. Speed and scale also influence the three threads introduced in Chapter 1. These threads capture the forces of change, points of contention, and emerging dynamics of China's capitalist transition. Each of the three threads further aims to integrate the themes and arguments contained in this volume's nine topical chapters, thus weaving their findings into an inclusive narrative.

The three threads

The incomplete nature of China's capitalist transition

The incomplete nature of China's capitalist transition represents the first and perhaps most influential thread. As one Chinese colleague put it, "China is both far away from socialism and far away from capitalism."[1] China's embryonic market economy remains highly politicized. With this, the institutional certainty and predictability necessary for private capital to expand is only partially established.

That China is in the midst of a monumental transition is in and of itself not a remarkable finding. Most of the academic literature on China's contemporary political economy expresses this fact in one way or another. This volume, though, applies the capitalist lens in the hope of providing a comprehensive and historically accurate picture of China's transition, thus adding explanatory power.

Specifically, Chapter 2 "measured" the progress of China's transition while employing a sufficiently general, yet precise definition of capitalism. In this manner, it elucidated how China continues to lack substantial institutional and legislative certainty. The bifurcation of secular authority – the rise of capital-owning social strata to political and social prominence – has only evolved in embryonic form.

The capitalist lens thus draws attention to the continued Leninist constitution of the Chinese state and the historical legacy of China's political economy. As Chapter 6 laid out, China's political economy remains characterized by a marked duality. Two processes – state-led development from above and network-based development from below – shape its distinct contours. While this structure has allowed local government officials and private entrepreneurs to cooperate and foster capitalist accumulation, state-capital relations remain highly idiosyncratic and localized. Private entrepreneurs tend to forge clientelistic ties with the local party-state, encouraging a myriad of corrupt practices.

In a similar vein, Chapter 3 speaks of three tiers in China's industrial economy, the first of which is state-dominated, the second characterized by a host of hybrid firms, and the third consisting of mostly small-scale private firms. It is in the middle tier that both domestic and international forces have contributed to the rapid emergence of a vibrant IT sector. This sector, the authors argue, forms the vanguard of China's industrial and technological transformation yet remains in many ways tied to the Chinese state by hybrid ownership and insider dealing.

Chapters 4 and 5 also feature the blurred borderlines between corporate and government sectors as a fundamental characteristic shaping China's venture capital industry and multinational corporations. The partial nature of market reforms is further highlighted in the analyses of Chapters 7 and 8. In particular, Chapter 7's analysis of the media sector notes how China's incomplete transition has created immense tensions between a capitalist logic predicated on maximizing commercial success and a state dominant logic focused on maximizing political control.

Looking at China's role in the global capitalist system, Chapters 9 through 11 similarly grapple with the incompleteness of China's transition. Especially Chapter 11 makes clear that although the "primacy of the economy" is influencing Chinese foreign policy, the CCP's future foreign policy orientation remains indeterminate. Political imperatives, such as assuring internal political control and regime stability, might very well limit the degree to which China will adopt a liberal and "internationalized" foreign policy stance.

All the topical chapters thus reflect how China remains a political economy in transition. More specifically, the capitalist lens illuminates how this system remains shaped by two fundamental logics that clash: a state dominant logic emphasizing political control; and a capitalist logic emphasizing efficiency and commercial success. The interaction of these two logics shapes a host of hybrid, intermediary, and often internally contradictory institutions.

State dominated capitalism in China actually fosters close ties between capital and the state. Rather than seeking autonomy, most capitalists seek to further enmesh themselves in state and party institutions, both for commercial and political reasons. China's emergent political economy thus remains dominated by the Chinese party-state, hampering the development of rule-based governance. This poses one fundamental question for the future of China's emergent political economy: will it become stuck in a form of "Chinese crony capitalism?" I will take this inquiry up in the last sections of this chapter, when I discuss the possible future scenarios facing China's capitalist transition.

China's unique variety of capitalism

The second thread infusing the narrative of China's capitalist transition is that China is undoubtedly generating a unique form of capitalism.

As noted above, standard features of capitalist development over the past 300 years are readily apparent in China, including urbanization, industrialization, environmental degradation, and social stratification. Nonetheless, China's transition is unfolding under historical, geographical, and external conditions that differ from earlier instances of capitalist development.

As a result, China is contributing to the generation of new capitalist institutions domestically and globally, something that is reflected in all chapters. Chapters 3 through 5 express succinctly how parts of China's corporate sector are melding cutting-edge features of corporate organization with China's unique national endowments. Chapter 3, for instance, argues that China is developing a multi-centric economy with considerable flexibility, international openness, and local diversity. Although many of China's IT firms continue to be characterized by close government-business ties and hybrid ownership, they are also showing patterns of organizational and strategic behavior that are likely to foster robust development.

Coming from a similar vantage point, Chapters 4 and 5 call attention to how China's rapid assimilation of global capitalist norms and practices is generating new forms of Chinese management. In fact, Chapter 5 notes that China's emerging multinationals are not building traditional corporate hierarchies but rather international knowledge networks. A global "learning effect" is taking place that allows Chinese companies to move into higher value activities while other aspects of China's domestic economy remain underdeveloped.

Chapters 6 through 8, while focusing on more politically charged dynamics, also find that the interplay of a state dominant logic with a capitalist logic is creating a host of hybrid institutions. This can be seen in China's budding network capitalism that combines some of the benefits of state-led development with networks of small-scale producers. Such "hybridization" has facilitated the infusion of Overseas Chinese capital into Chinese production networks, creating institutional synergies and instant access to world markets.

Chapter 7 notes another peculiar Chinese invention – the Chinese media conglomerate. Such conglomerates fulfill two purposes: one is quintessentially capitalist – to seek economies of scale; the other quintessentially Leninist – to simplify party oversight over media content. Indeed, these media conglomerates tend to use revenues from commercially oriented tabloids to support the promulgation of CCP propaganda in other less profitable news sources. Quite elegantly, this has allowed the CCP to combine Leninist and capitalist practices.

Chapter 8 maps the unique political dynamics facing China's capitalism. Unlike many earlier capitalist developers, China's transition has been initiated, guided, and controlled by an ideologically anticapitalist party-state. So far, the Leninist constitution of this state has not allowed for any significant separation of political and economic powers. Rather, social stratification and spiraling class conflicts have driven affluent Chinese into the arms of authoritarian stability. This is leading China's lower classes into an apparently revolutionary disposition, making a smooth transition toward democratic rule more remote.

Chapters 9 through 11 further elucidate several aspects of China's unique capitalism. Chapter 9, for instance, compares the different dynamics and features of China's export boom with those preceding it in East Asia. Another notable aspect is how China has built a highly internationalized export regime while limiting the influence of foreign investors and traders on much of its internal trading system. Again, a dualistic picture of China's emergent political economy emerges.

In sum, China has developed specific institutional features and organizational structures that are beginning to constitute a unique form of capitalism. In large part, the uniqueness of China's emergent capitalism stems from two sources. First, the combination of cutting-edge practices used under the new global capitalism with institutional arrangements necessitated by China's underdeveloped domestic economy. Venture capitalists in China, for example, need to both master the Chinese art of *guanxi* and have in-depth knowledge of new developments in global finance and corporate governance.

The second source are the deep tensions and opposing forces created by the two dominant logics shaping China's emergent capitalism: a state dominant logic seeking to assure the CCP's monopoly over political organization; and a capitalist logic creating a transformative push that expands capital's economic *and* political space. The result is a number of hybrid institutions, ranging from the dynamic telecommunications equipment manufacturer Huawei to Chinese state oil and shipping companies that distinctively intermingle commercial and political goals.

The clash of these two logics also lends China's institutional transformation a somewhat bizarre quality. Institutions, such as media conglomerates, often have dual purposes that are not readily apparent. This is further reflected in China's international posture. Chinese diplomats tend to note that they do not interfere in the political affairs of other sovereign nations, and that "business is business." In reality, though, economic and political interests are inextricably intermingled in many of China's institutional arrangements and commercial transactions. The international realm is no exception.

China's emergent capitalism and its global impact

The third thread permeating the chapters is an intense concern with how China's role in the global capitalist system is likely to evolve. Many of the chapters reflect that China's international ascent is already a reality. Due to its large size, fast developmental dynamics, and unique institutional arrangements, China is having an impact on the globe's economics and geopolitics at a very early stage in its transition. And if China's evolution roughly follows its present trajectory, then China's rise will reshape the 21st century.

On the positive, China's emergence could have a beneficial impact on the world economy, and especially on Asia. Already at an early stage in its capitalist transition China has become a force for regional economic integration. This is not only a result of its size but also of China's relative openness. At first, networks of ethnic Chinese investors built bridges linking China with Asia, but soon global production networks started to base assembly and innovation operations in the country. After WTO accession, these networks are upgrading and expanding. China thus figures prominently in the strategic decision-making of the world's largest corporations.

The relentless opening of sector after sector to foreign trade and investment has also made China one of the globe's most interdependent economies. As a result, China has now reached a point where it has become quantitatively significant as a force driving world economic growth. For instance, China's economic boom from 2002 to 2006 has benefited its Asian neighbors significantly by providing considerable economic stimulus.

In this manner, China's economic ascent could create a strong third node in the global capitalist system. This node is likely to integrate the economies of Japan, South Korea, Taiwan, and Southeast Asia with China's own, fostering deep regional economic interdependence. Indeed, China's ascent might define an era in which East Asia becomes the globe's largest and most dynamic growth pole.

While the potential of China in global economic terms is enormous, most chapters in this volume also convey some unease about the future of China's capitalist transition and its impact on the world. As with the rise of great powers before it, China's rise will be disruptive and difficult for the international system. First, China has already at an early stage in its transition produced internationally competitive corporations. Corporations like Pearl River Piano or Hai'er have managed to combine global best practices with China's unique endowments. This is also expressed in China's fast developing venture capital sector and the international competitiveness embedded in Chinese network capitalism.

As many Chinese companies move into more advanced industries, they will target the more sophisticated markets that Western nations and Japan have so far considered their sole preserve. In the not-too-distant future, therefore, jobs which were thought to be immune from Chinese competition will start to come under pressure in developed nations. Perceptions of "unfair" competition will be further aggravated by the incomplete nature of China's capitalist transition.

Chapter 5 situates this issue lucidly when Ming Zeng and Peter Williamson note that "the public in the developed world may be poorly prepared for the international repercussions of China's capitalist transition." Indeed, "the risks of protectionist or potentially retaliatory policies are aggravated by the fact that the key driver of overseas expansion by Chinese companies,

China's capitalist transition, remains far from complete." The incompleteness of China's transition generates opaque policy-making, an underdeveloped "soft" infrastructure of the economy, and significant distortions to market-driven resource allocation. Since the corporate practices of Chinese multinationals are being shaped by this incompleteness, their increasing weight in the global economy raises the specter of mounting frictions. China is already being accused by some in the West of exporting dysfunctional domestic practices, including corruption, bad lending, a disregard for labor rights, and poor environmental standards. In that sense, the present tensions over the exchange rate of the Chinese *yuan* might only be a prelude to even more contentious disputes.

This issue is further elucidated by analyses in Chapters 9 through 11. For example, Yinhong Shi in Chapter 11 argues that the incompleteness of China's capitalist transition circumscribes the "primacy of the economy" in influencing Chinese foreign policy. This raises a two-pronged problem: the dilemma of China's incomplete transition combined with the dilemma of China's huge size. China is emerging very rapidly as a very large global economic power, yet its internal institutional arrangements lack legislative and institutional certainty. Perhaps never has the global system had to deal with such a large power at such an early stage in its development.

China's continued international ascent is therefore doubly "threatening" to its neighbors and major world powers. First, as with the rise of any great power, China's ascent is fundamentally alarming because new powers tend to destabilize established international orders. Second, many of China's institutions remain underdeveloped and shaped by a one-party Leninist state with a historical legacy of empire. Add on Chapter 8's arguments on the potential for political instability if socio-economic disparities continue to widen, and it becomes clear why the world might be faced with a major capitalist power that is internally volatile. There is thus no certainty that China will adopt moderate foreign policies that support the international status quo in the future.

In one way or another, China's unrelenting rise will reshape the globe's geopolitical environment. It will complicate China's international relations and create uncertainties over the prospects for sustaining China's own development. Ironically, China's continued development might constitute the country's biggest geopolitical liability, since China's escalating international impact combined with an incomplete capitalist transition will undoubtedly challenge established economic and geopolitical balances.

Future scenarios

China is irrefutably in the process of a capitalist transition. But is this transition sustainable? And where will it lead? Answering these questions necessitates some futuristic thinking, an undertaking that is generally discouraged in the social sciences. Despite the pitfalls associated with peeking into the future, I will attempt an exercise of logical analysis and extrapolation. The hope is that this will allow me to put forward possible future scenarios concerning China's capitalist transition.

The capitalist lens adopted in this volume can shed some important light on the inherent tendencies in China's domestic political economy. As noted in Chapter 2, political imperatives could conceivably halt China's capitalist transition and roll back achievements to date. There are many historical examples of this. Clearly, there is a distinct danger that China's political economy could become stuck in a form of "Chinese crony capitalism," perpetuating the present situation in which most sizeable private firms must seek close clientelistic ties with government officials. In fact, to move beyond Chinese crony capitalism, China's political leadership will have to come to grips with major political trade-offs.

One of the key distinguishing aspects of capitalist systems is their potential to establish rule-based governance that restrains and reshapes state action. The result is the gradual construction of a relatively self-directing and autonomous realm of the economy. Since capital moves according to where the greatest returns and lowest risks are, states, in order to retain and generate wealth, must create favorable conditions for capital accumulation. These conditions include establishing secure property rights, functioning markets, and predictable policies. At the same time, capitalist development expands state power enormously. States can make use of the greater productive capacities unleashed by economic growth, therefore marshalling superior organizational, financial, technological, and human resources.

One of the most misunderstood aspects of capitalism in popular conceptions is that it is a purely "private" economic system. Quite to the contrary, the expansion of capital-owning classes serves to expand and reconstitute state power. In essence, capitalist development leads to a process of mutual empowerment whereby both the realm of the "economy" and that of the "state" gain in sophistication and governance capacity. The structural power of capital tends to keep in check the vagaries of state power, while the state tends to constrain the imperfections of markets and the avarice of humans.

The world's history, though, shows that few state elites are willing to strike this "deal" with capital. Since states are inclined to acquire a monopoly over the concentrated means of coercion within their territory, they tend to squash potential competitors for power. Capital represents such a competitor, because its possession of wealth can rival the influence of the state.

Therefore, capital remains at the mercy of state elites before capitalist political economies mature. Indeed, capital leads a highly precarious existence during the early stages of capitalist development. State elite's direct influence over property rights and exchange systems allows them to easily repress or subvert the growing power of capital-holding classes. The lack of widespread capitalist development in the world attests to this fact.

Evidently, one of the necessary conditions for capitalist development is a modicum of security provided by the state to capital. Otherwise, capitalists are likely to move their holdings to safe havens.

Stated differently, for capitalist development to advance, state leaders must be induced to institutionalize greater political sway for capital. Ultimately, real or perceived threats to national and/or regime survival are the most common forces pushing state elites in this direction. Judging from how China's communist leadership views the external environment (as basically hostile and intent on subverting its rule) there are some grounds for optimism.

Possible domestic scenarios

China's capitalist transition has unleashed enormous increases in productivity, drawn large segments of Chinese society into capitalist relations of production, and integrated China's economy with the global capitalist system. Over the past years, though, the strains and contradictions created by China's own successes have become increasingly evident. I already have mentioned some of these, including environmental degradation on a massive scale and the accumulation of inequalities between the winners and losers of reform. More specifically, China suffers from many of the excesses typically present during initial phases of capitalist accumulation. These include, for example, the eviction of poor people from their land and homes in order to commercialize more land for construction and real estate; mounting instances of corruption and popular dissatisfaction with state governance; rapid migration of rural residents to cities and the resulting stresses of urbanization; and the failure to adapt China's social security system to the country's changed conditions.

Faced with these challenges, what are the likely future trajectories of China's political economy? I will elaborate here three likely scenarios. This list is not exhaustive and at best tentative. The three scenarios, though, attempt to capture the range of possibilities without falling into extremes.

Scenario I: in-system tinkering

In the near future, the most likely scenario for China is that present arrangements stay in place. This implies that most reform efforts amount to in-system tinkering. One way to understand this scenario is to assume that the deep historical legacy of China's imperial and Leninist past would continue to hold sway. The state's dominance over private commercial and industrial capital would remain intact. The CCP party-state would also continue its aim of strengthening societal controls, especially over the generation and dissemination of information.

Under the present leadership of Hu Jintao and Wen Jiabao such moves are clearly evident. The idea of a "harmonious society" reflects, on one hand, an awareness of the massive stresses generated by China's capitalist transition. On the other, it expresses that the CCP wants to take the lead in addressing social inequalities and environmental pressures, thus bolstering its domestic legitimacy. In fact, the present leadership is implicitly using the contradictions of China's capitalist transition to foster a new governing ideology. Based on Chinese people's fear of social chaos (luan), the CCP is tacitly encouraging a come-back of Confucian precepts, aiming perhaps to establish a Neo-Confucian order under CCP tutelage.

This scenario does not preclude that certain aspects of the state's bureaucracy and regulatory apparatus continue to be refined. Moreover, China's corporate sector would continue its development and internationalization. Within system tinkering might even extend to changes in the tax code and in the social security system to afford the weakest and most vulnerable members of Chinese society better economic protection. However, this scenario does not involve fundamental changes to China's political economy, such as establishing a relatively autonomous system of courts or more independent governmental oversight institutions, such as Hong Kong's Independent Commission Against Corruption.

How long could China's political economy muddle through under institutional and political parameters assuring CCP dominance? In view of China's present social and environmental stresses the sustainability of the system is more likely to be measured in years than decades. For example, since 2003 the CCP has been tinkering with the cadre incentive system to press for greater social and environmental accountability on the part of local cadres. However, so far these efforts have not met with much success, reflecting the limits to in-system tinkering.

Scenario II: peaceful evolution

Most Chinese quietly admit that the very best scenario for China's future is peaceful evolution (*heping yanbian*). Under this scenario, institutional change in state administration, law, and other spheres would be sustained, supporting continued progress by China's capitalism. Most importantly, this would entail a strengthening of the rule of law, which would have to include a substantial reduction in the CCP's powers to oversee and direct court judgments.

Peaceful evolution would further imply that emerging political interests are effectively incorporated into the polity, enabling China to attain greater degrees of social and environmental justice. Under Jiang Zemin's "Three Represents," capital-owning social strata have already been given greater political recognition. However, as An Chen points out in Chapter 8, these new social interests remain under CCP tutelage. Members of China's weak middle classes and poor under classes also continue to feel politically powerless. When China's mounting social polarization is added to this mix, the prospect of heightened social tensions, even if mediated by China's

Confucian legacy, looms large. Political developments to date, therefore, amount to in-system tinkering.

In the end, peaceful evolution entails that China's Leninist party-state is gradually nudged towards becoming a "constitutional" state, something that will require far-reaching political reforms. For example, government interference in the economy would have to be diminished, ideally accompanied by higher standards of accountability and transparency on the part of local cadres. As mentioned above, structural political change would also need to include legal reforms, especially greater professionalism and independence of the courts. Lastly, reforms would have to include expanded channels for institutionalized policy input and feedback, such as those provided by effective government ombudsmen or an independent press.

The possibility that China might gradually develop a "constitutional" state should not be dismissed outright. There are, however, two caveats. First, if China continues to evolve politically, the system that emerges will most likely look quite different from existing polities under advanced capitalism. China's political structure will undoubtedly contain distinct Chinese characteristics.

Second, as Chapter 8 laid out in detail, opportunities for peaceful evolution might be slipping away. Such a transition could only occur with some degree of CCP blessing. Yet, the CCP seems far away from undertaking bold moves in political reform. In-system tinkering thus appears most likely for the foreseeable future. At some point, though, China's social, environmental, and political pressures might become so immense that social actors opt to employ more revolutionary methods to further their aims.

Scenario III: Chinese crony capitalism

A final option is that by seeking to retain its monopoly on legitimate political organization at any cost, the CCP acts to stall China's capitalist transition. As with peaceful evolution, this scenario is most likely to emerge after several additional years of in-system tinkering, though with a contrary outcome. Rather than outgrowing the dominant state model, limitations to the security of property rights and sway of markets would ossify, forcing Chinese entrepreneurs to continue their subservient ties with the party-state. As a result, China's variety of capitalism would become stuck in a form of Chinese crony capitalism.

As noted above, one of the key distinguishing aspects of capitalist systems is the potential for capital-owning social strata to restrain state action and construct a relatively autonomous realm of the economy. Alas, examples in world history show that the CCP might not be willing to yield the institutional and political space necessary for China's private entrepreneurs to continue their dynamism. As other state elites before it, the CCP seeks a monopoly over political organization and tends to suppress any potential competitors for power. The CCP might thus opt to continue its direct influence over property rights and with this private capital's reliance on state munificence. This, though, could start to undermine the dynamic economic change experienced by China and strengthen the crony capitalist tendencies of China's emergent political economy.[2]

Chinese crony capitalism would mean that private entrepreneurs, especially those overseeing large firms, continue to seek close personal ties with state and party officials. There would also be a tendency by the state to clamp down on independent investor interests and to strengthen control over foreign capital. This system would continue China's present infusion of corrupt practices, and strengthen the monopoly positions of many firms locally and nationally. Chinese crony capitalism thus implies that the political imperatives of the CCP "freeze" China's capitalist transition near its present state. Capital's state-subservient position would continue, engendering an alliance of weak capital with a strong Chinese party-state.

Would such a system be sustainable? Partially this depends on whether China is able to retain pockets of economic dynamism (as now in coastal areas) while the overall political economy remains under state tutelage. In the long term, though, Chinese crony capitalism is quite unlikely to be sustained. So far, the CCP has been able to harness capital accumulation for the purposes of party legitimacy. This process must at some point exhaust itself.

First and foremost, we do not live in a static world. Pressures emanating from the global capitalist system will necessitate that China's state and party continue to upgrade the investment climate. Moreover, Chinese leaders continue to perceive both internal and external threats to national and regime survival. Rapid capital accumulation within China's borders could serve to contain and even surmount these perceived threats. Continued economic growth thus holds the key to the CCP's internal legitimacy and China's enhanced standing in the world. CCP hegemony does not stand above any perceived need for economic expansion.

As a result, the CCP leadership might see itself forced to back the continuation of China's capitalist transition, fostering economic liberalization and increased political prominence for capital-owning social strata. Political reforms necessary to assure continued capital accumulation would then have to follow at some point. In a sense, the global system's capitalist logic would induce internal political change in China, not much unlike what already has taken place in a gradual manner over the past thirty years.

This logic implies that peaceful evolution is a more likely scenario than Chinese crony capitalism. As noted above, however, the CCP does not seem to be willing to give up its ultimate authority over political organization, at least so far. In-system tinkering is certainly the most realistic scenario for the near future; while the longer term future of China's capitalist transition remains indeterminate. The already visible strains of China's transition such as widening income gaps, massive environmental degradation, and plentiful instances of corruption could become too much for the system to bear. At a minimum, China's polity remains relatively insecure and volatile. The toughest challenge of a capitalist transition – the institutionalization of constraints on state action to construct a relatively autonomous realm of the economy – remains ahead.

International ramifications

Whichever of these three scenarios shapes China's future will have significant implications for the world. If China continues to muddle through and sustains its variety of capitalism under state tutelage, greater internal and external frictions are likely. Similarly, if Chinese crony capitalism emerges as the dominant feature of China's political economy, China could face a prolonged period of economic stagnation and social unrest.

Both of these scenarios imply that China continues a state-sponsored form of capitalism. On China's scale, this could prove to be highly destabilizing for the global capitalist system. Mounting financial and trade imbalances could trigger protectionist sentiments among both established and developing economies. Greater economic frictions, in turn, could alter China's international posture. One distinct possibility is that China's leadership, when faced with a protectionist backlash to its exports or slowing economic growth, might resort to encourage a stronger and more aggressive brand of nationalism. Stronger emphasis on nationalism could also be triggered by a large shock to China's system, such as a military conflict with Taiwan, a major world recession, or social upheaval within China.

A nationalist backlash, while temporarily bolstering the CCP's legitimacy, could easily snuff out China's forces of change, especially those fostering greater international openness. The limited advances made by China's private entrepreneurs and business leaders might then dissipate, making China's already somewhat insecure polity even more volatile. Political change in this direction also raises the specter of a form of Chinese fascism emerging. Although this must be regarded as a distant possibility, a move in this direction would express the CCP leadership's inability to progress politically.

The consequences of such developments would be dire for the world. China is already a giant trading and manufacturing power. It possesses rapidly advancing military capabilities and an expanding diplomatic and cultural reach. An upsurge of Chinese nationalism would create immense dangers for the Asia Pacific region and the world, ushering in a period of international conflict and economic instability. East Asia's economic boom of the early 21st century might then seem like a distant mirage.

Even without a nationalist backlash, the internal political situation in China could destabilize the country. The strains of China's capitalist transition are already palpable, such as widening income gaps and environmental degradation. Most importantly, though, China's leadership might just simply lack the political will to advance the country's transition. Reforms could stall, pushing China into an equilibrium characterized by increased corruption and continuing lapses in governance. Again, the world would be faced with a major economic power encompassing volatile internal conditions.

A more optimistic outlook would see China making continued advances in economic and political governance. This would involve the process of peaceful evolution by which China gradually develops a "constitutional" state, though most likely with distinct Chinese characteristics. China's budding capitalists could then emerge as a truly competitive force, fundamentally altering the nature and logic of global capitalism.

Under this scenario, China is likely to surface as a much more open political economy than those of Asia's earlier developers, especially Japan, South Korea, and Taiwan. Indeed, China's network capitalism facilitates economic integration among economies containing large segments of Overseas Chinese. In addition, China's political efforts to engage with the region, especially the establishment of a free trade area in East Asia, could further support China's emergence as a major trading power. China could then arise as a new center for global economic activity by the next decade, bolstering its position as the economic hub of East Asia.

Put differently, if China roughly follows the path of peaceful evolution, the prospects for the smooth integration of China into the global political economy improve. Some of the effects, however, might still be difficult to deal with. China's rapidly developing corporate sector would most likely emerge as a competitive threat to many established corporations and endanger jobs in the developing and developed world. Moreover, as China's power expands the potential for both China's leadership and other world powers to mismanage China's international ascent increases. As I noted above, both external and internal factors could derail China's capitalist transition, with reverberations ranging from virulent nationalism in China to greater political instability in East Asia. If events unfold rapidly, problems in China could even generate a global economic shock.

In the end, China is already a colossus at a very early stage in its capitalist transition. Since China's authoritarian political constitution is unlikely to change in the near future, the world will be faced with a large economic power that nonetheless contains substantial institutional and legislative instability. China's size and transitory nature could therefore have destabilizing influences, even if China continues to make political advances.

Undoubtedly, the emergence of China as a major capitalist political economy is starting to alter global institutional arrangements. And if China's economic trajectory does not change, the country will become a formidable economic player, heating up economic and geopolitical competition. Clear signs of this are visible. As China's international influence grows, regional powers will have to realign their foreign policies.

Already this is causing increased tensions between China and Japan, and will most likely create greater tensions between China and the United States in the near future.

As with the rise of other great powers before it, China's rise will be disruptive and difficult for the international system to absorb. Can the world accept and live with capitalism in the dragon's lair? This will be the major question for the geopolitics and economics of the early 21st century.

Notes

1 Informant 66, Beijing, 2005.
2 See Chapter 6 for a definition of crony capitalism.

References

China Economic Quarterly (2005) "Building Human Capital: Education in China," 10(4): 19–32.

Economy, E. (2004) *The River Runs Black: The Environmental Challenge to China's Future*, Ithaca, NY: Cornell University Press.

Fang, D. (2004) "Expressways Will Link Main Cities Across Country," *South China Morning Post*, 14 January, p. A4.

McGregor, J. (2005) *One Billion Customers: Lessons from the Front Lines of Doing Business in China*, New York: Free Press.

National Bureau of Statistics (2004) *China Statistical Yearbook 2004*, Beijing: China Statistics Press.

People's Daily (2005) "China to Push Forward Urbanization Steadily," May 12. Online. Available HTTP:english.people.com.cn/200505/12/print20050512_184776. html (accessed December 12, 2006).

Spencer, J. (2006) "Why Beijing Is Trying to Tally the Hidden Costs of Pollution as China's Economy Booms," *Wall Street Journal*, October 2, p. A2.

Index